Tony Chuang's research, analysis, and writing are a testament to the blend of academic rigor and real-world application, offering crucial insights for contextual gospel transmission in Taipei and similar contexts globally. In our shared journey at Trinity Evangelical Divinity School, I've seen Tony's profound understanding of intercultural studies, which he brilliantly demonstrates through this work. His study reveals various pivotal findings, such as how Taipei people's pluralistic worldview and utilitarian spirituality significantly hinder their understanding of confident Christian claims commonly used by Western evangelists and missionary endeavors.

In addition, this work provides several implications from its findings. It explains three main issues related to missiology in Taipei: issues with worldview, concepts of conversion, and religious pluralism. By tackling these issues, Tony is adding his voice to other missiologists, such as Paul Hiebert, in refining the understanding and application of contextualization. The study ends with seven suggestions for gospel presentations in Taipei, cementing the bridge of theoretical knowledge with practical application.

Tony's work is a looked-for contribution for missionaries and scholars alike, offering a new lens to view religious pluralism and spirituality in contexts akin to Taipei. As a colleague who has witnessed his journey, I am proud of his achievement and confident in his research's positive impact on the understanding and transmission of the gospel.

Yamil Acevedo, PhD
Executive Vice President,
Wesley Seminary, Indiana, USA

An excellent read! How is Taiwanese Chinese society best engaged with the gospel – a society that on the surface is largely irreligious, but on closer inspection is actually quite religious, albeit with a utilitarian bent? Raised in a non-Christian Taiwanese Chinese family and equally adept in both Chinese and English, the author has effectively drawn out the "lived religiosity" of the ordinary Taiwanese Chinese folks. Most importantly, this book offers practical guidelines on best approaches to presenting the gospel in the light of their culture and worldviews.

NamChen Chan, PhD
陳南振
Executive Director,
AsiaCMS, Malaysia

I am Chinese and came from a Chinese folk religion background similar to Tony's. Although I am in Southeast Asia, I could resonate with Tony's research. Tony's research crossed geographical limits as he focused on the most crucial issue – the Chinese worldview. Tony puts much effort into designing the methodology for research, and he is showing the outcome of being a very responsible researcher. Also the clear presentation of the outcome is intriguing. Tony's conclusion with the practical gospel steps for the Christian evangelizing person and the transforming non-Christian will be an innovation in sharing the gospel with friends from Chinese folk religious background.

Chia Choon Chuah, PhD
蔡家存
Dean of Doctoral Studies and Mission Initiatives,
Malaysia Baptist Theological Seminary, Penang

在基督教的世界中，已有大量的文獻研究在西方處境下的福音策略，但缺乏在非西方處境相對應的研究，而莊博士本書的研究恰恰彌補了這空隙。莊博士以居住台灣的華人社群作為研究對象，探究影響人們歸信特定宗教的關鍵因素，指認出緣分、宿命、功利、對今生的關注、孝道與祖先崇拜、以及宗教多元的現實，提出許多發人省思的洞見。莊博士提出的洞見，不只是對「傳福音」有意義，亦是對「福音」意涵的重新發現，進而促使今日的教會省思當下門徒培育和宣教工作的實踐。

In the Christian world, there is a large amount of literature studying evangelical strategies in Western contexts, but there is a lack of corresponding research in non-Western contexts. Dr. Chuang's research in this book exactly fills this gap. Dr. Chuang used the Chinese community living in Taiwan as the research focus to explore the key factors that influence people converting to specific religions. He identified predestined affinity, fate, utility, concern for this life, filial piety, and ancestor worship, as well as the reality of religious plurality, and proposed many thought-provoking insights. The insights provided by Dr. Chuang are not only meaningful for "evangelism," but also a rediscovery of the meaning of "gospel," which in turn prompts today's churches to reflect on the current practice of discipleship training and missionary work.

David Doong, PhD
董家驊
General Secretary,
Chinese Coordination Center of World Evangelization

In his field-based research, Tony Chuang asks why Christianity only makes up a small, underwhelming minority in Taiwan, a nation with religious freedom and many decades of evangelistic efforts, and what needs to be done to spread the gospel more. He finds the answers by delving into a world of folk religions practiced in Taiwan and carefully investigating the locals' nuanced spiritual and religious experiences. His analysis gives us concrete steps to advance the gospel among the research population. For Chuang, this research is not merely an academic exercise, it is deeply personal – it is about his life, family, and calling. The result is this unique volume in which Chuang successfully builds bridges between sound missiological theories and passionate practice of contextualized gospel ministry, between Western perspectives and a Majority World context. I applaud this terrific work, which points us toward a new direction in gospel transmission in Taiwan and gives us many hints for East Asia and beyond.

Peter T. Lee, PhD
이태훈
Associate Director of Korean DMin Program and
Affiliate Professor of Intercultural Studies,
Trinity Evangelical Divinity School, Illinois, USA

This is a timely book written by someone deeply passionate about evangelizing to Asians. Many Asian countries share Taiwan's contextual background. Much of the findings in this research will be useful for a deeper and grassroots understanding of Chinese religious beliefs in Asia. The book is useful for missiological researchers and practitioners to be more aware of the contextual issues when evangelizing to Taiwanese and Chinese people. Missionaries, church leaders, and anyone who has a heart for reaching the Chinese people ought to read this book.

Tat Yan Lee, PhD
李達恩
President,
Bible College of Malaysia, Selangor

How can we be more effective and loving when presenting the gospel to a common Chinese person? Chuang provides a convincing answer through this work. His valuable research confirms that religious pluralism rooted in practicality is in fact the lived experience of the Taiwanese in particular and Chinese in general. Hence, a "proclamation-only" type of gospel presentation may be deemed as impersonal, blunt, arrogant, and irrelevant, and is therefore far from effective for them. After examining a range of Chinese religious concepts, Chuang proposes an alternative. He helpfully proposes steps to present the gospel holistically and strategically – through understanding, honesty, proper conduct, and gradual stages which would be meaningful, thorough, and enriching to a typical Chinese person. This is a significant work and an important contribution to the conversation on missions to the Chinese people.

Khee-Vun Lin, DMin
凌啟文
Founder and Principal,
Anglican Training Institute, Malaysia

Despite the impact of globalization and modernization on societies in Asia, folk religious beliefs and practices continue to exert significant influence on many peoples' understanding and behavior. In this carefully crafted and informative study Dr. Chuang explores various expressions of folk religion among the Chinese in Taipei, Taiwan, and he offers helpful and innovative suggestions for more effective Christian ministry in such contexts. This is an important contribution to our understanding of mission in Asia today.

Harold A. Netland, PhD
Professor of Philosophy of Religion and Intercultural Studies,
Trinity Evangelical Divinity School, Illinois, USA

Religiosity and Gospel Transmission

Insights from Folk Religion in Taipei

Tony Chuang
莊智超

© 2024 Tony Chuang [莊智超]

Published 2024 by Langham Academic
An imprint of Langham Publishing
www.langhampublishing.org

Langham Publishing and its imprints are a ministry of Langham Partnership

Langham Partnership
PO Box 296, Carlisle, Cumbria, CA3 9WZ, UK
www.langham.org

ISBNs:
978-1-83973-919-4 Print
978-1-78641-063-4 ePub
978-1-78641-064-1 PDF

Tony Chuang [莊智超] has asserted his right under the Copyright, Designs and Patents Act, 1988 to be identified as the Author of this work.

All rights reserved. No part of this publication may be reproduced, stored in a retrieval system or transmitted, in any form or by any means, electronic, mechanical, photocopying, recording or otherwise, without the prior written permission of the publisher or the Copyright Licensing Agency.

Requests to reuse content from Langham Publishing are processed through PLSclear. Please visit www.plsclear.com to complete your request.

Scripture quotations are from The Holy Bible, English Standard Version® (ESV®), copyright © 2001 by Crossway, a publishing ministry of Good News Publishers. Used by permission. All rights reserved.

British Library Cataloguing-in-Publication Data
A catalogue record for this book is available from the British Library

ISBN: 978-1-83973-919-4

Cover & Book Design: projectluz.com

All photographs in this work have been taken by the author.

Langham Partnership actively supports theological dialogue and an author's right to publish but does not necessarily endorse the views and opinions set forth here or in works referenced within this publication, nor can we guarantee technical and grammatical correctness. Langham Partnership does not accept any responsibility or liability to persons or property as a consequence of the reading, use or interpretation of its published content.

To my wife, who is the first Dr. Chuang,
and to my ever-supportive parents

爸媽，這本書是獻給你們的

Contents

List of Tables...xv

List of Figures...xvi

Acknowledgments xvii

Abstract...xix

Chapter 1 1
   Introduction
      Background 2
      Research Problem 3
      Research Objective 4
         Research Questions 5
      Scope and Limitations...5
      Significance and Contribution...6
      Researcher Bias 7
      Definitions and Terms...8
      Overview of the Chapters 12

Chapter 2 13
   Folk Religion in Taiwan
      Folk Religion as a Concept...14
         Religion 15
         Traditional Religion..21
         Folk Religion 22
         Popular Religion 24
         Folk Belief...26
         Term of Choice...30
      Chinese Religiosity..31
         Ancient Beliefs 31
         Religious Behaviors 35
         Imperial Cults...37
      Folk Religion in Taiwan 38
         A Tentative Definition..38
         The Taiwanese Context 40
         Culture in Temples, Folk Beliefs, and Society............45
         Deities..47
      Summary of Folk Religion..52

Chapter 3 55
  Methodology
    Rationale 55
    Research Sample 57
      Sample Group 57
      Sample Size 59
      Data Saturation 59
    Overview of Information Needed 60
      Contextual Information 60
      Demographic Information 61
      Perceptual Information 61
      Theoretical Information 63
      Summary of Information Needed 64
    Research Design 64
      Research Process 64
      Contextualization 65
    Data Collection Method 67
      Interview Structure 67
      Interview Transcription 68
    Data Analysis 69
      Coding the Interviews 69
      Pattern Analysis 69
      Stages of Coding 71
      Summary of Data Analysis 72
    Ethical Considerations 72
      Participant Consent 72
      Protection of Human Rights 73
      Sharing the Researcher's Religious Experience 73
      Remuneration 74
    Issues of Trustworthiness 74
      Credibility 74
      Transferability 75
    Summary of Methodology 76

Chapter 4 77
  Findings on General Attitudes and Religiosity
    General Attitudes Toward the Unseen Realm 78
      Yuánfèn 78
      Ancestral Veneration 80
      Reincarnation 85
      Fortune Telling 87

- Amulets 90
- Atheists on Folk Religion Beliefs and Practices........................90
- Summary of General Attitudes 91
- Different Words to Express "Faith" 92
  - Believing in Something..93
  - Superstition..93
  - Familial Relationship..93
  - Relationship of Exchange..94
  - *Bài* (Small Worship) 96
  - Beseech...102
  - Summary of Words..105
- Being Part of a Religious System 105
  - Conversion...105
  - Utilitarian Perspective of Deities..112
  - Part of Life 115
  - Defining a Devout Person...116
  - Summary of Being Part of a Religious System........................121
- Summary of Findings on the Unseen Realm and General Religiosity 121

Chapter 5 123

Findings on Deities, Jesus, and Christianity

- Choosing a Deity 123
  - How to Have "Faith" in a Deity..123
  - Why People Choose a Deity..134
  - Assumed Belief in Multiple Deities...139
  - Summary of "Faith" in a Deity...147
- Interpreting "Believe in Jesus for Eternal Life" 148
  - Interpreting "Believe"..149
  - Interpreting "Eternal Life" 153
  - General Reactions to the Phrase..156
  - Summary of Interpretations 157
- Key Objections to Christianity 158
  - Evangelism Tactic 158
  - Lack of Unity..158
  - Narrow and Exclusive 159
  - Bad Morals of Christians 160
  - Religious Wars...160
  - Strict Requirements 160
  - Judgmental..161
- Summary of Findings on Deities, Jesus, and Christianity............162

Chapter 6 163
Key Issues in the Taiwanese Context
Issues with Worldview 164
Yuánfèn and Fatalism 165
This Life Versus the Next Life 167
Ancestors 169
Truth Claims..172
Relating to Deities and the Unseen Realm 174
Issues with Religious Boundary Crossing 175
What Needs to Change 176
Conversion as a Problematic Term....................................178
Transformation as an Alternative Term............................183
Issues with Religious Pluralism 185
Pluralism as a Concept...186
Pluralism as a Lived Reality..188
Power as the Special Factor 192
Pluralism in the New Testament Times 193
Interreligious Dialogue 196
Summary of Key Issues..201

Chapter 7 203
Gospel Transmission in Taipei
The Gospel in Light of Local Attitudes 204
The Gospel in Action..204
The Gospel for the Sinned-Against 206
The Gospel's Answer to a Relationship of Exchange.......211
The Gospel in Conversation with Deities and Ancestors..........214
The Gospel in Light of the Lived Reality...............................216
The Gospel through a Relationship Network...................217
The Gospel for the Middle Realm 220
The Gospel in Daily Life 222
Summary of Gospel Transmission in Taiwan 228

Chapter 8 229
Conclusion
Gospel Steps 229
Steps for the Christian Evangelizing Person 230
Steps for the Transforming Non-Christian 234
Summary of Gospel Steps..237
Recommendations for Future Research 237
Perception of Folk Religion in Taiwan..............................238

                Christian Conversion Stories Among Taiwanese 238
                Applicability Outside Taiwan 239
        Closing Remarks..239

Appendix 1 241
    Chinese Terms and Names
        Romanization..241
        Chinese Names 242
        Chinese Quotation from Interviews 243
        Chinese Citations in the Reference List................................244

Appendix 2 247
    Interview Protocol
        Basic Information 247
        What Is the General Attitude toward the Unseen Realm? 248
        What Does It Mean to Believe in a Deity?............................249
        What Does it Mean to Be in a Religious System?...............249
        How Does Folk Religion Influence Understandings of Faith? 250
        What Are Some Chinese Terms Used to Describe Faith? 251
        What Are Some of the Ways That 信 (Faith) is Used in Chinese? ...251
        How Is Faith Understood by Taiwanese Christians?...........251

Appendix 3 253
    Details of the Coding Process
        First Cycle Coding...253
            Coding for Key Words and Values 253
            Coding for Thinking and Believing................................254
        Second Cycle Coding 256
            Coding for Categories 256
            Coding for Theory 258
        Mixing the Stages..259

Bibliography 261

List of Tables

Table 1. Hiebert, Shaw, and Tiénou's framework for analysis of religious systems..17

Table 2. Classification of religions by F. Yang based on his categories................18

List of Photos

Figure 1. A red *bagua* symbol hanging above the garage door of an apartment 34

Figure 2. 台北霞海城隍廟 (Taipei Xiahai City God Temple) 41

Figure 3. An offering to the researcher's grandfather, right before burning incense 43

Figure 4. Parade at 西門町 (Ximending), a famous night market in Taipei, Taiwan 46

Figure 5. A Mazu temple next to modern buildings on a street in 新竹 (Hsinchu) 46

Figure 6. Offering to the Earth God outside a shoe store 49

Figure 7. Offering with paper money outside a restaurant 49

Figure 8. A well-frequented temple in Taipei with many offerings on the table 51

Figure 9. A row of fortune tellers grouped in close proximity 87

Figure 10. A digital instructional sign on how to *bài* and do other important rituals 97

Figure 11. A poster explaining how to conduct proper worship at this temple 98

Figure 12. The temple that Pei-Pei and Ms. Sha mentioned had long lines 126

Figure 13. People in a zigzag line, waiting for two *gūpós* to perform *shōu jīng* for them 131

Figure 14. The front of the temple 行天宮 (Hsing Tian Kong) in Taipei, Taiwan 142

Figure 15. People at the temple doing *bài* while a message was given 143

Figure 16. One of about six older ladies reciting out loud a religious text 143

Figure 17. Explanations of the deities' stories happen throughout the day 144

Figure 18. A billboard in red containing the *Namo Amitābha* chant 153

Figure 19. Visual picture of the most common codes for the research 257

Acknowledgments

I dropped out of Georgia Tech in 2007. In the same year, I was deported from the United States for overstaying my visa. I retreated to Taiwan, bringing so much shame to my family. After crying, being depressed, contemplating suicide, and hating God for half a year, I came to accept that my high school diploma would be my highest degree. However, this was not God's plan for my life. When I bounced back, my faith grew stronger than ever. I eventually completed a Bachelor of Science degree in Computer Science at a university in Canada, then worked briefly as a computer programmer. I then proceeded to get a Master of Divinity in the United States. Now, I have turned in a dissertation for a Doctor of Philosophy degree. Yes, a deported, college drop-out has earned a PhD in the very country from which he was deported.

I share all this to show that I could not have gotten this far without lots of help. I must acknowledge first and foremost using the words of the apostle Paul, "by the grace of God I am what I am, and his grace toward me was not in vain. On the contrary, I worked harder than any of them, though it was not I, but the grace of God that is with me" (1 Cor 15:10). Without God giving me a second chance, I would not have been able to do anything, let alone finish a terminal degree. He is my joy and my salvation. To God alone be the glory.

I must also acknowledge the patience and guidance of my parents. Without their emotional and financial support I would not be able to stay alive. Any amount of filial piety I can show to them is insufficient compared to the amount of sacrificial love they have shown me. My parents were and still are the means through which the Lord is good to me.

My wife, Dr. Esther Shin Chuang, has been a great source of comfort in those days when I felt overwhelmed by my many responsibilities and the difficulty of a PhD. Her cooking and her love have sustained me, not to mention her editorial help. She also took care of our two children during those long days and nights when I had to write.

My family in Taiwan has been invaluable during the qualitative research phase. My grandmother has tried to help me with the interviews. Other cousins, aunts, and uncles have given me valuable insight into Buddhism and folk religion. Their willingness to help me despite their feelings about Christianity has moved me deeply.

I would not be able to produce a scholarly work of this level without the advice of my dissertation committee members. Dr. Tite Tiénou has strengthened my work by helping me think and providing valuable insight. Dr. David Gustafson has indulged me in more than a few conversations about the gospel and evangelism. Dr. Harold Netland has challenged me on multiple issues, thus making the end product that much better. Dr. Craig Ott, some of the other faculty, and my PhD colleagues have all helped improve my work and my thinking.

I want to thank the people at my church, Hope Community Bible Church, who have allowed me to reduce my pastoral responsibilities so that I may focus more on writing. Their prayer and words of encouragement makes me feel blessed and loved. The kindness shown by my friends outside the church has also warmed my heart greatly. I would like to give a special thanks to Sarah Williams, whose speedy editorial services proved invaluable.

I cannot forget the interview participants, most of whom do not know me. I still do not know many of their names because I encountered them on the streets. These Taiwanese people in Taipei have agreed to participate in an hour-long interview with no remuneration. Yet many of them thanked me and some even offered to treat me to food. This Taiwanese 風情 (*fēngqíng*, elegant demeanor) is why I have and will continue to do research on this beautiful island nation.

Abstract

This work explores Taiwanese attitudes and lived reality regarding religiosity. The purpose is to develop a contextual approach to gospel transmission in Taipei, Taiwan. This study incorporates qualitative research in the form of twenty-five in-depth, semi-structured interviews about actual religious experiences. Participants were gathered through the snowball approach and at random on the streets and temples of Taipei. While this work is mostly written in English, all the interviews and some of the literature used are in Mandarin Chinese.

This study's literature about folk religion introduces Chinese religiosity and the context of folk religion in Taiwan. The conceptual framework employed is a mixture of the models proposed by Fenggang Yang, Paul Hiebert, Daniel Shaw, Tite Tiénou, and C. K. Yang. In terms of primary contextualization models, a transformative framework is utilized.

The qualitative findings of the research revealed the nuances of how Taipei people conceptualize religion and the unseen realm. One salient finding shows that Taipei people's daily interaction with the supposed "excluded middle" of the unseen realm is both normal and expected within the culture. Due to this worldview, many different words were used by the participants to express 信 ("faith"), revealing a deeply familial, informal, and relational conceptualization of religion.

These differences reflect the fluid and pluralistic nature of being part of a religious system in Taipei. The pluralism is compounded by people's "utilitarian perspective of deities,"[1] which makes choosing a deity a problematic concept and exclusivist claims repulsive to them. This worldview has led to

---

1. See Chapter 4: Being Part of a Religious System: Utilitarian Perspective of Deities, p 112.

Taipei people grossly misunderstanding Christian phrases like "believe in Jesus for eternal life" and voicing fundamental objections to Christianity itself.

As implications from the findings, this work explains three main issues related to missiology in Taipei: issues with worldview, concepts of conversion, and religious pluralism. The study ends with seven suggestions for gospel presentations in Taipei. A "gospel in daily life" and "gospel for the middle realm" are hypothesized as particularly fitting models. Practical gospel steps are given as a concrete approach to follow.

CHAPTER 1

Introduction

It was a school day like any other. A seven-year-old boy just finished school and starts running home so that he can play. He runs past bustling skyscrapers and motor vehicles crowding the streets of downtown Taipei. When he arrives home, he notices that his parents are still at work; so, his grandparents greet him. This is nothing unusual for the office workers of Taiwan's capital city. His grandmother tells him that he has to greet the ancestors first before he can go play. He walks over to the ancestral shrine in the middle of the living room, picks up a stick of incense, clamps his palms together, and prays a simple prayer. The idols on the shrine do not respond; they never do. But the boy is earnest and respectful because the ancestors may be watching somehow.

He remembers the proper ritual that his grandmother has taught him multiple times at home. He has also done it plenty of times in that temple down the street between a fried chicken fast-food restaurant and a car dealership. The boy beseeches for health, wealth, and good grades, the only three things in the world that are important. He then gets to eat some crackers that were given as an offering for the ancestors and for the other deities on the shrine. He thinks to himself, "Good thing we always have food offered to these idols, otherwise what would I eat?" After this tasty snack, he does his homework, then sits down in front of the television and plays the latest video game on the device he borrowed from his cousin. Life is good. He has hardworking parents who provide for him, grandparents who watch him, and ancestors who bless and protect him.

That little boy was me. I was like millions of other little boys in Taiwan who had never heard the gospel. What I had heard of Christianity at that time was mostly negative, namely that they were out to get our money and that it is simply "not our way." Some scholars characterize what I experienced as folk religion. I call it my lived reality. How much of it is the lived reality of Taiwan? What is this thing called folk religion that has shaped my worldview so much? Are my attitudes normal or unusual? How come I am a Christian but the rest of my cousins and extended family are not? And most importantly, how can more little boys and girls in Taiwan turn to Jesus the same way I did? These questions form the motivation for the entirety of this work.

Background

Taiwan is an island nation (35,980 km^2) to the east of China. The National Statistics lists the population as 23.5 million people.[1] The Pew Research Center estimates that in 2020, 43.8 percent of Taiwan's people will be classified as adhering to "Folk Religions."[2] Taiwan's number is unusually high as compared to the entire Asia-Pacific region, where only 8.6 percent adhere to folk religion. In the ranking for all 198 countries/territories, Taiwan ranks third. Pew Research Center has a category of religion called "Other," which includes "smaller faiths" like the Baháʼí faith, Sikhism, Daoism, and other religions which are presumably harder to define. Taiwan tops the list for "Other" at 15.5 percent, followed by North Korea and Palau.

The country with the highest percentage of folk religion adherents in Europe is Iceland at 0.5 percent. In North America, it is Bermuda at 3.0 percent.[3] The high contrast of folk religion adherents in Taiwan versus other places (especially the West) could be due to Taiwan's unique religious and political history. It also could be due to the classification of folk religion in these other places. Folk religion is often seen in association with traditional religion, which is associated with what economists perceive as poor, undeveloped countries.[4] Because of this stigma associated with folk religion, it is unusual to find Taiwan having so many folk religion adherents yet ranking

---

1. "Latest Indicators," National Statistics, Republic of China (Taiwan), February 2021, https://eng.stat.gov.tw/point.asp?index=9.

2. Pew Research Center, "Religious Composition by Country, 2010–2050," Pew Research Center, 2 April 2015, https://www.pewforum.org/2015/04/02/religious-projection-table/2020/percent/all/.

3. Pew Research Center, "Religious Composition by Country, 2010–2050."

4. Parrinder, *African Traditional Religion*; Burnett, *World of the Spirits*.

twentieth in the world's highest nominal GDP (Gross Domestic Product) at 682.7 billion US Dollars.⁵

The Christian population in Taiwan (including Protestants, Catholics, Mormons, and others) is 5.8 percent according to Pew Research Center and even lower according to others. This figure is much lower than folk religion. The freedom of belief that the Taiwanese government affords to its citizens allows any religious group to proselytize as they wish. However, the Christian population has remained largely the same over the past few decades. Apart from the Buddhist group (at 21.2 percent), other world religions see almost no adherents (e.g. Islam at less than 0.1 percent). This data highlights, through contrast, the popularity of folk religion in Taiwan.⁶

Research Problem

It is unfortunate that Pew Research Center, despite widespread use of its data, does not nuance the different kinds of religious beliefs and practices that make up the 43.8 percent of folk religion adherents in Taiwan. Pew does not say which deities are being worshipped, the requirement for being considered a folk religion adherent, the central belief system, organizational structure, or many other details that would shed light on this religious system making up almost half the country (or almost 60 percent if one includes the 15.5 percent from the "Other" category). The "Folk Religions" category seems to be a mix of many religious systems that do not have their own unique categories.

All this data raises a few questions: What is it about folk religion that draws so many adherents in Taiwan? In contrast, why are only 5.8 percent of people Christians in Taiwan despite being a religiously open country with decades of gospel work, both foreign and domestic? Surveying English literature from the past few decades, there was much interest in understanding folk religion in Taiwan.⁷ However, the intersection with gospel work was either absent or

---

5. International Monetary Fund, "IMF DataMapper," International Monetary Fund, April 2021, https://www.imf.org/external/datamapper/NGDPD@WEO/OEMDC/ADVEC/WEOWORLD.

6. Pew Research Center, "Religious Composition by Country, 2010–2050."

7. Jordan, *Gods, Ghosts, and Ancestors*; Overmyer, *Folk Buddhist Religion*.

downplayed in that period. 董芳苑,[8] seeing the lack of scholarly work on the topic, urged the community to take seriously the impact that folk religion has on gospel transmission in Taiwan.[9] Seemingly as a response to the call, a series of articles appeared in the journal *Taiwan Mission*.[10] But the question still remains, Since folk religion is so prevalent in Taiwan, how do we evangelize in this context? The question is not, What is it about folk religion that is framing Taiwanese people's understanding of faith, and could it be affecting gospel transmission on a more theoretical level? The problem is that some scholarly works address understanding folk religion, and others address gospel transmission. But almost none address the plausibility structure of the gospel itself in relationship to Taiwanese culture, which cannot be considered apart from its folk religion.[11]

There is abundant literature dealing with folk religion in Taiwan or Taiwanese religiosity in general.[12] But there is a paucity of literature dealing with how folk religion may affect a Taiwanese person's understanding of "faith," as well as how a Taiwanese person treats coming into a religion. This is a serious problem. To illustrate the issue, when a Taiwanese folk religion adherent says she has "faith" (信, *xin*) in a local deity, it can mean multiple things, such as intellectual consent, practicing rituals, faithfulness to teachings, or any mixture of these. Thus, popular statements like "faith in Jesus alone" may mean several things depending on the context. It is possible that Taiwan's relatively slow Christian growth is in part due to theoretical misunderstandings that could be improved by better contextualization.

Research Objective

This study takes a conceptual route to help Taiwan's gospel transmission efforts. Preliminary research on the topic indicates that the way Taiwanese

---

8. See appendix 1 for when and how Chinese will be used in the work. The reason for why some authors are shown with Chinese names while others are not is also explained in appendix 1.

9. Dong, "Táiwān Mínjiān Xìnyǎng Zhī Zhèngshì, 臺灣民間信仰之正視," 49–74.

10. Bolton, "Taiwan's Ancestor Cult," 5–12; Khong, "Idol Removal," 22–23.

11. Berger, *Sacred Canopy*.

12. Yang and Hu, "Mapping Chinese Folk Religion," 505–21; Hu, "Gifts of Money," 313–35; Liu, "Religious Coping Methods," 1138–45; Chang and Penny, *Religion in Taiwan*.

people understand religiosity affects how they perceive concepts like faith, belief, and conversion.[13] In light of this reality, one could analyze culture, political history, folk religion, or any number of areas. Through a better understanding of Taiwanese religiosity, this work contributes to current theories, practices, and theologies that inform a better contextual approach to gospel transmission in Taipei, specifically with some applicability to Taiwan as a whole.

Research Questions

This study can be said to have one main topic: What is Taiwanese religiosity like? Framed more specifically, the topic is: How do Taiwanese people living in Taipei understand coming into and being in a religion? Addressing this topic helps in achieving the research objective of improving Taipei's gospel transmission efforts. Addressing this topic required answering the following research questions:

- RQ1: What is the general attitude toward the unseen realm?
- RQ2: What does it mean to believe in a deity?
- RQ3: What does it mean to be in a religious system?
- RQ4: How does folk religion influence Taiwanese religiosity?
- RQ5: What are some Chinese terms used to describe faith in a deity?
- RQ6: How do Taiwanese living in Taipei understand the Christian concept of faith?

Scope and Limitations

The main topic that this study explores is how Taiwanese people understand religiosity. The grouping "Taiwanese people" does not mean that this work does qualitative research across the entire nation. This study researches only a sample of those living in Taipei, Taiwan. This is a delimitation due to funding as well as time.

This research analyzes certain types of folk religion in Taiwan, such as ancestral veneration, fortune telling, and Mazu. Due to the variety of beliefs

---

13. Chuang, "Chinese Modernity," 161–75.

and practices involved, it is impossible to cover them all with the depth required to make an adequate analysis. The goal of this study is not to better understand the depth and breadth of the various traditions classified as folk religion in Taiwan. The goal is to better understand the religiosity behind folk religion by exploring the specific concepts related to faith, which leads to a more contextual approach to gospel transmission. Detailed history, specific doctrine, and related practices behind each type of folk religion in Taiwan are covered insofar as they help accomplish this goal and inasmuch as they surfaced in the interviews.

Significance and Contribution

Most works on folk religion in Taiwan are of an exploratory nature – understanding what are all the types, the history behind the traditions, and the makeup of the adherents.[14] Most works deal with what folk religion is in Taiwan while almost none deal with what "faith" is to a Taiwanese person. Intersection with "faith" has been alluded to in some works,[15] but discourse on the topic is still rare.

Most works on gospel transmission in Taiwan focus on specific methods of evangelism or mission strategies. The approach taken in this study of focusing on the theoretical and theological issues is rare in comparison. The works that focus on those issues tend to be more general, without focusing on a specific country, let alone a specific city like Taipei. Few works exist on the contextual approach to gospel transmission derived from the cultural context of Taiwan. In studies in Chinese, the focus is often more practical rather than theoretical.

By addressing theoretical and theological issues, this study builds the foundation for better gospel transmission strategies for Taipei in the future. Ultimately, this research clarifies the conceptual issues so that local theologians, pastors, leaders, and laypeople can later fully apply it in their respective ministries. The result is that more people in Taipei may better respond to the gospel and in turn transmit the gospel to a family without Christ and who is still steeped in folk religion.

---

14. Overmyer, *Folk Buddhist Religion*; Yang and Hu, "Mapping Chinese Folk Religion."
15. Gao, "Impact of Contemporary Chinese," 170–81.

Researcher Bias

It is difficult if not impossible to be without researcher bias. Even seasoned researchers acknowledge this fact. 林茂賢 [Mao-Hsien Lin] is seen as one of the leading experts on folk religion in Taiwan. In his recent book detailing a "collection of Taiwanese folk practices," he started by explaining his motivation for the book. He wrote about how he grew up experiencing the traditional music and puppet shows in the temple courtyards, in a family who worshipped deities and Buddha, and following many traditional customs. M.-H. Lin said that folk religion along with all its artistic expressions and folk customs 「原本就是[他]生活的一部分」 ("has always been a part of [his] life"). He continued by saying that he 「沒有刻意去『研究』臺灣文化，……實踐民俗文化原本就是[他]的身活模式」 ("did not purposefully 'research' Taiwanese culture, . . . living and practicing folk culture has always been [his] lifestyle").[16]

I feel the same as M.-H. Lin when approaching this research. I became a Christian later in life. Before I met Christ, I grew up with my parents and grandparents in the same household in Taipei, Taiwan. I had an ancestral shrine filled with ancestors and deities of many kinds. I worshipped and prayed to these ancestors and deities every day when I came home, often eating the food that had been offered/sacrificed to them. I have gone to many temples and experienced many rituals. I have had my fortune told and worn amulets of protection. I am familiar with many deities and the proper way to conduct myself for certain ones.

Studying folk religion for me is not just studying this foreign religious system the same way an American anthropologist would study an ethnic group in Africa. Studying folk religion for me is exploring my own past as well as understanding the present reality of the majority of my family and extended family, with whom I am very close.

The topic of developing a contextual approach to gospel transmission is even more personal. I am not just doing it because I am in the department of mission and evangelism. I have shed many tears praying for my family to come to Christ. So far, four members of my extended family (including my father) have made professions of Christian faith. Many more remain uninterested and even hostile to my efforts at proclaiming the gospel to them.

---

16. Lin 林, *Dà Miào Chéng* 大廟埕, 13.

My own grandmother has told me that I have 「走火入魔」 (which means "becoming obsessed in a dangerous way" but literally translates to "walking into fire and entering into the demonic") because of my Christian faith.

I have often asked myself, "What am I doing wrong?" and "How can I share the gospel with them in a way that they will be more receptive to it?" This work is birthed out of that burning desire I have had since the day I became Christian. This research topic is thus extremely personal to me. I am above all interested in the gospel in Taipei. I passionately want the gospel to effectively reach my family and the millions of my Taiwanese kin.

I share all this to give more background to the reader of this work. I also share it to be upfront about my researcher bias. I do not pretend to be an "objective outsider" studying Taipei's context and contextualizing the gospel. As my family often points out to me because of my time in Malaysia, Canada, and the United States, I am not a complete insider either. My experience growing up in folk religion has informed much of the research, teaching me things that would be very difficult for an American researcher to find out. My background can be tremendously helpful to the research in finding the best questions to ask the interview participants and in figuring out what modes of gospel transmission tends to work better. My background can at the same time introduce researcher bias, in the sense that I may perceive the Taiwanese reality through my own eyes or skew the interview data to fit my own memories.

To the issue of bias, I can say that I have profited greatly from my prior knowledge and experience. It has allowed me to produce research questions relevant to Taipei. I can also say that I have been very diligent and careful in coding the data, spending close to nine months doing so just to make sure everything I wrote can be derived from the interviews. I have inserted copious amounts of interview quotations to ensure that the reader can see that every bit of qualitative data came from methodical research. As a human being, I cannot help that they have all been filtered through my lens, but hopefully the way I analyzed the data helped offset the negative effects as much as possible.

Definitions and Terms

Before moving on, it is useful to discuss some terms that are important to the study and that might have some ambiguity. Many of these terms are explored more fully in relevant sections throughout the work. However, in order to avoid confusion, a summary of potentially ambiguous terms is first discussed here. This study works on the basis of these definitions as presuppositions.

Taiwan. Today this is defined as the island nation to the east of the People's Republic of China. In 1949, the communist party led by Chairman Mao Zedong overthrew and drove the then-current government to the island of Taiwan, leading to a differentiation between what we today call "China" and "Taiwan." Before 1949, it was all one nation. The many deities revered, the Confucian values, and the influence of Buddhism were (and in many places, still are) similar. This is why in discussions of folk religion in Taiwan, many elements overlap with what many in the field call "Chinese folk religion." Literature is drawn from both sources.

Taiwanese. This work focuses on the specific context of Taipei City. Unless specified to be more general, the term "Taiwanese" as used in this study is an abbreviation for "Taiwanese people living in Taipei." This includes people born in Taipei as well as those born in southern Taiwan who moved up for various reasons. Additionally, there is a difference between the people who arrived in Taiwan from mainland China before 1949 and after 1949. They may all be Taiwanese in terms of nationality, but there are varying degrees of cultural and religious differences between those groups.

Chinese society. Chinese may be a nationality as well as an ethnicity. Popular and academic writing tend to treat "Chinese society" in the ethnic sense, as a broad umbrella covering many nationalities and a great diaspora. More accurately, it is better to write "Han Chinese society." Unless specified as Mainland Chinese, all references to Chinese made in this work are in the general, ethnic sense. In talking about the specifics of Taiwan, the term Chinese society still generally applies. For example, in addition to China and Taiwan, Singapore and certain regions in Malaysia are considered different Chinese societies.

Folk religion. The exact definition of this term is debated in academic literature. Most scholars define it by what it is not. Folk religion is often defined as a type of religion that is in contrast to institutionalized religions like Christianity, Islam, or Buddhism. It is put in parallel with traditional religions and is sometimes used interchangeably with the term *popular religion*. Scholarly consensus points to lower levels of organization and higher focus on practices in folk religion. The term *Chinese folk religion* refers to the broad category of folk religion that includes elements of Confucianism, Daoism, Chuang-Tzu, Tian, and other distinctly Chinese elements. Folk religion in Taiwan can either be a subset or an extension of Chinese folk religion. While some may prefer the term *folk religionists* to talk about people who self-identify under folk religion, this study prefers the term *folk religion adherents*. This term draws more attention to the fact that folk religion is not one unified religion for people to belong to but rather a conglomerate of deities and rituals that people adhere to either tightly or loosely. The *adherent* terminology is shared by Pew Research Center in their discussions on folk religion.[17]

The West. The West is an ambiguous term that can include many countries and regions. This work uses it to mean Europe and North America even though some countries in those two regions do not fit in, and even though other places like Australia may well belong in the category. Another reason for the use of the term in this study is that sources in Chinese, which are a significant part of the research, use the term frequently.

Bài. This is from the Chinese word 拜 that can be translated as worship. However, it is not the same way that Christians use the term worship. It is included here because this study uses *bài* instead of an English word. *Bài* refers to the action of bowing down and closing both palms together in reverence before an ancestor or deity. It is more a form of paying respect than it is an overflow of love or some other emotion. Chapter 4 deals with this word more comprehensively and explains why the Chinese transliteration is used.

Supernatural and the *unseen realm.* For the purposes of this study, *supernatural* refers to anything that is seen as operating from the unseen realm. The *unseen realm* refers to what Hiebert has called the "excluded middle," excluded by many in "the West" and part of the reality of the Taiwanese.[18] The language of *supernatural* does not mean that a phenomenon is somehow less (or more) real in the participants' minds or in the world. These two terms are drawn from Hiebert, Shaw, and Tiénou. The usage of language like the *natural*

---

17. Hackett and Huynh, "Second-Largest Religious Group," Pew Research Center, 22 June 2015, https://www.pewresearch.org/fact-tank/2015/06/22/what-is-each-countrys-second-largest-religious-group/; Hackett and McClendon, "World's Largest Religion," Pew Research Center, 5 April 2017, https://www.pewresearch.org/fact-tank/2017/04/05/christians-remain-worlds-largest-religious-group-but-they-are-declining-in-europe/; Kramer, "Key Findings," Pew Research Center, 13 December 2019, https://www.pewresearch.org/fact-tank/2019/12/13/key-findings-how-living-arrangements-vary-by-religious-affiliation-around-the-world/.

18. Hiebert, "The Flaw of the Excluded Middle."

and *supernatural, seen realm* and *unseen realm* is meant to draw attention to Hiebert, Shaw, and Tiénou's framework and thus to the "middle realm" that Taiwanese people seem to fall between as well as the ways that Taiwanese tend to blur the lines between categories like these. See chapter 2 for more details on Hiebert, Shaw, and Tiénou's framework and other frameworks for discussing religious concepts.

Gospel. Greg Gilbert defines the gospel more systematically or thematically, looking primarily at sin, God's righteousness, and Jesus's provision.[19] Scot McKnight frames the gospel using the idea of the kingdom, dividing common definitions of the gospel into two categories: the "soterian gospel" and the "apostolic gospel."[20] McKnight equates the afterlife-focused "soterians" with present-day evangelicals, and his critique of this popular evangelical view is that the gospel is bigger than the plan of salvation.[21] He articulates the big difference between the "gospeling of Acts" and the evangelism by evangelicals of today. For McKnight, he sees the apostolic gospel as one that fits the biblical narrative better. McKnight writes, "the gospeling of the apostles in the book of Acts is bold declaration that leads to a summons while much of evangelism today is crafty persuasion."[22] For the purposes of this study, McKnight's "apostolic gospel" will be used as the default definition for *gospel*. The "declaration" in McKnight's definition refers to the good news about Jesus Christ. This good news refers to the story of Jesus's life, death, and resurrection as well as its implications for human beings and the rest of creation.

Evangelizing person. The word *evangelizing* refers to the act of transmitting the gospel to a certain audience. The term *evangelizing person* is used as opposed to *evangelist* because of the unhelpful associations some people may have with the word *evangelist*. An evangelizing person is any person who attempts to transmit the gospel regardless of training, success, frequency, or methodology.

Evangelism. This is the act or study of evangelizing. In contemporary usage, *evangelism* is often defined as being the vertical dimension of the mission of God. There is always a goal associated with *evangelism* (i.e. that people accept the message), but proclamation of the gospel is sufficient for an act to be

---

19. Gilbert, *What Is the Gospel?*.
20. McKnight, *King Jesus Gospel*.
21. McKnight, 70.
22. McKnight, 134.

considered evangelism.[23] This work can be seen as the study of evangelism in Taiwan. *Evangelism* is sometimes presented in competition with social action for priority in organizational resources and focus. This historical debate and the term's association with verbal communication are why the term gospel transmission is preferred in this work.

Gospel transmission. This English term is derived from the Chinese term 「傳福音」 (*chuán fúyīn*, literally "passing the gospel"; other possible translations are "gospel-spreading" or "gospel-propagating"). Gospel transmission is used in this work to describe everything from street witnessing, relational evangelism, and even missions. For mission or missions, the word 「宣教」 (*xuānjiào*, literally "proclaiming religion") is used. However, *xuānjiào* is usually reserved more for special occasions, such as oversea mission trips. Gospel transmission is the default term to use for most other occasions.

LORD. This dissertation uses the term LORD to refer to the Christian deity as revealed in the Bible. The term *Shangdi* is not used, despite its popularity in Taiwan, in order to avoid confusion with the deity in ancient China. The term God is not used to avoid confusion with a god at a temple. The term Christian God is not used because it sounds too much like a description instead of a name or title.

Overview of the Chapters

In this chapter, the research problem, the research objectives, and some preliminary information that clarify the boundaries of the dissertation are introduced. In chapter 2, folk religion in Taiwan is discussed. Discussion includes the anthropology behind the terms, the specifics of the Chinese context, and the expressions of folk religion in Taiwan. In chapter 3, the methodology of the entire research is explained. In chapters 4 and 5, the rich findings from the qualitative research done in Taipei are revealed. In chapter 6, implications from the findings are used to discuss potential issues in gospel transmission in Taipei. In chapter 7, more implications are drawn to discuss possible approaches to gospel presentations in Taipei specifically and Taiwan as a whole. In chapter 8, the study concludes with some concrete suggestions for gospel work and some final remarks.

---

23. Gustafson, *Gospel Witness*.

CHAPTER 2

Folk Religion in Taiwan

In the introduction, we saw how popular folk religion is in Taiwan, namely that 43.8 percent of Taiwanese self-identify as folk religion adherents. This statistic ranks Taiwan as the third highest in the world in terms of percentage. The study's biggest question is, How does one contextualize the gospel in Taipei, Taiwan? Due to folk religion's popularity in Taiwan, one cannot study Taiwanese religiosity without at least a basic understanding of folk religion.

Even though it is important to understand the specifics of folk religion in Taiwan, it is impossible to do so without first understanding the concept of folk religion more broadly. This conceptual understanding is crucial because the direction of the dissertation is in exploring the Taiwanese *concept* of folk religion, not the Taiwanese *branches* of folk religion. As such, the study of folk religion, especially in anthropology, has a prominent place in this chapter.

In this study of folk religion, the terminology used does not just affect definitions, but it affects how this religious phenomenon is framed. Studying the Chinese context, 楊慶堃 [Ch'ing-k'un Yang] uses the term "diffused religion" to describe Chinese religiosity.[1] C. K. Yang contrasts the term with what he calls "institutional religion." Using data gathered from multiple fields in the study of Chinese society, C. K. Yang came to the conclusion that the religious element is "diffused into all major social institutions and into the organized life of every community in China. It was in its diffused form that people made their most intimate contact with religion."[2] His theory on diffused religiosity bears resemblance to what many scholars today call "folk religion."

---

1. Yang, *Religion in Chinese Society*, 294–340.
2. Yang, 296.

Folk religion is a category of religion that has seen many in-depth ethnographic and historical studies both older as well as more contemporary. A considerable amount of scholarly work has intersected studies of religion with studies of modernity and secularization. It is not uncommon to find many broader theories or implications about religiosity in general at the end of these studies on folk religion. The approach taken in this chapter is to explore concepts going from broad to narrow. First, this chapter examines the different terminologies used in studies of folk religion in order to have a better theoretical foundation. Second, this chapter explores a few types of religiosity found in Chinese societies. As such, the details of specific beliefs and practices of the wide spectrum of Chinese folk religions are largely left out. Third, this chapter explores the nuances of folk religion in Taiwan, with particular focus on thematic elements rather than on specific beliefs and practices. Specifics are discussed insofar as they help explain Taiwanese religiosity.

Folk Religion as a Concept

There are varying terms used to describe what this study has referred to as "folk religion." For example, Edward B. Tylor uses terms like "primitive religions" or "animism" in his book *Primitive Culture*.[3] Originally published in 1865, Tylor's aim was to understand religion at its most basic level. He believed that animism provided a "deep-lying doctrine" of spirituality and "embodies the very essence of [spiritual] philosophy."[4] For Tylor, the doctrine of the soul and of the other spirits is the main focus of animism. Tylor's chapters on language and mythology ground his research on the "primitive" people of his study. Of course, the concept of primitive has since then been seen as erroneous and unhelpful.[5] Seeing as his work seemed to have derived more from reading than fieldwork, this may be a legitimate criticism. Nevertheless, Tylor's main contribution was his insistence that all cultures are "religious" in some sense. He thus conceived the essentialist definition for religion as "the Belief in Spiritual Beings."[6]

---

3. Tylor, *Primitive Culture*.
4. Tylor, 425.
5. Tiénou, "Invention of the 'Primitive,'" 295–303.
6. Tylor, *Primitive Culture*, 424. Capitalization in original.

Tylor's understanding of primitive religions influenced the study of folk religion for many decades. Understandings of the field of folk religion studies, its close linkage to "premodern" societies, and concepts of "spiritual beings" have all been shaped by Tylor's work on animism. In contemporary scholarship, animism has often been described as attributing human-like qualities to non-human species and sometimes objects as well, resulting in having a sense of being more at peace with nature.[7] Animism has been seen as a part of beliefs and practices of some major world religions, a part that stresses the "spiritual" aspect of this world.[8]

But our topic is folk religion. We discuss animism because it shares some conceptual similarities with how scholars define folk religion today. One such similarity is the focus on agents in the non-material world as powerful influences in a person's daily life. Furthermore, recent scholarship seems to indicate a resurgence of the term animism without the negative connotations seen in Tylor's work.[9] However, scholarship on animism and scholarship on folk religion do not overlap significantly. Folk religion has enough distinctions of its own to be considered a separate field. In order to achieve more conceptual clarity on folk religion, this section considers four terms widely used by scholars to describe folk religion. The focus is not so much on the content of various studies, but their methodological approaches. Before discussing the four terms, we must first evaluate the term *religion*, which is the common factor in all four terms.

Religion

It is not uncommon for scholars of folk religion to situate the topic in the broader context of religion in general. Paul G. Hiebert, R. Daniel Shaw, and Tite Tiénou for example take a "system of systems" approach, studying the phenomenology of folk religion particularly in the cultural and social systems.[10] Hiebert, Shaw, and Tiénou critique understandings of religion like those of Tylor's as outdated and "fatally flawed."[11] Hiebert, Shaw, and Tiénou

---

7. Harvey, *Animism*.
8. Harvey, *Handbook of Contemporary Animism*.
9. Århem and Sprenger, *Animism in Southeast Asia*.
10. Hiebert, Shaw, and Tiénou, *Understanding Folk Religion*, 31–44.
11. Hiebert, Shaw, and Tiénou, 35.

see religion as "an essential component of culture;" thus, folk religion as one outflow of human religiosity is an inevitable and ubiquitous part of every culture.[12] They draw heavily from Clifford Geertz's definition of religion and approach to its study in their analytical model, looking at religion as a system of symbols given meaning by its participants. Hiebert, Shaw, and Tiénou prefer to think of religion as the "beliefs about the ultimate nature of things."[13]

Hiebert, Shaw, and Tiénou use "root metaphors" and "dimensions of scale" to analyze belief systems.[14] Root metaphors include organic metaphors and mechanical metaphors, the former seeing the world as composed of "living beings in relationship with one another" and the latter seeing the world as controlled by impersonal, amoral, and essentially deterministic forces.[15] Dimensions of scale divide the world between immanence and transcendence, with the former representing the empirical human senses and the latter representing "cosmic realms beyond human experience."[16] There is also an in-between stage, the "unseen or transempirical realities of this world."[17]

The lack of consideration for the middle realm is what Hiebert calls the "Flaw of the Excluded Middle."[18] Hiebert is concerned about the lack of engagement of many missionaries who ignore this in-between stage. Hiebert, Shaw, and Tiénou call this middle realm "folk or low religion" along with "magic and astrology."[19] They provide the full typology in their book, which is reproduced (with some explanations left out) in table 1.

---

12. Hiebert, Shaw, and Tiénou, 36.
13. Hiebert, Shaw, and Tiénou, 35.
14. Hiebert, Shaw, and Tiénou, 45–72.
15. Hiebert, Shaw, and Tiénou, 46.
16. Hiebert, Shaw, and Tiénou, 47.
17. Hiebert, Shaw, and Tiénou, 47.
18. Hiebert, "Flaw of the Excluded Middle," 35–47.
19. Hiebert, Shaw, and Tiénou, *Understanding Folk Religion*, 49.

Table 1. Hiebert, Shaw, and Tiénou's framework for analysis of religious systems[20]

Organic Analogy		Mechanical Analogy	
Unseen or Supernatural	**High Religion Based on Cosmic Beings:** cosmic gods, angels, demons, spirits of other worlds	**High Religion Based on Cosmic Forces:** Kismet, fate, Brahman and karma, impersonal cosmic forces	Other Worldly
	Folk or Low Religion: Local gods and goddesses, ancestors and ghosts, spirits, demons and evil spirits, dead saints	**Magic and Astrology:** Mana, astrological forces, charms, amulets, and magical rites, evil eye, evil tongue	This Worldly
Seen or Empirical	**Folk Social Science:** Interaction of living beings such as humans, possibly animals and plants	**Folk Natural Science:** interaction of natural objects based on natural forces	

Hiebert, Shaw, and Tiénou used their typology to briefly explain folk religion in the Chinese, Indian, and Muslim contexts. Hiebert, Shaw, and Tiénou also looked at Thailand, Korea, and places in Africa to illustrate how this model works.[21] The beauty of their model is the ability to use a simple grid with two variables to produce not the typical 4 by 4 categorizations, but something more elaborate and all-encompassing. One downside to this typology is that it seems to try to encompass religion, natural sciences, and everything in between. For our current study, it is useful to also look at a typology focused only on different kinds of religions.

楊鳳崗 [Fenggang Yang] provides such a typology specifically for religion. F. Yang, unhappy with the state of the study of religion in his early years, sought to come up with a better definition and classification of religion. The focus of F. Yang is on the sociological study of religion, specifically with the

---

20. Hiebert, Shaw, and Tiénou, 49
21. Hiebert, Shaw, and Tiénou, 50–72.

methodology used to conduct such studies. F. Yang sees four elements in religion: "(1) a belief in the supernatural, (2) a set of beliefs regarding life and the world, (3) a set of ritual practices manifesting the beliefs, and (4) a distinct social organization of moral community of believers and practitioners."[22] F. Yang includes a table that shows how his definition classifies different types of religions (see table 2).

Table 2. Classification of religions by F. Yang based on his categories[23]

	Supernatural	Beliefs	Practices	Organization	Examples
Full religion	Yes	Yes	Yes	Yes	Christianity, Buddhism, Islam
Semi-religion	Yes	Underdeveloped	Yes	Underdeveloped	Folk or popular religion, magic, spiritualities
Quasi-religion	Yes	Yes	Yes	Diffused	Civil religion, ancestor worship, guild cults
Pseudo-religion	No	Yes	Yes	Yes	Atheism, Confucianism, fetishism

The typology proposed by F. Yang classifies folk religion as a "semireligion." F. Yang does not consider folk religion a "full religion" the same way Christianity, Buddhism, and Islam would be. F. Yang does not treat full and semi-religions differently in inherent value, but only in the method of analysis. It seems that F. Yang wants to study each kind of religion properly, without overemphasizing beliefs over practices. F. Yang believes that the four categories he named better encompass and describe all facets of religious expression in society.

Moreover, F. Yang believes that "there are three major social forces contending to define religion: scholars, believers, and the government."[24] Though

---

22. Yang, *Religion in China*, 36.
23. Yang, 37.
24. Yang, 27.

he was writing in the context of religion in China, he sees universal applicability to this statement. As a scholar, he himself has tried to reshape the definition of religion in his pursuit of a better methodology for the scientific study of religion, a pursuit that has led him to start a journal of the same name and co-write an edited book with Graeme Lang.[25] F. Yang's biography influenced his own thinking as well. He was born in China to a father who is a lifelong Chinese communist party member; he now works as a scholar focusing on religious studies at Purdue University. His scholarly works provided him the reputation as an expert in religious studies in China.

F. Yang argues that for the past few decades, the Chinese government has shaped religious practices significantly in that country.[26] Xinzhong Yao and Yanxia Zhao make the same argument about the three social forces in China.[27] This close tie of the government to definitions and expressions of religions is related to the long history of the emperor cult in China. It is further exaggerated today by the communist party's control over religious definitions in China. Perhaps because of these factors, F. Yang has categorized China's blend of atheism and the emperor cult as "pseudo-religion," which not all scholars would agree on. What F. Yang, Hiebert, Shaw, and Tiénou do agree on is the necessity of using typologies like these to properly understand and study religion. They would argue that having proper typologies is even more important for studies of folk religion, which is often misunderstood and applied either too narrowly or too broadly.

The typologies proposed by Hiebert, Shaw, Tiénou, and F. Yang improve the methodology for religious studies. They help improve understanding of what constitutes folk religion through a more careful understanding of what constitutes religion itself. Scholars studying Chinese folk religion seem to agree with this approach, which is reflected in the many books that include at least one section dealing with Chinese understandings of religion. As just one example, Goosaert and Palmer start their study of China with an examination and redefinition of religion.[28] Like our present study, they seek to explain what folk religion is by explaining what it is not.

---

25. Yang and Lang, *Social Scientific Studies*.
26. Yang, *Religion in China*, 65–84.
27. Yao and Zhao, *Chinese Religion*, 123–45.
28. Goossaert and Palmer, *Religious Question*.

Combining Hiebert, Shaw, Tiénou, and F. Yang's typologies (see table 1 and table 2), we can use the same approach to begin to come to a typological definition of folk religion. F. Yang contrasts folk religion with what he calls "full religions" while Hiebert, Shaw, and Tiénou contrast the same concept with what they call "formal religions." F. Yang sees folk religion as having "underdeveloped" beliefs while Hiebert, Shaw, and Tiénou consider the beliefs to be focusing on different kinds of questions.[29] F. Yang sees an "underdeveloped" organization in folk religion while Hiebert, Shaw, and Tiénou see it as being on a different point on the path of "institutionalization."[30] Hiebert, Shaw, and Tiénou use an organic metaphor to describe folk religion, stressing the interactions between all living beings in relation to one another, a focus prevalent in many examples they studied. They place folk religion between the immanent and the transcendent, also known as the "middle realm."

Not surprisingly, these typologies are not without problems. F. Yang, in his endeavor to anchor the study of religion mainly in social science, misses the organic nature of all kinds of religions, something that Hiebert, Shaw, and Tiénou elaborate on. The terms F. Yang used can be problematic as well. The term *full religion* implies an ideal type for religion, something that is a debate of its own; the term *formal religion* overestimates the formality of religions like Christianity and underestimates the sacredness of some of folk religion's ceremonies. Nevertheless, better terms and typologies have not surfaced in the field; so, for this study's purposes, the present classification is sufficient.

Hiebert, Shaw, and Tiénou show that using root metaphors helps explain the way that folk religion takes shape in society. Hiebert's concept of the middle realm explains folk religion's popularity while giving insight into what to study and what questions to ask of folk religion adherents. F. Yang's four categories show the different aspects of religious expression in society without treating one aspect as superior or inferior. This combined theoretical framework shapes this research's theory and method of analysis with regard to folk religion.

---

29. See Hiebert, Shaw, and Tiénou, *Understanding Folk Religion*, 93–228 for a review of four such kinds of questions.

30. Hiebert, Shaw, and Tiénou, *Understanding Folk Religion*, 331–38.

Traditional Religion

We have looked at a definition of folk religion based on typologies. Now we explore some of the terminologies that scholars prefer to use in order to understand how it is studied. David Burnett prefers the term "traditional religion."[31] He sees the study of this religious system as classified into three phases: "travelers and missionaries, academic anthropologists, and African historians."[32] In Burnett's mind, scholarly understanding of whatever traditional religion constitutes is largely shaped by colonial and postcolonial discourse.

Burnett derives his terminology from Geoffrey Parrinder, who moved away from words like "tribal" or "primitive" and toward attributing the same level of academic importance to African traditional religions as Christianity and Islam.[33] Parrinder's term, while useful in its move away from primitive and derogatory connotations, is still too rooted in colonial studies to accurately describe the African contexts. Nevertheless, some Africans have utilized the term to improve scholarly understanding of religiosity on the continent.

Bọlaji Idowu is one such example. Studying the Yoruba in Nigeria, Idowu argues for a monotheism inherent in some traditional religions.[34] Idowu uses the term "diffused monotheism" to explain his thought. Idowu thinks that the different Yoruba divinities are "no more than conceptualizations of attributes of Olódùmarè."[35] He argues that this Olódùmarè controls all these lesser deities the same way God controls and uses angels to minister to humans. Both Parrinder and Idowu see a variety of beliefs and practices in traditional religions. By contrast, Rosalind Shaw describes the lumping of all these religious expressions into one category as an "invention" by those with Judeo-Christian roots.[36]

---

31. Burnett, *World of the Spirits*, 12.
32. Burnett, 13.
33. Parrinder, *African Traditional Religion*; Parrinder, *Africa's Three Religions*. The book *African Traditional Religion* was first published in 1954. Before Parrinder turned to teaching, he was a missionary in West Africa, having spent time in Côte d'Ivoire. His understanding of and respect for world religions is reflected in his writings, which influenced the study of traditional religion by scholars after him.
34. Idowu, *Olódùmarè*.
35. Idowu, vii.
36. Shaw, "African Traditional Religion," 339.

Nevertheless, some kind of categorization is needed to properly study this field. Invention or not, many belief systems do share broad similarities even if the particulars do not match. Burnett does an excellent job pointing out the problems and inconsistencies in defining traditional religions in the context of the world religions.[37] Universality, sacred texts, doctrines, and level of organization are all areas that scholars have used to point out the superiority of world religions over traditional religions, an evaluation that Burnett sees as problematic. These areas of contrast recall F. Yang's classifications. All in all, Burnett seems to view traditional religions as focusing on spirits, ancestors, and other expressions found in traditional/primitive societies.

In his book, *World of the Spirits*, Burnett spends many chapters dealing with how spirits fit within certain cultures. He has a whole chapter on spirit possession, in which he carefully analyzes the types of possessions encountered particularly in Africa and Micronesia.[38] His explanation of the differences between ghost and spirit was helpful because it clarified the terminology and explained various kinds of ancestral veneration that is prevalent in traditional religion. Burnett thinks that the kinship ties are what keeps an ancestor in contact with family members after death, making the ancestor a spirit instead of a ghost.[39] It is uncertain whether other scholars would define ghost and spirit similarly, but his push for clarity in definitions is a welcome contribution to the field.

Folk Religion

Some have used the term "folk religion" instead of traditional religion to talk about the topic of our study. Instead of stressing the traditional nature of the religious system, they highlight the beliefs and practices adhered to by the average person, the common folk.[40] This implies that folk religion deals with things that the common folk are concerned about, like health, wealth, and kinship. This can be reflected in beliefs and practices regarding the nature of souls, shamanism, divination, and other rituals.

---

37. Burnett, *World of the Spirits*, 22–24.
38. Burnett, 157–73.
39. Burnett, 60.
40. Hiebert, Shaw, and Tiénou, *Understanding Folk Religion*, 75.

The term itself is often said to derive from German Lutheran Paul Drews in 1901, who used the term "*religiöse Volkskund*," which can be translated as "the religious dimension of folk-culture, or the folk-cultural dimension of religion."[41] The term first referred to how Lutheranism may be practiced among the common people in the congregations that Lutheran ministers may encounter.[42] In American scholarship, this term largely developed throughout the twentieth century among cultural anthropologists to describe syncretism in non-American cultures.[43] The term "*religiöse Volkskund*" draws many similarities with what David Hall calls "lived religion"[44] and what Nancy Ammerman calls "everyday religion."[45] The difference in usage is that in non-American cultures, it is called folk religion while the same phenomenon in America is called "lived religion" or "everyday religion."

Burnett distinguishes between "high" and "low" religions. This roughly corresponds to the full and semi religion that F. Yang defines. Drawing on Norman Allison, Burnett sees high religion as answering "cosmic questions" and low religion as dealing with "everyday issues."[46] It is here that Burnett distinguishes between traditional and folk religion. For him, traditional religions are the religious beliefs and practices of a society (usually lower on the scale of modernity). When a major world religion like Christianity comes into contact with such societies, religious syncretism happens as part of the process of conversion; folk religion is the term that explains the resultant everyday beliefs and practices of the average person, the common "folk."[47]

Looking at this definition, Burnett seems to associate folk religion with syncretism and traditional religion with a less syncretistic religiosity. This draws attention to the role of the common people in defining beliefs and practices of a religion, a move that is better for a phenomenological or sociological study of religion. However, Burnett never really explains why he prefers the term *traditional religion* when others prefer the term *folk religion*.[48] Burnett

---

41. Yoder, "Towards a Definition," 2.
42. Yoder, 3.
43. Yoder, 5.
44. Hall, *Lived Religion in America*.
45. Ammerman, *Everyday Religion*.
46. Burnett, *World of the Spirits*, 228.
47. Burnett, 226–40.
48. Yang, *Religion in China*; Hiebert, Shaw, and Tiénou, *Understanding Folk Religion*.

does not explain the significance of using one term rather than the other. This is not a problem particular to Burnett. Many scholars do not spend much time (if any at all) explaining their preferred term. It is unfortunate because one is forced to guess at a scholar's position by reading between the lines. What is helpful is when scholars explain what they mean by their preferred term beyond a one-sentence definition. Hiebert, Shaw, and Tiénou, for example, spend a whole chapter explaining what they mean by folk religion and the detailed classification schemes they use for each type of folk religion.[49] They divide folk religion into two types based on whether it is a small-scale, kin-based society or a large-scale, complex society, a distinction that not many others draw.

Popular Religion

Popular religion is another term that is used. The term rose in popularity in the past few decades. Stephan Feuchtwang, as one of the most cited non-Chinese scholars of Chinese religiosity in the past few decades, is helpful here. Feuchtwang sees the boundaries of *popular religion* as so blurry that he questions whether this concept should even be called *religion*.[50] Burnett at one point uses the term *popular religion* seemingly interchangeably with the idea of folk religion.[51] The only difference was that the context in which he used the term *popular religion* was that of low-income people migrating to urban areas in the midst of modernization. Citing the ethnographic study of Barend J. Terwiel about Buddhists in central Thailand, Burnett sees a difference between the syncretistic popular religion of the uneducated lower class and the "compartmentalized" religiosity of the educated urbanites.[52]

Terwiel's study of folk Buddhism is helpful in understanding folk Buddhism in Taiwan. To better understand the texts, rituals, and overall life of a Buddhist monk, Terwiel wanted to be more than just a participant observer. Terwiel himself was ordained as a monk, practicing for six months before writing his famous work, *Monks and Magic*, originally published in 1975 and now in its fourth edition.

---

49. Hiebert, Shaw, and Tiénou, *Understanding Folk Religion*, 73–94.
50. Stephan Feuchtwang, *Popular Religion*, vi.
51. Burnett, *World of the Spirits*, 239.
52. Burnett, 238.

Terwiel sees Buddhism in his subject village, Wat Sanchao, as syncretistic and "magico-animistic."[53] Like many studies about animism and the usage of this term,[54] the subjects associated with animism are considered somehow less developed than others, at least in their socioeconomic status. Terwiel may see the village Buddhists as less educated, but he does not see village Buddhism as somehow less true than the Buddhism of the urban elites. Rather, it is a kind of Buddhism that pays greater attention to the supernatural, magical elements. Furthermore, it is the most popular kind of Buddhism in Wat Sanchao.

Terwiel's study is part of a larger discussion centered on Robert Redfield's idea of the "great tradition" and the "little tradition."[55] The former describes the religiosity of the societal elites formed by professional ministers while the latter describes the religiosity of the illiterate villagers, which may only bear some resemblance to the authoritative traditions. Therefore, Terwiel is not concerned with popular religion in the same way our present study is, but rather is concerned with how magic fits into the lived Buddhism of the village. Redfield's concept ultimately saw popular religion as the "popular" (widely-practiced) religious expressions of the people, as a "low religion" that builds on "little traditions." To be clear, the terminology involving "low" seems to be merely technical because the authors do not seem to have any kind of conscious derision toward folk religion adherents.

Terwiel's dichotomy of syncretistic village Buddhism and compartmentalized urban Buddhism, while accurate on some levels, has its problems. As many dichotomies go, there may be much more continuity than discontinuity. Even though for Terwiel, the educated urbanites can successfully compartmentalize their religious beliefs and practices from their daily routines, there may be more non-compartmentalization in the urbanites than Terwiel gives credit for. In other words, there may be more practice of "magico-animism," or simply "magic," than what appears on the surface.

This continuity can be illustrated with Jeaneane and Merv Fowler's study on Chinese religiosity. Fowler and Fowler combined their expertise in Daoism and Buddhism into a book meant as an introduction to Chinese religiosity for

---

53. Terwiel, *Monks and Magic*, 4.
54. Tylor, *Primitive Culture*.
55. Redfield, *Peasant Society*.

those with "no previous knowledge of China."[56] Looking at both Chinese and English literatures, they summarize the major beliefs and practices that make up this diverse field. Unlike Terwiel's view that links popular religion to the uneducated rural areas, Fowler and Fowler trace popular religion practiced by "the literati and nobility throughout Chinese history."[57] They define popular religion as "linked with lay belief . . . expressed in localities, and affect[ing] the whole gamut of society extraneous to specifically clerical beliefs and practices, though sometimes these two overlap."[58] Fowler and Fowler show that education and socioeconomic level do not necessarily predict one's adherence to folk religion.

There is much diversity in the popular religious practices in China seeing as they are results of combining local legends with varying interpretations of Chinese philosophy and various major world religions. For scholars studying this kind of religiosity, popular religion represents the beliefs and practices that are popular, that is to say, commonly adhered to and diffused by definition. This diffusion may be what led many authors writing on popular religion to spend considerable time exploring the deities worshipped by different localities in order to understand the essence of the concept.[59]

Folk Belief

We have looked at three popular terms in English. 姚新中 [Xinzhong Yao] and 趙艷霞 [Yanxia Zhao], the former a scholar of Confucianism and the latter of Daoism, see the importance of studying the field in Chinese as well. They take a contextual approach to studying Chinese religion. Like Hiebert, Shaw, and Tiénou, Yao and Zhao understand religion as one dimension of culture. They are careful to analyze the long histories of development for each of the so-called indigenous religions, the cultural changes during certain periods, and thematic crossovers between beliefs and practices. As such, their book *Chinese Religion* has no chapters on specific religions, but rather is organized around specific themes such as family, history, and state. The logic

---

56. Fowler and Fowler, *Chinese Religions*, ix.
57. Fowler and Fowler, 224.
58. Fowler and Fowler, 224.
59. See Fowler and Fowler, 227–38.

seems to be that this thematic approach is better than traditional approaches at explaining Chinese religiosity.

The English word religion has a Chinese counterpart: 宗教 (*zong jiao*). *Zong*, the first character for the word religion, refers to one's ancestors or ancestral traditions. Yao and Zhao write, "The character *zong* informs us that religion was perceived as something that was related to sacrifice or worship that took place in a roofed building."[60] The evolution of Chinese characters from the earliest 甲骨文 (*jiaguwen*, oracle bone script originating from writings on carapace bones) to our modern-day versions shows strong evidence of this link.

Jiao, the second character in the word religion, refers to some kind of teaching. The word commonly used today for religion therefore has meant "teaching of the ancestors" until recent times. Many believe it is not until the early twentieth century that *zong jiao* is used to be the equivalent of religion in English.[61] The close tie of religion and ancestors has been noticed by other scholars too.

Yao and Zhao describe folk religion, in part, as ancestral veneration and animistic cults. They subscribe to the diffused religion model proposed by C. K. Yang and add an element that describes the intentional conflation of categories.[62] They explain this conflation thus,

> religion in China is characterized by an ambiguity in differentiation or classification; in other words, the difference between the secular and the religious, or between the profane and the holy which is held highly in many other cultures, seems to have been either deliberately reduced to minimum or subconsciously left unclarified.[63]

They argue that in the ancient form found on oracle bone inscriptions, the first character used for culture, 文化 (*wenhua*), "portrays a frontal view of a man with tattoo on his chest," which relates to either nature or ancestral

---

60. Yao and Zhao, *Chinese Religion*, 31.
61. Thompson, *Chinese Religion*, xxiii.
62. Yao and Zhao, *Chinese Religion*, 2.
63. Yao and Zhao, 193. The sharp dichotomy that Yao and Zhao say is "held highly in many other cultures" is never given a clear source. They do not mention what other cultures do this. Context suggests that they are referring to the so-called "West."

veneration.[64] They conclude that the character's origin "speaks volumes for the primary position of religion in Chinese culture."[65]

Looking at the characters used in "religion" show that the home was central to Chinese religiosity at some point in time. Whether this continues today remains to be proven. Looking at the characters used in "culture" show that religion was central to Chinese culture at some point in time, if not today. The point is that Chinese culture has deep roots in religion, which often finds expression in people's homes and their daily lives. Put another way, the daily life of the general population shows aspects of Chinese religiosity, whether it is through seeking shamans or venerating ancestors.

This may be the reason that in Taiwan, the most popular term used to describe folk religion is 民間信仰 (*min jian xin yang*, "folk belief" or "beliefs held by the general population"). Popular usage of the term refers to a wide spectrum of beliefs and practices ranging from ancestral veneration to Mazu tours. Many of the practices are celebrated as part of Taiwanese culture regardless of a person's religious affiliation. Though there is general, popular consensus on preference for this term, scholars do nevertheless debate occasionally whether another term is preferable.[66]

謝國興 [Kuo-Hsing Hsieh] explains that the term 民間信仰 (folk belief) originated in Japanese literature in 1897.[67] In 1930, Chinese scholarly literature on the topic started adopting this same term to replace the then common term of 迷信 (*míxìn*, "superstition"). Origin aside, Hsieh explains that the term *folk belief* used in Chinese literature is used to cover the same field of scholarship that English literature calls folk religion. Both of those terms refer to the same field, namely a kind of religion that is distinctly different from organized religion.

The contours of folk belief in Taiwan are influenced by Shintoism in Japan. From 1895 to 1945, the island of Taiwan was a Japanese colony. 中島 三千男 [Michio Nakajima] explains the rise of Shintoism in Taiwan.[68] The first Shinto shrine in Taiwan was erected in July 1896. Local religions and beliefs

---

64. Yao and Zhao, 78.
65. Yao and Zhao, 78.
66. Wong, "Chinese Folk Religion," 153.
67. Hsieh 謝, *Pilgrimages, Sacrifice Offerings* 進香．醮．祭與社會文化變遷, 3.
68. Nakajima, "Shinto Deities that Crossed the Sea," 26–31.

were actively regulated, especially after the Xialaian Incident of 1915. After the Manchurian Incident of 1931, there was a 国民教化運動 (*Kokumin kyōka undo*, "Japanese national indoctrination movement"). The official government policy was to "emphasize worship at Shinto shrines while discouraging local religious customs and rituals."[69] All these efforts led to faster propagation of the Shinto idea of deities and worship in the public eye. During the entire Japanese colonial period in Taiwan, 68 shrines were erected and 116 semi-shrines were erected.

Japanese efforts of cultural assimilation, specifically in the area of religion, had a significant impact on Taiwanese religiosity and thinking. For example, some existing Buddhists temples were modified to introduce deities more popular in Japan (i.e. *Kṣitigarbha* [地藏]). However, at least one underlying aspect of religiosity is the same, namely that deities play an important role in the daily lives of people and in the cultural fabric of society. 菅 浩二 [Kōji Suga] cites influential Shinto scholar 小笠原 省三 [Shōzō Ogasawara], "Shinto shrines are 'sites for the performance of the state ritual' of course, but forcibly maintaining entities alienated from peoples' actual lives through state power would make shrines lose their religious nature."[70] Therefore, even though Japanese influence exists, the scope of this study as well as its qualitative nature makes further discussion on Shintoism unnecessary.

Even with some debates and regardless of its Japanese origin, folk belief seems to be the most used term in Chinese language literature in Taiwan. Even among people who use other terms like folk practice or folk religion in their English translations,[71] they still use folk belief in the original Chinese. If Thompson is right that the term religion was not part of Chinese vocabulary until the twentieth century, then the Chinese choice of terms makes perfect sense. Moreover, the term belief (the same word used for faith) versus religion may be indicative of the way that Chinese think of religion, specifically pointing out the diffused, unorganized nature of faith practices as opposed to religious doctrines.

---

69. Nakajima, "Shinto Deities that Crossed the Sea," 31
70. Suga, "Concept of 'Overseas Shinto Shrines,'" 51.
71. Lin 林, *Dà Miào Chéng* 大廟埕; Hsieh 謝, *Pilgrimages, Sacrifice Offerings* 進香．醮．祭與社會文化變遷; Lin 林, *Táiwān Mínjiān Xìnyǎng Yánjiū Shūmù* 台灣民間信仰研究書目.

Term of Choice

We have finally discussed four important terms that different scholars have used to discuss our topic. Considering the chapter title, it should be no surprise to the reader that this work's term of choice is folk religion. The rationale is explained here. The term religion is important to ground our entire study, especially considering Hiebert, Shaw, Tiénou, and F. Yang's typologies of religion. The term traditional religion, with its association with colonial discourse, is too outdated to be useful here. The term folk religion is the most common term in scholarly literature, drawing attention to the "folk-cultural dimension of religion."[72] The term popular religion draws attention to societal popularity instead of the educational or socioeconomic level of the common folk. In Chinese literature, 民間信仰 (folk belief) is the preferred term. There exists other terms, like *vernacular religion*,[73] that are not covered due to space. All these terms have their nuances but for the most part refer to the same body of literature. For example, Chinese scholarship on folk belief seems to reference the same body of literature from which scholarship on folk religion draws. Namely, both draw from what many in the field call Chinese folk religion.

This study uses the term folk religion. It does not treat folk religion as somehow a lower form of religion compared to institutionalized religion. The way folk religion is used is more akin to Hall's lived religion and Ammerman's everyday religion. The term *folk religion in Taiwan* refers to the type of lived, everyday religion that is commonly seen among Taiwanese people. Folk religion in Taiwan can be a subset of Chinese folk religion in the sense that there are many local expressions of folk religion in Chinese societies, with Taiwan's various localities being only a small percentage of the localities. Folk religion in Taiwan can be an extension of Chinese folk religion in the sense that many of the cultural-religious history (i.e. Daoism, Buddhism) and current social practices (i.e. ancestral veneration) are shared. Exactly how Chinese religiosity is expressed and how they fit with the lived reality of Taiwanese people are topics for the next section.

---

72. Yoder, "Towards a Definition," 2.
73. Primiano, "Vernacular Religion," 37–56.

Chinese Religiosity

Terminology aside, what does Chinese religiosity look like? Laurence Thompson is useful here as an influential scholar on Chinese religiosity. His book *Chinese Religion* is now in its fifth edition and widely cited. Thompson is insistent on the singular form "Chinese Religion" to describe the field rather than the plural form that others like Fowler and Fowler prefer. Scholars like Fowler and Fowler see the various religious traditions of Confucianism, Buddhism, and others as distinct entities to be studied separately as opposed to the unified whole that others like Thompson have proposed. Thompson prefers the singular because he believes that "the character of religious expression in China is above all a *manifestation of the Chinese culture*."[74]

Thompson's view is consistent with Feuchtwang, Yao and Zhao, and many other scholars of Chinese religion. Thompson uses the stronger phrase "manifestation of culture" as opposed to Hiebert, Shaw, and Tiénou's phrase "dimension of culture." By using the word "manifestation," Thompson highlights the "Chinese-ness" in every religious expression in Chinese societies. His chart at the beginning of the book that links many religious traditions to each other is a great example of this kind of thinking.[75] Thompson sees the diffused religiosity that C. K. Yang proposes. He thinks the insistence "Western" societies put on doctrine is unhelpful in understanding Chinese religiosity.[76] In Thompson's mind, what set the study of Chinese religiosity apart from other studies are the religious expressions Chinese people practice while not belonging to specific religious sects.

Ancient Beliefs

Many scholars of Chinese folk religion spend the first few chapters of their books dealing with the beliefs and associated worldview of the ancient Chinese. Thompson for example devotes two chapters to the topic. Even subsequent chapters that deal with subjects like Daoism or Confucianism detail their long histories back to the ancient times that birthed these beliefs

---

74. Thompson, *Chinese Religion*, xxiii, emphasis in original.
75. Thompson, xx–xxi.
76. Since Thompson does not specify what he means by "Western," one has to guess that Thompson is likely referring to North America and Western Europe.

and worldviews. This chapter follows that trend and explores two significant beliefs dating back to ancient China.

Highest in the Heavens

Thompson explains that the Chinese viewed the world as having a "law without a lawgiver."[77] At the same time, there is a "personalized power of conspicuous importance" that people have referred to as 上帝 (*Shangdi/Shang Ti*). This *Shangdi* represents the supreme ruler of the heavens. The heavens, or 天 (*Tien*) in Chinese, was an even higher, more ambiguous, and more transcendent power than *Shangdi*.[78] In modern usage, *tien* often means the sky or the heavens; however, its religious idea of transcendent power is still in popular usage.

Tien became synonymous with the concept of *Shangdi* sometime in the 周 (Zhou) dynasty.[79] Some see *Shangdi* as reflecting a monotheism in Chinese religiosity, which would make it similar to Idowu's diffused monotheism concept. In this view, all the other deities would be "ministers" of the one God *Shangdi*. However, others see *Shangdi* as reflecting pantheism due to how many deities are "ministering." Commenting on the various views, Yao and Zhao do not give a definitive answer but rather write, "the Chinese compound of beliefs is multi-layered or multi-dimensional; these different layers and dimensions may be in harmony or may seem to be in opposition to each other, but together they are highly functional."[80] In other words, the monotheism or polytheism does not matter to the Chinese; what matters is functionality and utility in life. Whatever the conclusion, scholars agree that folk religion in Chinese societies is ultimately rooted in the ancient beliefs of *Tien* and the accompanying worldview.

Shangdi is still a big part of Chinese religious thinking, especially in folk religions. Popularity can be attested by the fact that the word *Shangdi* is used in translations for God in the Bible. Sangkeun Kim details the history of why Matteo Ricci and others came to this decision.[81] Today *Shangdi* is revered for

---

77. Thompson, *Chinese Religion*, 1–2.
78. Yao and Zhao, *Chinese Religion*, 154–55.
79. The Zhou dynasty was from the eleventh to the third centuries BC, which is the third earliest dynasty in China. Thompson, *Chinese Religion*, 3.
80. Yao and Zhao, *Chinese Religion*, 149.
81. Kim, *Strange Names of God*.

most types of folk religion that adherents practice. Because it is nigh impossible to commune with *Shangdi*, people still rely on local deities and shamans. Each emperor of China is said to be able to commune with the heavenly realm, hence the other name for emperors 天子 (*Tiānzǐ*, Son of *Tien*). Beginning with the legendary 黃帝 (*Huangdi*, Yellow Emperor), each of the subsequent 皇帝 (*Huangdi*, royal emperor) have earthly authority because of the divine lineage, namely by having ancestors who dwell with *Shangdi* himself.[82] This may not have technically given the emperors divinity, but they were treated as such. Coupled with their identities as sons of the dragon, this naturally explains the continuing influence of the imperial cult through the ages.[83] The same imperial cult is reflected in the ancestral cult, both being rooted in the reverence of a higher power who has influence over one's life.

Oldest of the Classic Texts

Thompson gathered the information from 書經 (*Shujing*), also known as 尚書 (*shangshu*), which is one of the five classic texts. The oldest of the five classics is the 易經 (*Yijing/I Ching*), which is the main interest for Fowler and Fowler. The *Yijing* began as a divination text not associated with any religious tradition but has since been used and interpreted in such a way that scholars believe Chinese culture is heavily influenced by it. It is a book of philosophy and explains the inter-relationship of things in the cosmos.

The words *yi* and *jing* themselves can be interpreted to mean a number of things. Fowler and Fowler interpret *yi* as "transformation" and *jing* as "warp."[84] Fowler and Fowler have accurately interpreted the first word, but the second word most likely means "famous work" or "classic." Since the *Yijing* is readily seen as the first of the "Five Classics," a fact that Fowler and Fowler themselves agree with, the "classic" translation makes more sense.[85] The term *Yijing* is thus best translated as "Classic of Changes" (a popular translation).

The *Yijing* has a section called the book of oracles that talks about something called 八卦 (*bagua*, eight trigrams). One *bagua* can be combined with another *bagua* to form an octagonal shape with sixty-four different

---

82. Thompson, *Chinese Religion*, 69.
83. Priest, "'Who Am I?,'" 175–92.
84. Fowler and Fowler, *Chinese Religions*, 39.
85. Fowler and Fowler, 39.

combinations.⁸⁶ *Bagua* is a series of eight symbols representing different parts of the cosmos (heaven, fire, lightning, wind, water, etc.). They also represent health, Chinese zodiac, body parts, direction, the elements, and family members. For example, the symbol ☰ represents heaven, father, south, gold, and other things depending on the context and the combination with another *bagua*. As a powerful tool for oracles, bagua is used to divine everything from the weather to the alignment of the heavens to the fortune of a person. Living up to its name, this method of divination is still widely used today in Taiwan by specialists.⁸⁷ See figure 1 for a picture of *bagua* in the streets of Taipei.

Figure 1. A red *bagua* symbol hanging above the garage door of an apartment

As a popular slang word, *bagua* means "gossip." It is usually used in the context of some story about a celebrity or comprehensive information about said celebrity. The idea is that this word, which originates from the *Yijing* and

---

86. Fowler and Fowler, 44–47.
87. Fowler and Fowler, 244; Yao and Zhao, *Chinese Religion*, 185–92.

has deep philosophical and religious elements, is still widely used today. Based on the *Yijing*, proper usage of *bagua* can generate comprehensive information about a person, including the person's future. Whether it is divining one's future through a shaman or divining a celebrity's secret through a paparazzi, *bagua* still retains the idea of divination. The term is popularly used in both senses depending on the context. This shows another example of the prevalence of religion in Chinese popular culture, namely that even words like "gossip" have religious connotations.

Religious Behaviors

Many scholars of Chinese folk religion note the impact of the ancient beliefs of *Tien* and *Shangdi* along with documents like *Shujing* or *Yijing* in various contemporary folk religion's practices and beliefs.[88] Of particular note is Meir Shahar and Robert Weller's edited volume *Unruly Gods*, which notes in detail how these ancient beliefs are seen today.[89] For example, the idea of 陰 (*yin*, dark/negative) and 陽 (*yang*, bright/positive) along with 太極 (*Taiji/Tai Chi*, the source) comes from the *Yijing*. The concept of 孝 (*xiao*, filial piety) is also derived from the *Yijing*. Thompson notes that *xiao* is so pervasive in Chinese culture that he calls it the "motivating ideal."[90] It is an ideal that perpetuates the cult of the ancestors, leading to the ancestral veneration still happening today.[91] Xinzhong Yao and Paul Badham found in their own four-year study of religion in China that, despite the fact that only 8.7 percent of people claim to be religious, 28.9 percent believe in receiving rewards due to proper ancestral veneration and 77.2 percent believe in the changing of fortunes through accumulating virtues (like diligently practicing *xiao*).[92] Yao and Baham's data show that self-ascribed religious identity can sometimes be very different from actual religious behavior.

Most see the linkage of *xiao* with Confucian teaching. However, the concept itself dates back even further. 焦國成 [Guocheng Jiao] and 趙艷霞 [Yanxia Zhao] examined the evolution of the character *xiao* in various

---

88. Clart, "Chinese Tradition," 84–97; Weller, "Matricidal Magistrates," 250–68; Shahar and Weller, *Unruly Gods*.
89. Shahar and Weller, *Unruly Gods*.
90. Thompson, *Chinese Religion*, 36.
91. Thompson, 40–52.
92. Yao and Badham, *Religious Experience*, 153–64.

writings, including ancient oracle bones, to trace the etymology of the word.[93] They also looked at certain historical documents, particularly from the 周 (Zhou) dynasty. Jiao and Zhao determined that the word *xiao* does not originally refer to filial piety, but rather to 「繼志述事」 ("worshipping ancestors and carrying out their behest").[94] Their central thesis is that *xiao* has evolved from god-orientation to people-orientation over time. Their conclusion is that *xiao* itself is loaded with religious history. Especially at home, in addition to the myriad of gods that one may place at the family shrine, the ancestors always retain a place on the altar.[95] Yao and Zhao see ancestral veneration as "a bedrock belief running through all stages of Chinese civilization and playing a crucial part in the state as well as folk religion."[96]

Scholars note that other religious behaviors can be seen in folk religion's many temples, especially in Taiwan. These temples are oftentimes organized and run by the laity, who provide the funding, administration, and sometimes even the services.[97] Richard Madsen traces the political history of Taiwan to stress just how important folk religion's temples have become in establishing Taiwan's national identity.[98] Folk religion is thus, at least for Taiwan, not just a religious question but a political one as well. These scholars agree that the continuing practice of offering incense to deities and ancestors is an aspect of Chinese religiosity that is as old as the *Yijing* and strengthened by political forces since then. The whole endeavor serves to guide Chinese societies to do two things: be moral and pass on important cultural elements. It is no wonder that 范麗珠 [Lizhu Fan] calls Chinese religiosity "moralization by sacred ways."[99]

---

93. Jiao 焦 and Zhao 趙, "'Xiào'de Lìshǐ Mìngyùn Jí Qí Yuánshǐ Yìyùn," '孝'的歷史命運及其原始意蘊, 5–10.

94. Today, 「繼志述事」 is best translated as "continuing the legacy of the past in living out the present." Jiao and Zhao were likely referring to what the phrase meant in more ancient times.

95. Fowler and Fowler, *Chinese Religions*, 246–49.

96. Yao and Zhao, *Chinese Religion*, 111–12.

97. Fowler and Fowler, *Chinese Religions*, 242.

98. Madsen, "Secular State," 291–94.

99. Fan, "Chinese Religious Studies," 90.

Imperial Cults

One such political force is again religious in nature, namely the imperial cult. Feuchtwang spends much time explaining how politics played a role in shaping Chinese folk religion.[100] Elsewhere, he tackles how the politics of mainland China and Taiwan affected folk religion. The cult of Mao stands out as particularly blurring the line between what is considered religion versus secular. The irony noted is that, despite being an officially atheist state, the near-deified status of Chairman Mao means that politics play a big factor in understanding religion in China. F. Yang notes the same phenomenon in the veneration of Chairman Mao both before and after his death.[101] F. Yang tackles the bigger phenomenon of how religion not just survived, but revived under communist rule.[102]

郭承天 [Cheng-Tian Kuo] looks at the same idea in Taiwan. A professor of political science, his main research interest is religion in politics. He employed case studies of more than seventy interviews along with statistical analysis to find out how religion affected democracy, and vice versa. Kuo found that a particular religion's influence on democracy depended on its "political theology, ecclesiology, and interaction with the state."[103] Presbyterians in Taiwan were especially influential in propagating much of the democratic ideals in the early days of the republican government (Kuomintang, KMT). Regardless of influence, Kuo notes how every religion seems to draw out and emphasize aspects of the Taiwanese democratic ideals, showing influence both ways.

The political aspect of folk religion continues in Taiwan today. Every year, political candidates appear in many religious ceremonies around election times, seemingly to draw the approval and vote of Taiwanese people. House Gongon, one of the interview participants, drew attention to this trend, specifically with a particular Mazu festival. He is very unhappy with the trend but understands it as part of election campaigning. In other words, just like praying to the Christian deity is a widely accepted positive action for American politicians, showing reverence to folk religion deities like Mazu is a widely accepted positive action for Taiwanese politicians.

---

100. Feuchtwang, *Popular Religion in China*, 27–95.
101. Yang, "Exceptionalism or Chinamerica," 18.
102. Yang, *Religion in China*.
103. Kuo, *Religion and Democracy*, 115.

Folk Religion in Taiwan

So far, we have explored several terminologies used to describe what is referred to as "folk religion." We have also explored Chinese religiosity. This next section focuses on how this religiosity is expressed in the context of Taiwan, which sets the foundation for what is folk religion in Taiwan.

A Tentative Definition

Thus far, this chapter has not clearly explained the following: what is Chinese religiosity and what defines folk religion in Taiwan? Fenggang Yang and Anning Hu, in the article "Chinese Folk Religion in Mainland China and Taiwan," used surveys to map out folk religion into three types: communal, sectarian, and individual.[104] Yang and Hu treat "Chinese folk religion" as a field of study with particular localities (i.e. Taiwan) having particular expressions. Most scholars in the field note the commonality of Taiwan and China on a worldview level (i.e. how adherents view the cosmos). The differences exist in how well accepted folk religion is in the two countries, the popularity level of various deities, and the local deities unique to each country.

To better suit the Taiwanese context, Mei-Rong Lin [林美容] classifies folk religion in Taiwan into three main categories:「民間信仰」("folk belief"),「民間教派」("folk religion sect"), and「民間俗信」("folk customs").[105] Throughout the book, M.-R. Lin includes multiple subtypes in each category, detailing numerous deities, temples, rituals, festivities, operas, folk songs, and more. The idea is that folk religion in Taiwan should not be seen as one religion, but rather as various expressions of Taiwanese religiosity based on different beliefs. Moreover, these expressions show up in different forms and are directed at different deities. Over time, they result in cultural customs that influence every person in society.

To use M.-R. Lin's typology, ancestral veneration is one expression of folk religion in Taiwan; so is Mazu worship; so are the many temples dedicated to many deities; so is a belief in the effects of *yin-yang* in one's daily life; so is any kind of religious expression not classified as a "world religion." Even some established religions, including Christianity, see only a blended, "folk"

---

104. Yang and Hu, "Mapping Chinese Folk Religion."
105. Lin 林, *Táiwān Mínjiān Xìnyǎng Yánjiū Shūmù* 台灣民間信仰研究書目, xiii.

expression in Taiwan.[106] All the aforementioned possible expressions of folk religion in Taiwan see parallels in different places in China.[107] So, even though this chapter focuses specifically on folk religion in Taiwan, it has drawn from the larger corpus of literature about Chinese folk religion.

As for a more precise, all-encompassing definition, Tamney's definition of what constitutes folk religion is used for this work:

> Chinese Folk Religion, in its present form dating back to the Sung Dynasty (960–1279), includes elements traceable to prehistoric times (ancestor worship, shamanism, divination, a belief in ghosts, and sacrificial rituals to the spirits of sacred objects and places) as well as aspects of Buddhism, Confucianism, and Taoism. Buddhist elements include believing in karma and rebirth, accepting Buddha and other bodhisattvas as gods, and using Buddhist meditational techniques. The Confucian influence is the concept of filial piety and associated practices. The numerous gods are organized into a hierarchy headed by the Jade Emperor, a deity borrowed from Taoism. Important annual rituals reflect their origin in an agrarian way of life (e.g., a harvesttime festival) but have been given new or additional meaning to accord with the ancestral cult or Buddhism. The religion is not centrally organized and lacks a formal canon. Rituals take place before home altars or at temples, which have no fixed congregations. Adherents vary considerably in belief and practice. Generally, folk religionists are fatalistic yet believe that one's luck can be affected by pleasing ancestors or gods, by locating graves and buildings in places where vital natural forces are located (geomancy), and by balancing opposing forces (yin, yang) within one's body.[108]

This definition accurately and succinctly captures the essence as well as the scope of folk religion. While speaking specifically about Chinese folk religion,

---

106. Brown and Cheng, "Religious Relations," 68.
107. Yang and Hu, "Mapping Chinese Folk Religion."
108. Tamney, "Asian Popular Religions."

Tamney's definition applies to Chinese societies more broadly, including Taiwan. The next section shows why that is true.

The Taiwanese Context

Recall the discussion on the ancient oracle bone scripts revealing the evolution of certain words in Chinese. These words, the belief about *Tien*, the veneration of ancestors, the nature of religiosity, Confucianism, Buddhism, and many more elements are shared between China and Taiwan. After all, before 1949, the two countries were just one. In terms of politics and certain parts of culture, China and Taiwan has diverged since 1949. However, the religious elements that predate 1949 are shared. Many scholars have picked up on this, and thus either conflate or compare certain findings about folk religion and the religious market using data from both countries.[109]

These findings are sometimes categorized specifically as folk religion while other times as Chinese religion(s). Laurence Thompson is insistent on the singular form "Chinese Religion"[110] to describe the field rather than the plural form that others like Jeaneane and Merv Fowler prefer.[111] Fowler and Fowler see the various religious traditions of Confucianism, Buddhism, and others as distinct entities to be studied separately. But Thompson prefers the singular form because he believes that one cannot truly understand Chinese religiosity until one understands the shared foundation of all the different expressions, namely Chinese culture.

In Taiwan, the cultural element of folk religion is even more pronounced. Folk religion and the many temples associated with it form an important part of Taiwanese culture.[112] M.-H. Lin describes the temple courtyard as a social as well as religious center, a place where older people sit to play Chinese chess while younger children play educational games, a place where important news is heralded while holidays are celebrated. There are artistic displays at temples, including 布袋戲 (puppet plays) and 歌仔戲 (Chinese operas). The way M.-H. Lin describes it, most temples in Taiwan function more as a community center than a worship center. 台北霞海城隍廟 (Taipei Xiahai City

---

109. Zhai, "Contrasting Trends," 94–111; Madsen, "Secular State"; Yang and Hu, "Mapping Chinese Folk Religion"; Chang and Penny, *Religion in Taiwan*.

110. Thompson, *Chinese Religion*, xxiii.

111. Fowler and Fowler, *Chinese Religions*.

112. Lin 林, *Dà Miào Chéng* 大廟埕.

God Temple) is one such example. As figure 2 shows, the temple is always packed with people. This temple has a website that lists the multiple events happening at this temple, usually on major holidays like the Lantern Festival or deity birthdays.[113] The events include puppet shows, dancing, parades, and multiple fun celebrations in which people from all over Taipei participate.

Figure 2. 台北霞海城隍廟 **(Taipei Xiahai City God Temple)**

Nevertheless, religious rituals abound in these temples, varying in specific expressions depending on the deity. Among the Taiwanese deities worshipped, Mazu tops the list in popularity. Some scholars have used certain Mazu temples or rituals as a religious model to explain Taiwanese religiosity in general. M.-R. Lin and Chen explain that the Makang Mazu Temple (located on a small island north of Taiwan) likely originated because of a drifting corpse.[114] They argue that the common saying 「浮屍立廟」 (*fúshī lì miào*, "see a drifting corpse, build a temple") sees its real-life occurrence not only

---

113. See http://www.tpecitygod.org/en-about-xia-hai01.html#en-xiahia-e00.

114. Lin 林 and Chen 陳, "Mǎzǔ Lièdǎo de Fúshī Lì Miào Yánjiū, 馬祖列島的浮屍立廟研究： 從馬港天后宮談起," 127.

at Makang, but on many cities in eastern China as well. M.-R. Lin and Chen believe that the saying *fúshī lì miào* represents a more deep-rooted idea of the cosmos, typifying Chinese people's beliefs about *yin-yang*, stability, and death. The very act of building a temple, in light of this concept, signifies wanting to turn a dark/negative (*yin*) situation into a bright/positive (*yang*) situation. M.-R. Lin and Chen used a specific locality to show how many elements of folk religion in Taiwan play out in wider society. The implication is that the origin of many temples, if not the origin of many deities themselves, come from dark/negative occurrences in the world.

蔡怡佳 [Yi-Jia Tsai] broadens the scope to argue that elements of folk religion are found within "world religions" like Buddhism and Christianity.[115] Using qualitative interviews, Y.-J. Tsai saw the same attitude on 修行 [*xiūxíng*, cultivating oneself] in both Buddhists and Christians in Taiwan. The detailed comparison between this same concept in the two religions reveals a Taiwanese worldview that treats "the divine" in a certain way, described by Y.-J. Tsai as 「祭神而有所求」 (*jìshén ér yǒu suǒ qiú*, "worship god because there is a need").[116] This utilitarian perspective of deities is very important and was seen repeatedly in the qualitative interviews.

Most interviewees expressed this utilitarian viewpoint as they discussed their participation in ancestral veneration. This research revealed a straightforward reciprocity in their practices. People pray and make offerings to ancestors in hopes of gaining their continued blessings and protection in current endeavors. For some scholars, ancestral veneration is the archetype for Chinese folk religion.[117] For others, the prominence of ancestral veneration is itself an interesting topic of study, shaping Taiwanese culture and identity.[118] Culturally speaking, 孝 (*xiao*, filial piety), influenced by Confucianism, is one of the most prominent ethics in Taiwan. In this case, the ethic is rooted in religious ideology and is expressed through veneration or worship. See figure 3 for an ancestral veneration offering that includes paper money and some of the deceased's favorite foods.

---

115. Tsai 蔡, "Yǔ Fú Xiāngyìng, Yǔ Shén Xiāng Qì, 與佛相應，與神相契：臺灣佛教徒與基督徒的祈禱修行體驗," 51–78.

116. Tsai 蔡, 52.

117. Yao and Zhao, *Chinese Religion*.

118. Nadeau and Chang, "Gods, Ghosts, and Ancestors," 280–99.

Figure 3. An offering to the researcher's grandfather, right before burning incense

Janet Scott details the acts involved in "worshipping ancestors," which has many parallels with how folk religion in Taiwan treats gods and ghosts.[119] The acts include paper money offerings, food offerings, and incense burning. They serve to either honor the gods, care for the ancestors, or protect against the ghosts. Scott outlines in detail many other acts and rituals, which shows the depth of this widespread folk religion ritual.

Folk religion in Taiwan adds modern day adaptations to a long history of traditional practices based on ancient beliefs. For example, ancestral veneration can be seen as an extension of the importance of filial piety, a concept that Confucianism stresses. The burning of incense and silver paper money can thus be seen as societal incarnations of filial piety. Few temples explain the theology of ancestors, their role in the everyday lives of individuals, and our role in their well-being in the afterlife. Yet people hold on to these ideas despite having no centralized theology. People uphold ancestral

---

119. Scott, *For Gods, Ghosts and Ancestors*.

veneration's importance as a tradition that is an essential part of being an ethically "good" person.

In light of this reality, 范麗珠 [Lizhu Fan] argues that Chinese religiosity is best seen not as following a list of doctrines given by a supernatural being but rather as living a moral life in light of the assumed existence of the supernatural. Fan calls this the "moralization by sacred way."[120] Fan points out that living morally is more important than discerning what is sacred or supernatural. In other words, behaving rightly in this world is the focus of Chinese religiosity, not understanding or worshipping whatever may lie beyond this world. The latter is acted on only insofar as it helps the former.

Chinese religiosity expresses itself very strongly in folk religion in Taiwan. The average person does not need to understand much theology about a local expression of folk religion. To borrow Fan's terms, this person just needs to "moralize by sacred ways," with the "way" being a local deity in a local temple. 鄭志明 [Chih Ming Cheng] explains how this "way" intersects with the average person's lived reality,

> 非組織性的民間信仰，其宗教理念與儀式混合在生活制度與風俗習慣之中，成為民眾習以為常的宗教情感與宗教經驗，學界慣稱為「民間信仰」，意旨民眾生活下的信仰系統，發展出百姓日用而不知的心靈價值世界 (Non-organized folk belief, whose religious concepts and rituals are mixed in the regimen of life and social customs, become the religious sentiments and religious experiences that people are accustomed to. Academia calls it "folk belief," meaning the belief system that frames the everyday living of the common people. It expresses a value system in the spiritual world that people are unaware of but nevertheless apply in daily life).[121]

Cheng's explanation of folk religion in Taiwan highlights, above all, that "everyday living" in "the regimen of life" is the focus of folk belief.

---

120. Fan, "Chinese Religious Studies," 90.

121. Cheng 鄭, "Jìn wǔshí niánlái táiwān dìqū mínjiān zōngjiào zhī yánjiū yǔ qiánzhān, 近五十年來臺灣地區民間宗教之研究與前瞻," 127.

Culture in Temples, Folk Beliefs, and Society

林茂賢 [Mao-Hsien Lin] wrote an influential book on the myriad of folk religion expressions in Taiwan.[122] These expressions have different deities, have different beliefs linked to them, are varied in popularity depending on the geographic locations, and reflect different aspects of Taiwanese culture. The title of his book is 《大廟埕: 林茂賢臺灣民俗選集》 [*Big Temple Courtyard: Selected Works of Lin Mao-Hsien on Taiwanese Folk Practices*].

Both explicitly and implicitly, M.-H. Lin argues for the close relationship of culture and folk religion in Taiwan, namely that folk religion is often an expression of culture. M.-H. Lin explains, 「廟會文化是台灣文化的縮影，在廟會中可以看到台灣人民的人文、藝術、信仰的呈現，也反映台灣民間的價值觀」 ("Temple culture is a microcosm of Taiwanese culture; in temples, one can see the portrayal of Taiwanese humanities, arts, and religiosity. This also reflects the Taiwanese folk value system").[123] Temples are not just religious centers that show a particular religion or belief system, but rather they have influenced Taiwanese culture to the extent that both are reflections of each other. This explains why M.-H. Lin, who at one time was a professor of cultural studies, is a leading expert on folk religion in Taiwan with a special focus on the folk religion's customs and artistic expressions.

Randall Nadeau and Hsun Chang make the linkage between Taiwanese culture and religion even more explicit, making folk religion an essential part of Taiwanese identity.[124] Wai Yip Wong sees the same interchangeability of culture and folk religion, "Chinese folk religion can be understood as a social cultural mixture of religiously [sic] traditions."[125] To scholars like M.-H. Lin, Nadeau, Chang, and Wong, Chinese folk religion is best described as a term that points not to institutional tradition, but rather to the culture shaped by folk belief over thousands of years. Perhaps there is something to be said for the inextricable relationship between culture and religion, especially folk religion.[126] See figure 4 for an example of a parade with Guan Shengdijun (the person with a red face) in a famous night market in Taipei. See figure 5 for

---

122. Lin 林, *Dà Miào Chéng* 大廟埕.
123. Lin 林, 443.
124. Nadeau and Chang, "Gods, Ghosts, and Ancestors."
125. Wong, "Chinese Folk Religion," 154.
126. Yang, *Religion in Chinese Society*, 294.

a temple located next to looming buildings, showing that temples in Taiwan co-exist with modern architecture.

Figure 4. Parade at 西門町 (Ximending), a famous night market in Taipei, Taiwan

Figure 5. A Mazu temple next to modern buildings on a street in 新竹 (Hsinchu)

Especially in a place like Taiwan, the link between culture and religion means that sometimes people do not or cannot separate the two. In Taiwan especially, folk religion's customs are deeply ingrained in society. M.-H. Lin explains,

> 民俗是人民生活文化的表徵。……名俗的形成是一個族群的生活體驗，經過長期的累積、整合、形成共識，最後才成為社會大眾普遍認同且共同遵循的風俗習慣。……民俗呈現一個族群的生活方式，反映族群的價值觀。……而且無關真假是非，是否合理，民眾都會遵守。 (Folk custom is a symbol of a people's living culture . . . The formation of a folk custom is a group's lived experience, [which] after a long time of accumulation, integration, and building consensus, finally becomes a social custom and habit that all of society's population commonly agrees on and together complies with . . . Folk customs demonstrate a group's lifestyle, [and] reflect a group's value system . . . Furthermore, it does not matter if it is true or false, logical or not, the populace will abide by it.)[127]

M.-H. Lin gives many examples, such as how even those who claim they do not think ghosts exist, refuse to get married during the seventh month of the lunar calendar (which is when the "ghost door" opens). Another example given is that those who are not superstitious still do not wear red to a funeral (which reflects one is celebrating a person's death, possibly bringing bad fortune to the wearer). Regardless of whether the person self-identifies as a "folk religion adherent" or whether the person habitually practices aspects of folk religion, many of these customs are still practiced.

Deities

We have discussed many cultural influences of folk religion in Taiwan. But it is important now to discuss how the deities themselves are viewed. Deities in Taiwan are more functional than they are historical. M.-H. Lin explains,「不同的神明有不同的身分和職務」 ("Different deities have different identities and jobs").[128] Depending on whether one requires protection, romance, career

---

127. Lin 林, *Dà Miào Chéng* 大廟埕, 248.
128. Lin 林, 250.

advancement, or a myriad of other issues, there are countless folk religion deities that do those specific jobs.

Some deities are in higher tiers than others, meaning that not all the gods are equal. One of the deities that is on the lower levels is 土地公 (*Tǔdì Gong*, Earth God or Lord of the Soil and the Ground). M.-H. Lin explains that Earth God's idol is one of the most common throughout Taiwan, found on the ground floor of many apartment buildings, restaurants, and offices. He is seen as the guardian for different localities.[129] The size of the region being watched over by an Earth God can be as big as a whole neighborhood and as small as a single apartment. As one might imagine, there are multiple Earth Gods throughout Taiwan. It is possible to have multiple because *Tǔdì Gong* is a title, not a name. Oftentimes, an idol of Earth God is displayed with offerings to the front of it, all enclosed within a shrine. Sizes vary, but the most common height of the idol seems to be around 30–50 centimeters (1–1.6 feet).

There are a few ways that the Earth God is treated. Because they are seen to protect the land, many a new office and new construction project worship the Earth God. The set days of worship are the second and the sixteenth of each lunar month. During the field research in Taiwan, the researcher encountered multiple sites that were in the middle of a worship ritual for the Earth God. See figure 6 for an offering dedicated to the Earth God outside a shoe store (without the idol) and figure 7 for an offering with paper money outside a restaurant.

The Earth God may be the most commonly seen deity in Taiwan, but 媽祖 (Mazu) is the most popular on the island. There are many origin stories of Mazu but no definitive historical evidence for any of the stories. The following details about Mazu are from what M.-H. Lin presents as the most likely origin story. Mazu's birth name is commonly known as 林默娘 (Quiet Lady Lin).[130] It is widely believed that Mazu was born around 宋朝 (Song dynasty, circa 960–1127) in Fujian, China. Her intelligence, quiet nature, unmarried status, and strength in the mystic arts are all common attributes associated with Mazu.

---

129. Lin 林, 320.
130. Lin 林, 332–33.

Figure 6. Offering to the Earth God outside a shoe store

Figure 7. Offering with paper money outside a restaurant

The name "Mazu" (literally meaning "Mother Ancestor") came from her being seen as a caring mother who watches over many people in tumultuous times. Due to many legends of her historical and mystical deeds, she is especially seen as a goddess of the sea. Thus, many fishermen seek her favor. Her sphere of influence has grown since those early days. For many decades or even centuries, Mazu has been sought by people with a wide variety of problems, including health, career, academics, and romance.

Today, Mazu has become synonymous with Taiwan's guardian deity. Taiwan is an island nation surrounded by the sea. In the days after 1949, when the Republican government fled the mainland into the island of Taiwan, it was a tumultuous time. The government was in disarray, the economy was struggling, the farming industry was unprepared for the changing population, and fishermen became busier than ever. Due to all these reasons, M.-H. Lin believes that Mazu cemented herself as the guardian deity due to an unprecedented desire for stability and protection. M.-H. Lin writes,「在人心最徬徨、無助的時候，媽祖婆的慈愛是臺灣人民心靈最重要的依靠」("When the human heart was the most uncertain and helpless, Mazu Grandma's compassionate love was the most important support for Taiwan's people").[131]

Another very popular deity in Taiwan is 月下老人 (*Yuè Xià Lǎorén*, Old Man Under the Moon), often shortened to 月老 (Yue Lao). Yue Lao is officially one of the deities in Daoism; however, people who pray to Yue Lao do not consider themselves Daoists. In both popular and academic classifications, Yue Lao is considered as part of folk religion in Taiwan. This is no surprise as Chinese folk religion is itself seen as a mix of Daoism, Buddhism, Confucianism, and ancient beliefs about ancestral veneration, shamanism, divination, ghosts, and other sacred rituals.[132] Yue Lao is a deity who is known for helping people with romantic issues, whether it is finding a boyfriend or settling down with a wife.

We have just seen a brief snippet on the Earth God, Mazu, and Yue Lao. Many other deities exist in Taiwan. M.-H. Lin includes more detailed profiles

---

131. Lin 林, 333.

132. Jordan, *Gods, Ghosts, and Ancestors*; Overmyer, *Folk Buddhist Religion*; Nadeau and Chang, "Gods, Ghosts, and Ancestors"; Yang and Tamney, *Confucianism*; Hu and Yang, "Trajectories of Folk Religion," 80–100.

of eleven deities even after leaving many out.[133] Popular counts on the internet list the number of deities worshipped in Taiwan as ranging from 160 to upward of 36,000. Offerings made to these deities can include snacks, soda, gold paper money, fruit, whole chicken, and essentially anything that is valuable. See figure 8 for offerings made to a deity in a popular temple in Taipei.

Figure 8. A well-frequented temple in Taipei with many offerings on the table

As have been stated previously, this study is not intended to explore folk religion in Taiwan. The intent is to understand the way that Taiwanese people view and treat the supernatural. In light of that understanding, this work starts the development of a contextual approach to gospel transmission. For the purposes of this study, it is sufficient to share this glimpse of what kind of popular deities exist and the deities' backgrounds. This gives enough context for readers unfamiliar with the religious environment of Taiwan so that the findings presented in the next few chapters make more sense.

---

133. Lin 林, *Dà Miào Chéng* 大廟埕, 324–49.

Summary of Folk Religion

In the first section, we have explored four terms used to describe the topic of our current study: traditional religion, folk religion, popular religion, and folk belief. Burnett, Parrinder, and others prefer the first term. Hiebert, Shaw, and Tiénou prefer the second. Feuchtwang, Fowler, and Fowler prefer the third. Taiwanese scholars like M.-H. Lin and M.-R. Lin prefer the fourth. C. K. Yang would likely prefer the term "diffused religion" rather than any of the four because of the term's socially and culturally descriptive properties. F. Yang does not commit himself to a particular term because he is more interested in methodology.

The term traditional religion has the benefit of pointing to cultural traditions that have been passed down for many generations. In the context of postcolonial discourse, this term adds more dignity to the field, which is part of the motivation for many scholars' usage of it. The term folk religion draws attention to the prevalence of the associated beliefs and practices among the common "folk." Unfortunately, this may have some pejorative connotations about the lower education and superstition of common people. The term popular religion draws attention to a phenomenological approach by focusing on what is popular among the people. The term folk belief moves away from preunderstandings about religion and draws attention to a more complex religiosity.

As Burnett shows, many terms can be used by the same scholar in the same book, so the importance of choosing one may not be important. Folk religion is currently the term that is used most broadly by scholars in the field. However, its overlap with "religion proper" is attested by many of the authors reviewed. Our survey of some terminologies used reveals the useful and outdated aspects of each terminology. One wonders why there are not more discussions on the terminology itself and the unintended consequences of using different terms.

In the second section, we have looked at Chinese religiosity. Feuchtwang, F. Yang, and Kuo stress the same inter-relatedness that Yao and Zhao mention as well. All these scholars note the intricate tie of politics to religion in Chinese societies. In fact, the most common factor in all these studies of Chinese folk religion is in their emphasis on the influence of one folk religion to another. If this research had to summarize Chinese folk religion based on all these authors, it would be "various localized manifestations of Chinese culture stretching back to the *Yijing*, more defined by behavior instead of belief, and with a distinct view of the supernatural rooted in the organic inter-relatedness of all things in the cosmos." Fowler and Fowler readily admit the overlap of religions in China, citing mutual influence and "concepts that are common to all" (e.g. *Yijing, bagua*).[134] Likewise, Yao and Zhao see the "syncretic and multidimensional" nature of Chinese religiosity.[135] They understand Chinese religiosity as distinctly non-institutional in nature and thus abounding in local expressions.

These scholars seem to point at a perception of religion that is neither institutional nor understood with creeds, but diffused and understood with practices. Granted, as globalization continues, scholars like Anna Sun are already noting the different ways that Chinese religiosity is slowly changing.[136] However, change seems to be slow. C. K. Yang writing in 1961 seems to come to the same conclusion as F. Yang in 2011 and Sun in 2015.[137] Fowler and Fowler, from a European perspective, agree as well. Folk religion remains a complex field of study rife with implications for the religious experience of "everyday believers." Chinese folk religion, with its added complexity due to Chinese history and thinking, is a field that demands much more scholarly interaction.

In the third section, we have looked more specifically at folk religion in Taiwan. A tentative definition from Tamney was given. M.-R. Lin's typology dividing folk religion into three subsets is helpful for understanding how it is perceived in Taiwan. We have also reviewed several scholars on their understanding of folk religion in Taiwan. Some of the location-based studies have informed the research, revealing beliefs about *yin-yang* and have shown that Taiwanese people "worship God because there is a need."[138] This needs-based, utilitarian approach reflects a Taiwanese worldview that sees the

---

134. Fowler and Fowler, *Chinese Religions*, 2.

135. Yao and Zhao, *Chinese Religion*, ix.

136. Sun, *Confucianism*, 120–33. Sun points out the problem with both old and new categories of conversion when discussing Confucianism due to the rapidly changing world. She also points out the problems with the concept of "world religion" a few chapters prior. See Sun, 160–66 for a fascinating account of the modern relevance of Confucianism as a world religion and the revival of certain ritual practices that see their roots in the *Yijing*.

137. Yang, *Religion in Chinese Society*; Yang, *Religion in China*; Sun, *Confucianism*.

138. Tsai 蔡, "Yǔ Fú Xiāngyìng, 與佛相應, 與神相契：臺灣佛教徒與基督徒的祈禱修行體驗," 52.

supernatural as part of daily life. Supernatural things like gods, ghosts, and ancestors are not part of a so-called "excluded middle" for those who engage with it every day. On the contrary, people focus the thinking and practice of their religious lives in this middle, unseen realm. Fan, Chen, Hu, and F. Yang all see the role of folk religion as helping people live in light of the assumed existence of the middle realm.

This shared worldview among Taiwanese led to the proliferation of temples in Taiwan. M.-H. Lin details the extent to which this temple culture has impacted all of Taiwanese culture, regardless of whether the person is religious or not. The fact that there are many deities in Taiwan seem to indicate that being "religious" is not a requirement for respecting deities. People have all kinds of very fascinating ways in which they view and treat deities in Taiwan. These fascinating accounts are revealed in the two chapters on the qualitative research findings. In order to get to that, we must first examine the methodology used. This methodology is the focus of the next chapter.

CHAPTER 3

Methodology

This chapter discusses the methodology used to conduct the research for this study. Discussion of research findings is very limited and reserved for the next chapter. Talking about essential elements of a qualitative research methodology, Linda Bloomberg and Marie Volpe outline nine elements. The elements are: (1) Rationale for approach and choice of methodology, (2) research sample, (3) overview of information needed, (4) research design, (5) methods and theoretical basis of data collection, (6) data analysis and synthesis, (7) ethical considerations, (8) issues of trustworthiness, and (9) limitations and delimitations of the study.[1] Except for the ninth element, which was discussed in the introduction, these form the structure of this chapter.

Rationale

We begin by explaining the rationale for choosing the methodology used to explore the study's main topic: understanding religious thinking among the Taiwanese in Taipei. To do so, it is necessary to study the "lived realities of actual religious communities"[2] in Taipei. The study is interested not in a better understanding of what folk religion looks like in Taipei but in the specific concept of faith in a deity. An ethnography helps with establishing a better understanding of folk religion and a case study helps with comparing it to something else. But to explore how Taiwanese people in Taipei relate to deities, it seemed best to use qualitative interviews – to ask individual

---

1. Bloomberg and Volpe, *Qualitative Dissertation*, 183.
2. Netland, *Christianity and Religious Diversity*, 9.

Taiwanese what they think about faith and how the many deities in Taiwan intersect with their everyday lives.

Because the goal was to develop a framework to help understand attitudes and religious thinking, it was best to use a grounded theory approach. Defined initially by Barney Glaser and Anselm Strauss, grounded theory is meant to help the researcher inductively develop a theory based on observations and other data.[3] This is different from deductive inquiry that tests if a previously established theory fits observation. Using the constructivist grounded theory approach that Kathy Charmaz describes, data from the interviews was interpreted to help in creating categories of understandings related to religious thinking.[4] This has resulted in a qualitative study.

Qualitative research can seem subjective, especially when compared to quantitative research. Saldaña explains the difference between the two, "Quantitative analysis calculates the mean. Qualitative analysis calculates meaning."[5] The topic of the work, how Taiwanese understand faith, requires analysis of meaning. No amount of quantitative analysis can adequately explain the way that Taiwanese people in Taipei think about, talk about, and act in relation to religion. As the literature review in the previous chapter shows, the category of religion as used in Taiwan is different from how many scholars of religion view it.

This study explores how Taiwanese people in Taipei think about religion. What does "faith" mean to Taiwanese? How is it used in daily life and in the context of religion? How are deities perceived? In other words, this work aims to answer a question of "meaning," of what "faith/believing in a religion" means to people. This quest for meaning is best taken using qualitative tools. The initial literature review in chapter 2 unpacks the scholarly perspective as well as builds the general foundation for the topic. The qualitative research in some ways verifies and in other ways nuances the data derived from books and articles. Without the qualitative data, there is no way to ground the theoretical development that is at the heart of this work. The result of having a qualitative portion is a better, more grounded picture of how Taiwanese

---

3. Glaser and Strauss, *Discovery of Grounded Theory*.
4. Charmaz, "Constructivist Grounded Theory," 299–300.
5. Saldaña, *Coding Manual*, 10.

people in Taipei think about religion and how folk religion has influenced that understanding.

As mentioned above, the qualitative data adds to available research found in books and articles. In that way, the literature serves as a review of the field or a foundation set before the qualitative research. For the literature review, a mixture of sources in English and Chinese were utilized, looking at the fields of both religious studies and cultural studies. The literature in this field mostly served to ground the field research. The majority of the literature found in the study was thus surveyed before any fieldwork began. This is reflected in the ordering of the chapters. While in Taipei, the researcher did converse with some professors of missiology and spent some time at libraries to procure additional literature from the most respected scholars in the field. This addition enriched the literature review further.

The next two sections focus on the particular steps of the qualitative research that was conducted from January through March of 2020. We begin with the research sample, how the participants were chosen.

Research Sample

The participants were chosen according to theoretical sampling, as is consistent with many grounded theory studies.[6] This is a type of purposive sampling, which also involves choosing participants based on certain characteristics.[7] The slight difference is that theoretical sampling stresses the selection of participants who both advance the theory and who may be deviant cases.[8] This helps create a more nuanced end result. A small group is selected in the beginning and a feedback loop informs the selection of future participants. The sample size is somewhat determined by the feedback loop. While there is an initial sample size estimate, the final sample size depends on data saturation.

Sample Group

For this study, the sample group was composed only of participants who have at least practiced some form of folk religion (e.g. ancestral veneration)

---

6. Emmel, *Sampling and Choosing*, 45–66.
7. Merriam, *Qualitative Research*.
8. Emmel, *Sampling and Choosing*, 11–32.

in the past. Despite actual experience, the participants' self-ascribed religious identities were noted. Yao and Badham did a survey of Chinese societies; the result indicated that self-ascribed religious identity and actual practice of folk religion can be drastically different.[9] A survey of Taiwan discovered that as high as 83.4 percent of Taiwanese adhere to Buddhist teachings and that even among atheists 38.3 percent believe in the supernatural.[10] To gather more data on the possible differences between religious identity and religious practice, participants were taken from three sample groups based on their self-ascribed identity: (1) Current folk religion adherents (including folk Buddhists or Daoists); (2) converts to Christianity; and (3) atheists. The research can also be described as having only one group composed of people who are varied in self-identification with folk religion despite having all practiced it to some degree. Having the deviant groups helps establish the deviant cases that Emmel mentions.

Participants for the research were chosen first via the researcher's contacts in Taipei. Then, using the snowball approach, other participants were interviewed. To diversify the participants, "spontaneous interviews" were conducted at locations of interest.[11] The researcher spent a few days going to 行天宮 (Hsing Tian Kong), the most frequented temple in Taipei, and looked for people to interview. This resulted in numerous good conversations (e.g. with a security officer) and important observations (e.g. practices of older ladies driving out evil spirits). However, it was not possible to obtain a full, recorded interview due to temple regulations. Nevertheless, the researcher was directed to a senior disciple of the temple who turned into one of the research participants. Combining spontaneous interviews with the snowball approach, all the data was collected.

The sample group was composed of people of varying ages, occupations, and education levels. Sometimes people may assume that folk religion is more for the uneducated masses. The sample group indicates otherwise. Out of the participants, four of them had associate degrees, fifteen had bachelor's degrees, and four had master's degrees. Only one of them stopped at high

---

9. Yao and Badham, *Religious Experience*, 153–64.

10. Tsai 蔡, "Táiwān Dìqū Zōngjiào Jīngyàn Zhī Bǐjiào Yánjiū-Jiǎnjiè Yīgè Kuà Xuékē Yánjiū de Ànlì, 臺灣地區宗教經驗之比較研究－簡介一個跨學科研究的案例," 179.

11. Leiter, "Bricolage of Urban Sidewalks," 13–28.

school and another one stopped at middle school. The researcher interviewed some tour guides, a tattoo artist, a housewife, many office workers, engineers, an actor, a temple disciple, corporate executives, and a retired CEO of a multinational corporation. All of the aforementioned people were very involved with folk religion in Taipei.

Sample Size

The total sample size estimate, before field research began, was twenty. The goal was to have twelve participants from group one, five from group two, and three from group three. Consistent with theoretical sampling, the sample size changed slightly as the research continued; in this case, the sample size increased to twenty-five. There were many more folk religion adherents compared to the other sample groups because that was the primary group of analysis. The inclusion of sample group three was for cross-analysis only. The Christian group, sample group two, allowed the researcher to ask questions related to conversion.

The sample size was sufficient for the following two reasons. First, the interview protocol has twenty-one questions, making the interviews in depth and potentially data-rich. Second, the goal of the study is the formation of theory about a specific concept (i.e. faith), not detailed information about a whole religious system (i.e. folk religion).

Data Saturation

Many qualitative handbooks mention or hint that data analysis never truly ends, not even after the research is completed.[12] There comes a time when one must move on. There are, however, markers that signal when one has done sufficient work that honors the data, or as some call it "theoretical saturation." The analysis was stopped after generating enough material for the study. The unplumbed depths of the rest of the data will be reserved for future work.

For this research, theoretical saturation happened after collecting twenty-five interviews, five more than planned. The originally intended twenty interviews were insufficient because data saturation has not been reached yet. At twenty interviews, there were still some lingering questions that needed to

---

12. Strauss, *Qualitative Analysis*; Merriam, *Qualitative Research*; Saldaña, *Coding Manual*; Denzin and Lincoln, *SAGE Handbook*.

be asked. It was also necessary to confirm whether certain thought patterns were present in other people. By participant 23, it began to be possible to predict many of the responses to the questions (e.g. attitude behind practicing ancestral veneration and reason for going to temples). The final two interviews did not yield significant new information, but repeated concepts similar to previous interviews. There were minor variations that added more depth to the data, but nothing new was added regarding religious understandings. Now, we turn our attention to what types of questions were asked and what kinds of information were needed.

Overview of Information Needed

Bloomberg and Volpe list four types of information that are needed in the research: contextual, demographic, perceptual, and theoretical.[13] This section goes through each of the four types of information gathered during this research in that order.

Contextual Information

Contextual information is any information on the participant's context, including their geographic location and broader culture. It can also be more specific, like their workplace, place of residence, affiliated organization, or any other relevant information regarding the participant's environment.

Much of the contextual information was gathered during casual conversation before the interviews officially started. Each participant picked the place of interview. Because of that, many picked places near their workplace or residence. A few of them were interviewed in the conference room of their company. Before the interview began, much was gathered just from careful observation. These were noted next to the participant profile kept in a password-protected file.

The broader cultural context was gathered before the interview began. The religious context of Taiwan was examined in previous study. Some dealt with the role that folk religion plays in the nation, others dealt with how modernity is viewed in Taiwan. The previous chapter on folk religion covered most of this information. The contextual information gleaned from the literature helped

---

13. Bloomberg and Volpe, *Qualitative Dissertation*, 187–90.

the researcher build better interview questions. The questions themselves helped establish the context to improve analysis of the data.

Demographic Information

Demographic information includes participant information like age, gender, background, education, and occupation. Education history and religious background were asked in the first two questions of the interview. These were the only two that were included in the interview protocol because they seemed to be most relevant. More importantly, it would be imprudent to ask too many personal questions because, from the researcher's experience, Taiwanese people are wary of sharing information with strangers. For this reason, the researcher did not even ask the names of some of the research participants.

Gender and age were visually estimated by the researcher before the interview began. For many of the interviews, casual conversation continued after the interview stopped. The participants often willingly shared any demographic information that was missing. Much of the demographic information ended up playing only a minor part in the data analysis. Nevertheless, it helped in understanding how certain groups of people might be predisposed toward certain understandings about religion.

Perceptual Information

Perceptual information formed the meat of the interview, requiring inquiry that reveals how the participant perceives religion. Perception is the main focus of the whole work. Perception is "rooted in long-held assumptions and one's own view of the world or frame of reference."[14] In other words, this was information on the participant's worldview, specifically on the part relating to religion.

Matters of perception are not always gathered in a straightforward manner. For example, asking questions like, "How do you understand faith?" or "How do you express religiosity?" likely would not produce the responses needed. Nevertheless, questions were still included in the interview protocol that asked the participant to define and describe "faith" (i.e. questions 14 and 15). To help their response, multiple Chinese words that people use to talk about the concept were included. Even with the added help, the vast majority

---
14. Bloomberg and Volpe, 188.

of participants could not answer the question easily. One participant, after the interview finished, told the interviewer that hard questions like these should not be asked because the majority of people would not be able to answer.

Since it was difficult to find out how Taiwanese understand religiosity through a direct question, interview questions that creatively explore the topic through roundabout ways were needed. To write these kinds of interview questions, a substantive frame was employed; that is, a sense of the type of material one is looking for.[15] The result was spending thirteen out of eighteen questions indirectly asking about the participant's thoughts about various aspects of folk religion. The following paragraphs explain the information desired from each type of question in the interview protocol.

The researcher asked questions (1–3) relating to the participant's experience in anything remotely religious to explore their motivation for practicing folk religion. This helped the researcher distinguish how their self-ascribed religious identities related to their actual religious practices. The researcher was looking for understandings of "faith" and religion, especially in the context of folk religion. To explore the mindset, specific questions relating to specific practices or ideas were asked (e.g. Why do you practice ancestral veneration? What happens when a person dies?). Those questions elicited responses that point to pre-understandings about "faith," religion, and believing in something. Those pre-understandings were what this research was really looking for. How the actual religious rituals were done is not relevant to this work.

Questions were asked about what a person says or does when a person believes in a deity (4–5). These types of questions helped distinguish the nuance between "faith" and "belief." There was probing in different ways regarding what the person meant by believing in a deity. For example, after asking what deity the person worships or believes in right now, the participant was asked, "How does this deity dictate how you live or influence your life?" and "Why do you believe in this deity?" Through this line of questioning, there was better understanding of what it means to believe in a deity. Special attention was paid to the terms that were used and the concepts that were employed.

Questions were asked relating to how one becomes an adherent of a certain religious system (6–9). Do people become part of the "Mazu religion" when they go to a Mazu temple? What does it mean to officially be a part

---

15. Weiss, *Learning from Strangers*, 29–31.

of a religion? What boundaries are crossed? What artefacts of the old religious system are left behind in the case of conversion to Christianity? These questions explore the usefulness of categories and boundaries for Taiwanese religious expressions. The most useful data from questions 6–9 arose when a participant self-identified as a Christian convert. In those cases, much information surfaced about how a participant defined the key moments in this change of religious system, or whether there was even a change to begin with.

Questions were asked exploring how folk religion affects Taiwanese understandings of "faith" (10–13). A previous line of questioning explored general understandings about "faith" (4–5). This line of questioning nuanced the responses from questions 4–5 by inserting folk religion into the context and asking the same questions in a different way. For example, instead of asking what it means to believe in a deity, the researcher asked the participants to name a favorite deity and why that deity stands out to them. The researcher also asked the participants to explain their thoughts about deities they might not believe in (e.g. Jesus). That particular question about Jesus (12) turned out to be a key question producing very rich data, as the next chapter will show.

As mentioned earlier, the researcher asked questions that were more theoretical, dealing with definitions of the word "faith" (14–15). These were useful for some participants in giving the researcher a bigger vocabulary to talk about the concept. But data saturation was reached by the tenth interview for these two questions, which led to skipping them for the rest of the interviews.

The last line of questioning (16–18) was reserved for Christians only. It was important to explore how Taiwanese Christians' understandings of faith compare to Taiwanese non-Christians' understandings of faith. The resulting analysis was not as rich as originally envisioned, but still gave helpful data. The complete list of questions can be found in appendix 2.

Theoretical Information

We have discussed contextual, demographic, and perceptual information. Theoretical information is the last element of information needed. Theoretical information refers to information that informs methodology, provides conceptual frameworks, supports findings, and gives credence to the conclusions.[16] Merriam cautions that the findings can often "reflect the constructs, concepts,

---

16. Bloomberg and Volpe, *Qualitative Dissertation*, 189.

language, models, and theories that structured the study in the first place."[17] The bulk of the theoretical information was gathered before the interview process through literature-based research on Taiwan and folk religion.

Though most of the literature was gathered before going to Taipei, much of the information was also gathered while spending time in Taipei. When not giving interviews or visiting temples, many public libraries were visited to consult scholarly and popular resources on folk religion. For example, Taiwan Theological Seminary's library provided useful material on the topic of Christian reflection on folk religion and on articulation of the gospel from Taiwanese authors. In addition, invaluable help came from conversations with multiple Christian leaders in Taipei, including professors of seminaries, the president of Taiwan Theological Seminary, and the national director of Cru in Taiwan.

Summary of Information Needed

In summary, among the four different types of information gathered, only two of them were gathered in the interviews while the other two were gathered mainly through literature. The next section unpacks the details of the research design.

Research Design

Bloomberg and Volpe define research design as "the plan for conducting the study."[18] The key is to have "methodological congruence" so that the various parts of the study are cohesive rather than disjointed. Moreover, it is important to have a systematic approach in the design so as to have a methodology that clearly explains the process of the research. First, the process of the field research is defined. Second, the approach to contextualization is outlined.

Research Process

The design of the field research is as follows: (1) literature review of folk religion in Taiwan that builds a theoretical foundation in crafting good interview questions; (2) interview of a group of about five participants; (3) basic

---

17. Merriam, *Qualitative Research*, 70.
18. Bloomberg and Volpe, *Qualitative Dissertation*, 190.

analysis of the data gathered so far in order to form categories and to refine questions; (4) interview of next group of about five participants; (5) repeat of steps 2 through 4 as necessary until sample size or data saturation is reached, whichever is the greater number; (6) analysis of data to interpret findings; and (7) synthesize all the work done thus far to start developing a contextual approach to gospel transmission.

The grounded theory approach utilizes a feedback loop in the data collection phase, which is reflected in step 5 of the research design. The loop occurred three times, once at five interviews, ten interviews, and nineteen interviews. Sometimes questions were modified while other times questions were removed altogether. Having the loop built into the research design provided the researcher with richer data in the later interviews as categories became clearer.

Another clarification that needs to be made is that the duration of step 3 was only as long as it was required to improve the interview protocol. An ideal step 3 would have required full transcription and in-depth coding of all the interviews up to that point. However, that was difficult to do while in the field due to time constraints. Analytic memos were thus used to make necessary revisions. The analytic memos included reviews of the interviews, highlights on points of interests, basic coding that only noted repeated themes, and what was classified as "unclear questions." Though it was not ideal, step 3 gave the researcher time to pause and reflect.

Contextualization

In analyzing and drawing implications from the research findings, the study draws from Paul Hiebert's methodology for critical contextualization. Hiebert outlines the steps as the following: (1) gather information about old practices (exegesis of the culture); (2) study what the Bible teaches relating to the issue (exegesis of Scripture); (3) critical evaluation; and (4) create a new contextualized practice.[19] While Hiebert was concerned with contextualizing specific practices, this work is concerned more with contextualizing a general approach. The goal may be different, but the process shares many similarities.

In this study, the chapters on folk religion and qualitative findings mirror Hiebert's step 1. The context of folk religion in Taiwan and the data from the

---

19. Hiebert, "Critical Contextualization," 75–92.

interviews deepen understandings of Taiwanese culture. Step 2 was mirrored in the analysis of data. Steps 3 and 4 are mirrored in chapter 6, where implications from the data are drawn and a contextualized approach was outlined.

The task of critically evaluating the context in light of Scripture (step 3) is one of the most important parts of critical contextualization. Dean Flemming, in *Contextualization in the New Testament*, gives a prime example of how this may have looked like for people like Paul and how it may look like today.[20] Others like Charles Kraft use terms like "biblical relativism" to discuss how God has dealt with humanity by "accepting and even endorsing" their culture (i.e. Old Testament practices) before starting to transform them.[21] Kraft argues that this "supracultural principle" is the model that Christian evangelizing people ought to embrace today. Ultimately, Flemming and others stress that contextualization is more of a process that we follow rather than a "finished theological product" that we can ship out to people.[22]

The concept of contextualization is further problematized when one considers that globalization has led to few cultures being "pure" and cultural hybridity being increasingly common. This postcolonial reality has led to people like Homi Bhabha saying that the "liminal space" between cultural identities is where increasingly more people find their true identity.[23] As a result, the "purity of cultures" becomes more of an essentializing claim to power. Craig Ott, writing on globalization and contextualization, argues that the process of globalization has led to more cultural hybridization, meaning that each context is "ever shifting under the contextualizer's feet."[24] This means that the work of contextualizing never ends, that we must always be trying to understand the "other." This is a humble and needed attitude. Ott's use of hybridization should remind us that the cultural identity of this "other" is increasingly hybridized and therefore blurred.

For the purposes of this study, three points relevant to the task of developing a contextual approach to gospel transmission are understood: (1) the biblical text and the human context are both important; (2) it is okay to

---

20. Flemming, *Contextualization*.
21. Kraft, *Christianity in Culture*, 99.
22. Flemming, *Contextualization*, 296.
23. Bhabha, *Location of Culture*.
24. Ott, "Globalization," 52.

"embrace" (à la Kraft) certain aspects of Taiwanese religious culture in an approach to gospel transmission. Embracing certain parts of religious culture does not mean accepting the elements contrary to Scripture; and (3) in a highly modern country like Taiwan where multiple global influences converge, cultural hybridity is prevalent. Any analysis of gospel transmission in this context must be carefully nuanced and easy "evangelism packages" ought to be avoided. These three points were carefully followed in discussing the implications of the findings.

Data Collection Method

We have just covered the qualitative research process and the process used for analysis of the findings. The means of data collection is the next topic. This study used qualitative interviews as the primary means of data collection. To ensure the usefulness of the interview questions, the researcher sought feedback from a Taiwanese contact with significant experience in folk religion before research began and made necessary adjustments.

Interview Structure

For the interviews that were set up ahead of time, the participants were allowed to choose where they wanted to be interviewed. This had the benefit of letting participants be at places where they felt most comfortable. Most of the interviews were at the quietest corners of public coffee shops. A few interviews were at the company where the participant worked. A few interviews were at the headquarters of a religious organization. Others were at the participants' homes, which allowed the researcher to observe some artefacts in addition to conducting the interview. In one case, the interview was conducted at a jazz bar.

The interview itself was semi-structured. That is, the interviewer allowed the interviewee to talk about particular themes that the interviewee brought up. Nevertheless, eleven to thirteen questions were prepared to help guide the discussion (sixteen to eighteen questions for Christian participants). There were twelve follow-up questions that were or were not asked depending on each participant's responses to certain preceding questions. The interviews were expected to last up to sixty minutes each. Two interviews went over by a few minutes and three interviews were on the shorter side (less than thirty minutes). But most interviews were well within expectation. The shortest interview was twenty minutes and the longest sixty-five minutes. The median interview length was forty-nine minutes, and the average length was fifty minutes.

The interview audio was recorded using a phone. No written notes were taken during the interview in order for the researcher to give participants complete attention. Instead of writing notes, points of particular importance were verbally repeated, both as a way to draw attention in the transcript during the data analysis stage and as a way to verify with the participant that they were understood correctly. Right after most of the interviews, "analytic memos"[25] were written about points of interests, insights gained, questions raised, similarity to other participants, key differences, and how the interview might fit in the research. These memos were mostly done standing on the street holding a smartphone on the way home from the interviews. They ended up being invaluable notes for the research. The analytic memos were written using a mixture of Mandarin Chinese and English.

Interview Transcription

A Taiwanese company was hired for the transcription of all interviews. Each interview and all qualitative components were conducted in Mandarin Chinese mixed with some Taiwanese and English. Taiwanese terms were usually used for key religious terms (e.g. adopted son of Mazu). In the interviews, Taiwanese was more commonly spoken among those sixty to eighty years old. English words were used for terms related to Christianity and certain concepts in the social sciences (e.g. "Barnum effect" mentioned by a psychologist participant). For the most part, Mandarin Chinese was the language used.

The researcher is comfortable enough in all three languages that he could read one language (i.e. Mandarin Chinese) while forming concepts and coding in another (i.e. English). Thus, the interview transcripts were kept in Mandarin Chinese and were not translated because this greatly cut down on the time required to conduct the research. The data was translated into English only when presenting the findings in the work.

---

25. Saldaña, *Coding Manual*, 22.

Data Analysis

The findings in the study resulted from careful data analysis. This section lays out the process that was used to analyze the interviews. Specifically, the following three areas are explained: (1) basics of coding, (2) method of pattern analysis, and (3) stages of coding.

Coding the Interviews

Anselm Strauss stated, "The excellence of the research rests in large part on the excellence of the coding."[26] Though the interviews were in Mandarin Chinese, the coding was done in English. The codes used, definitions for the codes, and certain renaming of the codes were documented in NVivo. At key points of the data analysis process, the codes were reviewed, which led to several redefinitions and renaming of the codes.

The codes were first developed by reading the interview transcripts and highlighting themes that occurred repeatedly (open coding). As more interviews were analyzed, the preliminary codes were revised. As analysis continued, some codes rose to become categories with sub-categories filled with sub-codes (axial coding). The aim was to come up with themes that help describe how Taiwanese understand faith in a religion. The following sections detail how coding was accomplished in the research.

Pattern Analysis

Coding requires reading over the contents of the qualitative fieldwork multiple times. To help the researcher analyze everything, the first step was establishing patterns in the data. Hatch mentions six basic patterns that serve as the guidelines for initial coding in this study: "Similarity (things happen the same way), difference (they happen in predictably different ways), frequency (they happen often or seldom), sequence (they happen in a certain order), correspondence (they happen in relation to other activities or events), and causation (one appears to cause another)."[27]

The researcher looked for similarity in the way people talked about deities. Attention was given to similar vocabulary used about things like consistently going to a particular deity at a particular temple or deciding to be Christian.

---

26. Strauss, *Qualitative Analysis*, 27.
27. Hatch, *Doing Qualitative Research*, 155.

It was important to know whether there is a pattern to how Taiwanese people in Taipei respond to the unseen realm or at least how they think is the appropriate response to the unseen realm.

Differences were examined between how Taiwanese people in Taipei understand faith/belief in a deity versus how faith/belief in Jesus is talked about in evangelical circles in the United States. Particular attention was paid to what people think was meant by the statement "believe in Jesus for eternal life."

Notes were made of the frequency that intellectual beliefs and actions were mentioned during conversations about one's relationship to a religious system. In addition, attention was paid to other terms' frequency in the data to better understand the religious worldview of Taiwanese people in Taipei, or at least to better understand the language through which they think about religious concepts.

The sequence of religious events in the participants' narratives was examined. It was noteworthy especially if a certain belief led to a certain action in the participants' minds, or vice versa. The logical order of the participants' religious thinking is a key part of the qualitative research. The sequence helped the researcher figure out what having faith meant in observable, everyday ways and whether there are common sequences in a person's faith experience.

The fifth element of correspondence in the participants' description of their religious experiences was also important. What did they associate with a deity? In describing their relationships to the deities, what terms did they use and what actions or beliefs were usually involved?

Last, participant-attributed causation of their religious experiences was noted. As a researcher, it was important to guard against falsely attributing causation, especially in the early stages of data analysis. However, whenever the participants attributed causation themselves, special notice was taken. For example, many participants attributed "respect for family" as the reason for doing many religious rituals. These kinds of participant-attributed causations significantly helped with forming theories.

It is worth mentioning that there were a few participants whose responses did not match the previously established patterns. Instead of discarding these cases, they were highlighted as a way to do a negative case analysis. In several instances, these outliers helped nuance the findings significantly.

Stages of Coding

Coding is not synonymous with category formation. It is when patterns are seen, connections are made, and stories are formed that categories emerge. Saldaña sees codes as "essence-capturing and essential elements of the research story."[28] In some cases, the codes used developed into certain categories. But primarily, coding was a tool to help data analysis, not the end point of data analysis.

Strauss and Corbin define coding more procedurally, referring to coding as "going through data" and to analysis as "the concept and the thought processes that go behind assigning meaning to data."[29] Coding ends with a list of codes and concepts while analysis ends with the "meaning" behind the data.

Glaser divides the whole process into substantive coding and theoretical coding. Glaser defines the difference thus, "Theoretical codes implicitly conceptualize how the substantive codes relate to each other as interrelated multivariate hypotheses in accounting for resolving the main concern."[30] Strauss and Corbin divide substantive coding into open and axial coding.[31] Some use "selective coding" as a way to describe what goes on in theoretical coding.[32] Others prefer to explain theoretical coding using terms like "linking categories" or "integrating categories."[33] Still others forego these names and use "first-cycle coding" and "second-cycle coding" to describe the entire process.[34]

In general, these authors agree on what needs to happen regardless of the name assigned to the process. This research follows Saldaña's more generic naming convention of first and second cycle coding for the sake of simplicity. He uses those two cycles to categorize the thirty-three coding methods he lists.[35] This research's data analysis did not employ all thirty-three coding methods but is nonetheless influenced by Saldaña's step-by-step guidelines.

All the coding in this research was done according to first and second cycle coding. First cycle coding included coding for key words and values, which

---

28. Saldaña, *Coding Manual*, 9.
29. Strauss and Corbin, *Basics of Qualitative Research*, 58.
30. Glaser, *Doing Grounded Theory*, 163.
31. Strauss and Corbin, *Basics of Qualitative Research*, 220–82.
32. Teppo, "Grounded Theory Methods," 8.
33. Strauss and Corbin, *Basics of Qualitative Research*, 295–310.
34. Saldaña, *Coding Manual*.
35. Saldaña, 74.

helped the researcher become more familiar with the data. The first cycle also included coding for thinking and believing, which revealed the thought patterns and motivation of the participants. Second cycle coding included coding for categories, which synthesized the sub-categories revealed in the first cycle. The second cycle also included coding for theory, which allowed central or core categories to emerge. More details of the coding process can be found in appendix 3.

Summary of Data Analysis

Overall, following the aforementioned steps of data analysis ensured that the data from the interviews were accurately represented. This stage of the research took seven months of full-time coding. This resulted in robust findings, many of which were not included in this work. In chapters 4 and 5, the details of the findings are revealed.

Ethical Considerations

The previous section explored how the data was analyzed, showing that the coding was done correctly. In a research project, doing things ethically is just as important as doing things correctly. This section lists the steps taken to ensure the research adhered to proper ethics during the whole process.

Participant Consent

One of the most important ethical considerations to keep is to ensure participant consent. Before each interview, the researcher read an "informed consent form" to the participants explaining the purpose of the research as well as the existence of the audio recording. See appendix 4 for the entire text read to the participants. The participant did not sign the form. Instead, verbal consent was recorded and stored. In Taiwan, giving one's signature is unusual and might have raised unnecessary barriers to research. Gathering the verbal consent ended up having an additional benefit of showing the participants the seriousness of the research, according to some participant feedback. The consent form listed the main precautions taken to ensure anonymity and confidentiality; this promise seemed to relieve concerns about privacy for the participants.

Most interviews conducted were with people who had already given consent prior to meeting the researcher and were very happy to help. As alluded to earlier, there was one place where potential participants could not consent. This was at the temple called Hsing Tian Kong, where the volunteers and new disciples were not allowed to be interviewed. They said that the temple has a rule that only certain disciples of the temple could participate in interviews. No visitors at the temple were interviewed for that reason. Disciple Wong, being the only authorized person, was the sole interviewee at the temple.

Protection of Human Rights

At the temple, permission was given to take photographs. They allowed as many photographs as needed, with the only condition being that there be no close-up shots. All research participants are referred to using pseudonyms to ensure anonymity. There were some interview participants whose names were not known; instead of making up a name, the researcher used either a location or a trait to write an identifier (e.g. Tour Guide Man, Bookstore Lady).

Sharing the Researcher's Religious Experience

In addition to acquiring consent, ensuring confidentiality, and keeping anonymity, the researcher had to be careful about proselytizing. Most of the research participants were not aware of the researcher's religious background. The researcher made a strong effort to conceal it to allow them to have the freedom to share. In two cases, the participants pushed for the researcher to talk about his religious experience. In both cases, the researcher insisted on not sharing by citing the human rights protocol. However, in one of the cases, the participant insisted that he answers after the interview was over. She felt that it was only fair after an hour of telling the researcher about her religious experience, that the researcher shares about his. Since the researcher did not want to offend her, he shared his own religious experience. She was thankful and happy that he was willing to share. The researcher believes it would have been rude not to share after her multiple insistences.

The only other case in which the researcher talked about his own religious experience was no more than the researcher being pushed to answer what religion he identifies with. It was a similar situation to the first, where it would have been rude to hold back the answer in light of the participant's openness during the interview. In this case, it was actually quite revealing after the researcher shared that he was a Christian. It was about three quarters through the interview when he shared. The participant became embarrassed after the researcher shared because she had said some "disrespectful" things about Christianity. This led to questions about what it means to be respectful or disrespectful to a deity. This concept ended up being a key finding in the research. This participant's strong reaction to finding out the researcher being Christian served as a lens to help reinterpret some of the data. Nevertheless, as an ethical consideration, the researcher avoided sharing about himself other than these two cases where it would have been culturally offensive to hold back.

Remuneration

No participants were paid any money for participating in the research. In most of the cases, the interviews were in public places like coffee shops. At those places, a small drink or a light meal (e.g. coffee or bento box) was purchased for the participant. This was one way of thanking the participants. This was the only form of remuneration that any participant received.

Issues of Trustworthiness

Ethical considerations deal with how the interviews were conducted. Issues of trustworthiness deal more with the research findings.[36] Bloomberg and Volpe mention four main issues that must be addressed: credibility, dependability, confirmability, and transferability.[37] Dependability was explained in the Data Analysis section. Confirmability, which compares findings with other researchers, is not relevant to this research. This section explains the remaining two issues.

Credibility

Credibility refers to whether the participant's views are accurately portrayed without the researcher's own biases skewing the data. The researcher's own filters and lenses affect the research in many ways. In fact, one's own biography affects the research. Filters affect the questions that are asked in the

---

36. The term validity is also used sometimes.
37. Bloomberg and Volpe, *Qualitative Dissertation*, 202–6.

first place, which in turn affects the type of responses that researchers get. Examples of lenses are the "gender, social class, and race/ethnicity" of both the participant and the researcher.[38]

Sunstein and Chiseri-Strater suggest that researchers need to keep in front of them three questions at all points of the research as a way to "check in on yourself" – "What surprised me? What intrigued me? What disturbed me?"[39] This process helped the researcher revise some of the research questions and synthesize parts of the coding scheme. Sunstein and Chiseri-Strater indicate that these questions serve to make the researcher aware of the researcher's positions and preconceptions. This was a constant reminder to be aware of researcher bias. To ensure credibility, the researcher was upfront with preconceived understandings in the introduction of the work.

Transferability

Transferability refers to whether the analysis can apply to a wider context. The research topic is about understanding how Taiwanese people in Taipei view and treat the unseen realm (in light of the prevalence of folk religion in Taiwan) in order to better transmit the gospel. Based on similar research,[40] some parts of the data could be transferable across not just Taiwan, but China as well.

Madsen has written extensively on secularism, particularly in Asia.[41] Madsen is also knowledgeable about Taiwan's religious context, with special attention to its Buddhist and political elements.[42] He often describes the modernization for the Taiwanese context as "hybrid modernity."[43] Madsen's works make references to the role of temples and allude to different religious terms and understandings. Combined with Yang and Hu's work on Chinese folk religion, it seems to indicate that such understandings have deeper cultural roots. As such, because the interviews ask questions about worldview and understanding, it is easily transferable across Taiwanese culture.

---

38. Saldaña, *Coding Manual*, 8.
39. Sunstein and Chiseri-Strater, *FieldWorking*, 115.
40. Madsen, "Secular State"; Yang and Hu, "Mapping Chinese Folk Religion"; Chang and Penny, *Religion in Taiwan*.
41. Madsen "Secularism, Religious Change," 248–69.
42. Madsen, *Democracy's Dharma*.
43. Madsen, 16–50, 131–58.

Moreover, Madsen, Yang and Hu, Chang and Penny, and many others writing on Chinese religion tend to analyze China and Taiwan together. Madsen for example has tested Charles Taylor's definition of secularism against both China and Taiwan to see if they apply to these cultures in addition to "the North Atlantic world" (i.e. "the West"). Despite the differences in politics, historical development, and current religious diversity in both places, Madsen and these other scholars saw enough similarities in the two cultures that they could use the same religious concepts to discuss both countries.

There are always nuances that have to be made to account for the differences. For example, the openness to folk religious practices is one major difference between the two countries. Mainland China has myriad political policies that hamper open religious expressions of many kinds, whereas Taiwan lacks these constraints. Some of these distinctions were accounted for in the discussion on the development of the contextual approach to gospel transmission. However, in both places there seem to be similar levels of acceptance of more fundamental concepts such as filial piety, ancestral veneration, feng shui, and belief in ghosts and spirits.[44] This points to a potentially high level of transferability of some of the findings of this research from Taiwan to China, given some differences in regional contexts. For a more detailed view of Chinese folk religion, refer to the chapter on folk religion in Taiwan.

Summary of Methodology

This methodology chapter reviewed various topics, including the rationale for choosing a qualitative approach to research and the process of the analysis of the data. In the next two chapters, the research findings from this field research are discussed.

---

44. Yao and Badham, *Religious Experience*; Yang and Hu, "Mapping Chinese Folk Religion."

CHAPTER 4

Findings on General Attitudes and Religiosity

We have just looked at the methodology that was used to conduct the research. This chapter and the next chapter unpack the findings of the qualitative portion of the research. This study investigates how Taiwanese people in Taipei view and treat the unseen realm. For the first five participants, considerable time was spent asking them directly what they thought the word 信 (xìn, "faith") meant. Future participants were still asked that question, but it was heavily downplayed. The reason was that most people could not answer this question easily. Mr. Rich, an interviewee who was an accomplished business consultant, told the researcher that he should eliminate this question in future interviews because of how difficult it was to answer for him. This was not the only interview question the researcher had to adjust or in some cases, leave out.

There were numerous data on how certain rituals are accomplished, including the incense used, timing of the ritual, the location of shrines, differences between rituals to ancestors and deities, and the like. Almost all of these kinds of information were left out from this work. The reason is because this study is answering the question of why people do certain things, not how they do them. This research is interested in the ways that people think about deities; how people interact with deities is only relevant insofar as they help us understand how they think about them. In this chapter, we discuss three main categories of data: (1) general attitudes toward the supernatural, (2) different words to express "faith," and (3) what it means to be a part of a religious system. We now begin discussion starting with the first category.

General Attitudes Toward the Unseen Realm

This section sets the foundation of the rest of the findings. The data presented here both verifies parts of the literature review on folk religion as well as builds a real-world context for better discussion.

Yuánfèn

The most mentioned concept throughout the interviews was the idea of 緣分 (*yuánfèn*, fateful coincidence or destiny), mentioned 104 times in total.[1] *Yuánfèn* presupposes a universe of interconnecting parts. Moreover, these parts interact not based on random chance, but rather on some special plan conceived by a higher power. Colloquially, the term is often simplified by using just the word *yuán*, which by itself carries the whole meaning of the term. A wooden translation of *yuánfèn* would be "a piece of *yuán*."

Mommy Farong, a businesswoman in her fifties, referred to the same concept *yuánfèn*, but with a Buddhist twist, when she talked about 因緣 (*yīnyuán*). This carries the same idea of *yuánfèn* but with a strong relationship to "karmic cause" (*yīn*). One translation of *yīnyuán* could be: "fateful coincidence due to karmic cause." Participants, regardless of whether they were Buddhists or not, used the terms *yuán*, *yuánfèn*, and *yīnyuán* interchangeably.

Yuánfèn is like fate in that it is not something that a person can control. It assumes that one's path in life is largely predetermined (though not completely unchangeable according to a few participants). It presupposes a fatalistic worldview where everything is interconnected, from the first cause to the last effect. Mr. Rich said that he did not have the *yuánfèn* to understand Buddhism and other religions. He was talking about not being fated to believe in some religion. Coe Bei, a retired CEO of a multinational corporation, said that she is not a Christian because of *yuan*, specifically, 「只是因為我沒有因緣進到這一個……這一個宗教裡面，我的因緣在佛教」 ("It is just because I do not have the *yuán* to enter this . . . this religion [Christianity], my *yīnyuán* is with Buddhism").

Mommy Farong said that she would not be in this particular branch of Buddhism if not for the *yīnyuán* of her devoted grandma. In another instance, she mentioned seeing a supernatural phenomenon of the moon's appearance becoming a 「蓮花座」 ("lotus seat"), a sacred image associated with

---

1. The term was used regardless of the question asked or the type of participant.

Guanyin Buddha. Even though there were many people with her at the time, only she and one other disciple were able to see the image. One disciple told her that not everyone has the *yīnyuán* to see this image. This touched her deeply because she treated it as a gift from a compassionate Buddha. In all these instances, *yīnyuán* was not just random chance, but related to karma from herself or those around her.

Bookstore Lady, a dedicated housewife in her sixties, said that no deities should be ranked in order of importance or worthiness to worship. She said that the only thing that matters is whether we have the *yīnyuán* to meet the deity. That *yīnyuán* determines whether the person meets the deity and even determines whether the person believes in the deity. *Yīnyuán* is used in this context as a mystical force to determine one's fated religion.

Yuánfèn is also like a coincidence in that the observer or participant often sees the event as a coincidence, something that is not due to a particular action or will of the person involved. In common usage, people explain missing a concert or breaking up with a person using *yuánfèn*. One did not get the chance to do something, therefore it was due to *yuánfèn*. Mountain Pi, a tanned hiker, explained that *yuánfèn* cannot be forced, but it should happen on its own. Even in these contexts of coincidence, the idea of fate is present. For Bookstore Lady and Shi Gu, they both explained that they did not get the chance to become Christians because it was not fated to be so.

In religious contexts, the idea of *yuánfèn* was used to explain why a certain deity or religion is more popular in a region. Coe Bei said that Guanyin is so popular in Taiwan because 「觀世音菩薩是跟我們最有緣分的」 ("Guanyin Buddha has the most *yuánfèn* with us"). Bookstore Lady went further and said that believing in or even visiting a temple of Mazu, Jesus, or any deity requires *yuán*. She explained, 「因為你跟他有緣，你才能進入到他的國度，受他庇佑」 ("Because you have *yuán* with him [a deity], only then can you enter into his kingdom, be protected and blessed by him").

Even Christians used *yuánfèn* to explain their religious events. For example, Coffee Girl, a stranger who self-identified as a strong Christian, said that she became a Christian due to *yuánfèn*. She did mention a teacher at her school being instrumental and a summer camp that was particularly influential; but ultimately, she ascribed the root cause to the simple concept of *yuánfèn*.

Ancestral Veneration

The chapter on folk religion explored how ancestral veneration (also called ancestor worship) is a big part of Chinese culture. Every single one of the twenty-five participants mentioned having done some kind of ancestral veneration in their lives. Almost all of them began by mentioning 清明節 (Qingming Festival), a tomb sweeping day that usually occurs in April. As one of the four biggest holidays in Chinese societies, it is not surprising that the participants all had some kind of experience with Qingming Festival. In many cases, the participants mentioned multiple reasons for practicing ancestral veneration. The reasons were divided into natural reasons and supernatural reasons to show how they both contribute to motivating Taiwanese people in Taipei toward ancestral veneration and how the lines can be blurred in their minds.

Natural Reasons

Natural reasons include reasons that can be understood without any understandings about the unseen realm. There were many reasons given by the participants. The reasons fall under five broad categories.

Childhood Habits

Most of the participants mentioned having started ancestral veneration as a child. Fishu, a young Christian small group leader at church, said that ever since she could remember, she always did ancestral veneration. Pei-Pei and Police Lady said that they just went along with the adults. Tour Guide Man, a quiet man in his thirties, said that he never used to think about why he did it as a child. Curu, a Christian church multiplication specialist, said that she did not know any better as a child and just did as she was told by her parents and other elders. This extended beyond ancestral veneration and included religious rituals with other deities. For example, Curu has experience with religious rituals involving 「鬼神」 (*guǐshén*, "ghost deities"), who are essentially ghosts with more power. Curu shared about her ample experience with deities like 「天公」 (*Tiāngōng*, "Heaven Father").[2] Smoker Ang, a truck driver who had children himself, said that he still visits many temples because his parents still bring him along.

---

2. This deity evolved from the concept of 天 (*Tien*). See chapter 2 for more information on the significance of this deity in the development of folk religion in Taiwan.

Healthy Chen, a young engineer in downtown Taipei, said that he did not have a choice in doing ancestral veneration. He jokingly said that he probably would have been hit by his father if he refused to participate. Healthy Chen, despite being an adult now, said that he still participates in the ancestral veneration rituals yearly at the behest of his family. He said that he does not see any significance in the rituals, but nevertheless treasures the opportunity for a yearly reunion of the whole extended family at the gravesite of the ancestors who have passed on.

Childhood habits extend beyond ancestral veneration to many kinds of religious encounters. Religious rituals, festivals, and exposure to certain temples or deities often began when the participants were young. Some participants came to worship certain deities because of this. House Gongon, a retired civil engineer, said that he 「自然而然就接受這一些神」 ("naturally accepted these deities") because he had been exposed to them ever since he was a child.

Because ancestral veneration had been practiced since childhood, the vast majority of participants mentioned still practicing it today. This applied to all the participants regardless of their self-ascribed religious identity. For example, Coffee Girl said she still practices ancestral veneration every Chinese New Year. She said these practices are nothing more than 「例行公事」 ("doing routine business") that is devoid of special meaning beyond the fact that it is a tradition she must uphold. House Gongon explained that this tradition is in turn something that must be passed on to the next generation, then the generation after, and so on. Smoker Ang said that the reason for passing on the tradition is that otherwise, when it is his turn to pass away, no one would be there to venerate him.

Visiting Family

For some, ancestral veneration is akin to visiting family. Tattoo Ju, a tattoo artist in her twenties, said that even though she does not have strong memories of her paternal grandmother, she still visits her grave and goes through the ancestral veneration rituals. She said it is because the grandmother is family, and we are supposed to visit family. To Tattoo Ju, ancestral veneration was a logical conclusion for expressing filial piety to one's elders, whether living or dead.

Others like Healthy Chen and Company Woman focused mainly on visiting the living family members. These people said that the special ancestral veneration rituals that occur on specific days are their chances to see family members that they might not otherwise see. Company Woman, a single office worker in her late thirties, said that she likes finding out how her cousins, uncles, and aunts are doing. She said that because people are required to gather at a site for ancestral veneration, the gathering can get quite big and festive.

Remembrance and Thankfulness

Many participants used proverbs to explain their reasoning for ancestral veneration, much more so than any of the other interview questions. The repetition of many of the same proverbs points to the influence of the Taiwanese education system. Mommy Farong, Chi, Shi Gu, Mr. Rich, House Gongon, and Disciple Wong all said that they have been taught to practice 「飲水思源」 ("When drinking water, think of the source"). This proverb means that one must never forget the source of a blessing, that one must be thinking of it and be thankful for it. Others like Bookstore Lady and College Hua talked about the same concept of remembrance and thankfulness without using the proverb.

Mommy Farong, Mrs. Ting, Coe Bei, Disciple Wong, and Hsiang Wu used another proverb, saying that we must 「慎終追遠」 ("carefully attend to the funeral rites [of parents] and follow [in ancestral veneration] to the distant future"). The main idea is summarized well by Mommy Farong and Mrs. Ting, who said that we cannot 「忘本」 (wàngběn, "forget where we come from").

Inner Sustenance

Bookstore Lady mentioned that sometimes ancestral veneration is important for 「精神的寄託」 ("inner sustenance"). She said that this action can cause the heart to be comforted for many people, especially older people.

Willpower

When asked how the act of ancestral veneration influences her daily life, Mommy Farong brought up the idea of karma. However, it was not simply good deeds leading to good fortune. She believed that having 「善念」 (shàn niàn, "goodwill") leads to these good actions which leads to good fortune. Ultimately, she understood good fortune as coming from 「信念」 (xìn niàn, "faith will," often translated as willpower, conviction, or belief) to influence the surroundings. The idea of xìn is again placed on the forefront. It is as if "faith" is not just a belief one holds, but a willpower that affects one's present and future.

Supernatural Reasons

The supernatural reasons given by participants for doing ancestral veneration are reasons that require an understanding of or belief in some aspect in the unseen realm to make sense. These fall under two broad categories, the positive and the negative.

Protection and Blessing

A common reason given by almost all participants was that the ancestor would 「庇佑」 (*bìyòu*, protect and bless) the family if consistent ancestral veneration is carried out. Conversely, if one is not diligent in ancestral veneration, bad things can happen. A very important part of ancestral veneration is taking care of the gravesite, including cleaning the tombstone area and making sure to visit the ancestor's resting place. Qingming Festival is a day that is often dedicated to these tasks. This holiday falls on the fifteenth day after the Spring equinox, which usually places it in the beginning of April.

Chi was an actor who self-identified as an ex-Christian and ex-Buddhist. Chi, even though he did not believe that ancestors directly impact his daily life, mentioned that sometimes they may protect and bless in other ways. He recounted this traffic accident he had where his maternal grandfather's name popped into his head right as the accident was happening. He said that he felt fearless and felt an unseen protective aura around himself as the accident happened. In the end, he was not hurt at all. Chi presently self-identifies as having no religious thoughts or practices, but he talked about the existence of many supernatural occurrences that cannot be explained scientifically. To him, even if ancestral veneration is mainly about venerating "the source of the water," there is an underlying supernatural aspect that should not be discounted.

Tour Guide Man said that the ancestors mainly have an indirect 「心靈層面」 ("emotional level") effect on him. Nevertheless, like Chi, he was not willing to 「否定這個事實」 ("deny the fact") that supernatural influences could be present. Mountain Pi was like them too, unwilling to say with certainty that supernatural blessings exist. She was more unwilling to deny that there might be some unknown blessing when a person performs ancestral veneration properly. Fishu said that at times when no human could seem to help her, she would turn to the next best thing, which were humans she used to know (i.e. parents, grandparents, aunts, and uncles) who became ancestors living in another realm. She felt that somehow, the ancestors had more control of the outcome of situations than she did. It seems that her ancestral veneration was borne out of a sense of helplessness.

This idea of protection and blessing was one of the most efficacious things that ancestors are thought to provide. Genie, a freelancer the researcher met at a bar, said that, unlike deities who are able to help with a variety of things, ancestors are much more limited in their abilities. She believed that being able to protect and bless is the upper limit of ancestors' abilities. Interestingly, Genie also thought that "protecting and blessing" is one of the primary things that Jesus offers to those who believe in him.

Negative Effects Due to Neglect

Venerating ancestors may have positive outcomes; but not doing so may have negative outcomes. Mrs. Ting, a fast-talking Buddhist, said that if there is a crack on the tombstone and it is not fixed, it can have deadly consequences for one's future or one's progeny. Car crash and early death were two events specifically mentioned. Mrs. Ting's husband had an ancestor tombstone that had a crack. Everyone in the family was scared because there was a person in the family who got into a car accident around the same time. They quickly fixed the tombstone and hired a shaman to do 超渡 (*chāo dù*, literally "super crossing"). *Chāo dù* is a ceremony that helps a soul lingering on earth for whatever reason to cross over into the afterlife. Mrs. Ting especially stressed the importance of *chāo dù* in avoiding continued bad fortune for the family.

Bookstore Lady also alluded to negative effects if one does not take care of the ancestor's gravestone. However, she was hesitant to say more, possibly due to the subject being somewhat of a taboo. Shi Gu, a practicing Buddhist who also identifies as a Daoist, alluded to negative effects as well and did not elaborate at first. Upon further questioning, Shi Gu revealed that these negative effects often involve the body, including getting sick or something even more serious. That is why for her own ancestors, anytime there were incidents related to the gravestone, she took care of it speedily.

Company Woman admitted to having experienced these negative effects herself but did not want to share more. She did share that after she took care of the cracks in the tombstone, the negative effects dissipated. She shared that her friend had a similar experience where the whole family went from being wealthy landowners to being farmhands on the same land they used to own. This friend consulted a Daoism specialist, who found that the gravesite revealed an improper treatment of the corpse. After taking care of the issue, the family started prospering again to the point where at the time of the interview, they had already bought back pieces of the land they used to own.

Summary of Ancestral Veneration and Implications

There were many reasons given for why people practice ancestral veneration. The natural reasons seem to stem from Taiwanese culture. Parents have taught their children to always behave this way. This behavior leads to pleasant family gatherings. The behavior is reinforced by proverbs in Chinese. The supernatural reasons can be summarized thus: "Practice ancestral veneration and good things may happen. Neglect it and bad things may happen." The key word is *may* because no one was completely sure of either the positive or negative; however, no one wanted to take a risk, and everyone did not mind the positive possibilities. Participants commonly repeated both natural and supernatural reasons, meaning either that these categories were both valid parts of their reality or that they did not perceive the world through categories like the supernatural and the natural. Either way, this points to the participants living in the so-called middle realm.

Ultimately, no matter the main reasons given, the majority of participants said that they do ancestral veneration in order to 「感謝」 (*gǎnxiè*, "give thanks") to their ancestors, particularly parents. Mrs. Ting saw it not just as a duty that she must carry out, but a 「美德」 (*měidé*, "virtue"). Perhaps because of the thanksgiving aspect of ancestral veneration, Chi practiced it even when he was a Christian and did not see anything wrong with doing so. His reasoning is that 「一個人的文化是非常重要的」 ("a person's culture is very important"). The implication is that ancestral veneration is part of his culture and it is unacceptable to neglect it just because of a new religion.

Reincarnation

The vast majority of the participants believed in some form of reincarnation. Many people "half-believed" in reincarnation. Some neither believed it was real nor did they think it was fake. Pei-Pei, a non-religious administrative staff who was working in a Buddhist organization, described herself as 「介於相信跟不相信之間」 ("between belief and unbelief"). There were people like Curu who did not believe in reincarnation but at the same time, she was scared of the concept. There were also people like Company Woman who believed in reincarnation but hoped it was not true.

Mommy Farong, after explaining reincarnation in depth, said matter-of-factly, 「那當然有因果就有輪迴」 ("Of course since we have [the law of] cause and effect, we have reincarnation"). This was the concluding argument to a discourse on reincarnation. She seemed to perceive reincarnation as an obvious conclusion if we accept that there is a law of cause and effect (also translated as karma). Mrs. Ting cited cause and effect as the reason why 「我們要種善因才會有好的結果」 ("we have to plant a good cause in order to get a good effect"). Her internal logic involved referencing the concept of cause and effect from the study of physics, using its scientific context to reinforce the truth of it, and then applying it to morality, reincarnation, and the supernatural.

Mommy Farong based her worldview firmly within the context of Buddhism and illustrated it using the famous Buddhist saying, 「欲知前世因，今生受者是，欲知來世果，今生作者是」 ("to know the cause of the past life, the recipient of this life is; to know the fruits of the next life, the author of this life is"). In other words, if we want to know what our past life was like, we look at the situation in our present life. Likewise, if we want to know what our next life would be like, we look at how we live our present life.

The idea of reincarnation is not mainly answering the question of what happens after we die. Rather, it answers the question of why our current life is like this. Life after death was not the main concern for Mommy Farong; rather, this life was more important to her. In all the conversations with participants who believed in reincarnation, the focus was more on how to work off the negative karma accumulated in the past life rather than to build up merit for the next life. Life before birth was discussed much more than life after death.

Another interesting point is that everything she explained was very behavior oriented. Karma itself is based on specific actions having specific consequences. Mommy Farong explained that to be reincarnated as a Buddha (the highest of six possible levels), we have to do special spiritual training. Every situation is based on actions in this life or the previous life. There was no mention of concepts relating to free promotions to a high reincarnation level.

To put it another way, the traditional Protestant understanding of "grace" was not talked about; good outcomes must be earned.

Mrs. Ting cited "doing good" as a measurement of where one reincarnates. However, she added the possibility of becoming a 「孤魂野鬼」 (*gū hún yě guǐ*, "lonely soul wild ghost"). These are people who could not reincarnate into another life and remain on this earth in the unseen realm, interacting with this world in sometimes beneficial but often maleficent ways.

Fortune Telling

Among the participants, some thought fortune telling works while most were not so sure. Nevertheless, almost all the participants have done some form of fortune telling or another. The only exception was Curu, who became a Christian at a young age. In Taiwan, fortune telling is easily accessible. One can go to a number of special areas that have multiple fortune tellers grouped in close proximity. See figure 9 for the famous 「命理大街」 ("Street of Fortune Telling") near the temple Hsing Tian Kong.[3]

Figure 9. A row of fortune tellers grouped in close proximity

---

3. The fee can be as low as USD$80 and as high as USD$300 for simple fortune telling. More specific fortune telling and the ones aimed at corporate customers seem to have different pricing structures.

This section has been divided into two, separating the participants who thought fortune telling works and those who did not. Both provide useful data on Taiwanese religious thinking. The most popular type of fortune telling mentioned by the participants was palm reading and using the eight trigrams. What is most relevant to us is not the type of fortune telling they did, but their motivations and expectations, both of which reveal more about their religious worldview.

Why Fortune Telling Works

Among those who thought fortune telling works, here are the reasons they did it. Mommy Farong did it because her parents did it for her. She herself believed it because she believed that our fate is determined when we are born. However, a few sentences later, she retracted her statement and said that in Buddhism, one can change one's fate through training. Mrs. Ting echoed this sentiment, saying,「命運不是用算出來的，我其實是從我的腦袋和行為去產生我自己的命運」("fate is not something we get divined, I think it is actually my brain and actions that create my own fate"). Others like Bookstore Lady shared the same sentiment.

Company Woman also believed that fortune telling works. She too talked about fate being something that can be changed, but not through religious training. She believed that the moment a fortune teller tells someone her fate along with the actions necessary to change it, that person's fate can now be changed. Despite believing that a fortune teller can help her change her fate, Company Woman did not go to fortune tellers anymore. She said that in her last encounter with a fortune teller, the fortune teller told her that changing one's fate may result in losing heaven's favor. So, even though she believed fate can be changed, she accepted whatever fate throws at her. In other words, she adopted a more fatalistic view.

For Mommy Farong, Mrs. Ting, Company Woman, and Bookstore Lady, they believed that fate can be changed. Their reason for visiting the fortune tellers was to determine their fate and learn how to change it. However, many of them ceased visiting the fortune tellers. Mrs. Ting's story gave a glimpse as to why. She recounted that before she was deep into Buddhism, she was really into various kinds of fortune telling. She estimated that half of the things spoken became true. Reconciling this belief in the efficacy of fortune telling and her stance, it seemed to indicate that she did not stop believing in the accuracy of fortune telling, but stopped seeing the necessity of relying on it.

Others like Shi Gu said about fortune telling, 「好的不準，壞的很準」 ("the good is not accurate, the bad is very accurate"). In her experience, some fortune tellers can tell a person's fate not only with palm reading (which is very common) but by just looking at one's face. Shi Gu explained that these people pay a price for such accuracy because what they are doing is 「洩漏天機」 ("leaking the secrets of heaven"). This is a popular concept told and retold across many media types. The person who leaks these secrets is often despised by the heavenly beings and are persecuted by them. Many times, this person loses people close to them.

Bookstore Lady spent a good deal of time speaking about how accurate fortune telling is. She recounted a story of her brother-in-law passing away within six months of a fortune telling master saying so. But like Mrs. Ting, she stopped seeking it out because she did not see a need to. In fact, all of them likely stopped because of the same reason of not seeing a need anymore. Disciple Wong, a senior disciple at Hsing Tian Kong, specifically stated how he stopped because it was no longer necessary for him. However, none of them stopped believing in the accuracy of fortune telling.

Smoker Ang was one of the few people in the interview who still regularly visited fortune tellers. He said that he does it to ask for pointers in this life, to know what to watch out for and to know how to improve his luck. To him, it was a tool to help him navigate the difficulties of life.

Why Fortune Telling Does Not Work

Among those who did not fully believe in fortune telling, most of them did it simply out of curiosity. They wanted to see if it was accurate and wanted to have some fun. Pei-Pei was one example; when asked about the accuracy of her last fortune telling experience, she said, 「我覺得會看到一些我需要被提醒的事情，這好像無所謂準不準」 ("I think I saw some things I needed to be reminded of, it does not matter if it is accurate or inaccurate"). Others like Police Lady, a reserved lady in her early twenties, did not really believe it works but nevertheless liked to do it, because she was curious about these things that are outside her control. Yet others like Coffee Girl did not believe it works but had a family that did it without her involvement and reported back to her regularly.

Mr. Rich did it to hear something good about himself. He wanted the fortune teller to praise him. Chi explained fortune telling as just part of going through life, as if he did not need a reason for why he does it. Chi's rationale was echoed by many of the participants. Most of them were going through life. Fishu had a work situation and needed advice. Tattoo Ju felt like nothing was going smoothly and wanted to know why. Lon Le, a manager in a big company, did not even fully believe in fortune telling but figured that it would only help him in life, not harm anything. Participants did not seem to need to believe in fortune telling in order to do it. It was seen as something one simply does if one encounters a difficult moment in life.

Amulets

Many of the participants had amulets of protection at multiple points in their lives. Pei-Pei wore one before her trip to Indonesia. Mountain Pi wore one on a recent trip simply because a parent asked her to. Mountain Pi half-believed it, but mainly wanted to give her mother a peace of mind. Authentic amulets (i.e. those that are perceived to be efficacious) are only acquired at temples after a few set rituals and some monetary offering. They are always tied to some deity or another. Pei-Pei for example got an amulet from a Mazu temple while her friend got one from Guanyin. This again points to the idea of different deities co-existing peacefully. Pei-Pei did not remember which temple she visited, nor did she frequent the temple she got the amulet from. This shows that deity allegiance is more based on need than it is based on truth (another point that Pei-Pei herself made).

Atheists on Folk Religion Beliefs and Practices

A few self-identified atheists were interviewed to see how their general orientation toward the unseen realm may be similar or different. The results showed that their general orientation is remarkably similar to the other group. Moreover, despite claiming to be atheists, they held onto beliefs that those who practice folk religion hold onto. Mr. Rich was a good example of this point. Mr. Rich, despite being a self-proclaimed atheist, still believed in some form of reincarnation. He subscribed to the Buddhist teaching that talked about the seven categories that people can reincarnate into. He seemed to see a contradiction in his own belief, saying,「雖然無神論者，不過我還是比較傾向好像有輪迴」("Even though [I am] an atheist, I still lean toward there having reincarnation"). The implication is that as an atheist, one is not supposed to believe in forces in the unseen realm. Even though Mr. Rich recognized the incongruency, he insisted that this was his view.

Another interesting belief of Mr. Rich was the power of 念力 (*niànlì*). The idea of *niànlì* comes from Buddhist teaching. He stated that as an atheist,「我相信從自心……自身內心發出來的念力有一天可以成真」("I believe that from the heart . . . from the whole being of the body, we produce a *niànlì* that allows [our dream] to become reality"). *Niànlì* is best described as the ability of the person to "will" something into being, whether it is a victory in a sparring match, good grades on an exam, or success in one's career. This concept of *niànlì* is very common in East Asian popular culture, appearing in movies, TV shows, self-help books, cartoons, and children's books. One example is a children's book that teaches that one could use *niànlì* to influence future events.[4] In other words, many aspects of folk religion have affected the worldview and religious thinking of Taiwanese people in Taipei. The more self-aware people like Mr. Rich recognized it, but many do not. Mr. Rich's example shows that regardless of how strongly one accepts the natural laws of physics as the only truth, people sometimes still find it hard to reject concepts popular in religions in Taiwan (that trace their roots to the unseen realm).

Summary of General Attitudes

We have examined many ways that Taiwanese people in Taipei view and treat the unseen realm. The general orientation is that supernatural phenomena in the unseen realm are just as normal and expected as events in the physical realm. This is demonstrated in the way that people talk about *yuánfèn*, fortune telling, and amulets. We have seen that ancestral veneration and issues of reincarnation blur the line between what exactly is natural and what is supernatural. For example, for each natural reason that the participant gave for practicing ancestral veneration, there was often also a supernatural reason given. It is as if the natural and supernatural are intertwined to form this complete reality that is taken as truth for the Taiwanese person. Stated another way, ancestral veneration is good for reuniting family and for providing supernatural protection and blessing. The interviews show that Taiwanese people in Taipei see the material world as containing invisible,

---

4. Shi 施, *Niànlì Shéngōng* 念力神功.

complex properties that the natural sciences cannot explain. Moreover, they are comfortable with this view of the world; most participants talked about forces in the unseen realm as everyday realities.

The blurring of lines between the seen and unseen realm is further demonstrated by how even self-identifying atheists like Mr. Rich believed in reincarnation. In the interview questions about general orientation and attitudes toward the supernatural, there was very little difference in how the participants responded. The Buddhists responded similarly to the Daoists, atheists, folk religion adherents, and Christians too. Some of the Christians made sure to talk about these attitudes in the past tense, implying that they think differently now. However, in terms of ancestors providing supernatural blessings and protection, even some of the Christians held to this view.

Now that we have covered how Taiwanese people in Taipei view and treat the unseen realm, it is time to be more specific and discuss what "faith" in a deity means and looks like. This is the topic for the next section.

Different Words to Express "Faith"

The semantic range of a word is the breadth of meaning for that word. According to BDAG, a Greek word like πίστις (*pisits*) has a semantic range that encompasses English words like "believing," "faithfulness," and some others.[5] A word's semantic range does not necessarily mean that in each usage, it encompasses all those meanings. However, it does mean that it could potentially be any of those meanings; sometimes a word encompasses one or more of those meanings in any given context. This is a basic tenet of philological criticism, part of a broader push circulating in biblical criticism. One of this research's main goals is to uncover the semantic range for the Chinese word *xìn* in order to uncover how people relate to a deity or a religion. It is difficult to translate some words into English without losing some of their meanings. Therefore, a few Chinese words were kept in their original forms to prevent this loss of meaning.

A few words were discovered by directly asking the participants what 信 (*xìn*, "faith") meant to them. They were then asked for alternative words they used to relate to their deities. These direct questions generated many

---

5. Bauer, Danker, Arndt, and Gingrich, *Greek-English Lexicon*.

responses. The data were categorized into realms of behavior and thinking to discover what people associated with *xìn*. Indirect ways were also employed to find ways that people related to deities. Special attention was paid to the way people were using the word *xìn* and other words that they used when discussing allegiance toward a deity. This section shows the main words or concepts used by the participants.

Believing in Something

The most widely used word in faith-related conversations was *xìn*. The most common meaning related to *xìn* is "to believe in the existence or reality of something." Tour Guide Man used it as the penultimate step before fully accepting the reality of a religion. Mommy Farong and Mrs. Ting used the term to refer to believing in the usefulness of a religion. Shi Gu used the term to refer to being careful about the power of ancestors to influence our lives. Tattoo Ju used the term to refer to trusting in how Mazu has taken care of her. Christians like Fishu and Coffee Girl used it in relation to accepting Jesus Christ into their lives. Each of these participants also used *xìn* in many other contexts. Nevertheless, this first meaning of "believing in something" remains the most widely used meaning of *xìn* in the interviews.

Superstition

One term that appeared in a few interviews was 迷信 (*mí xìn*, superstition). Tour Guide Man differentiated between "normal" faith (*xìn*) and superstition (*mí xìn*) by what is acceptable in culture. He used his own example of visiting the deity Lord Superior Wen Chang to explain. He said that visiting one temple to *bài* (worship) Lord Superior Wen Chang is normal faith whereas visiting five temples to *bài* the same deity reflects a little bit of superstition. For him, visiting ten temples for the same request was a sure sign of deep superstition. The main point was not on the number of temples, but on one's level of reliance on religion and forces in the unseen realm. It seemed that for Tour Guide Man, deities are there for us humans to ask help from, but not to overly rely on.

Familial Relationship

To others, having "faith" in a deity was more of a familial relationship. Curu recognized a father-daughter relationship in her own religion, Christianity.

Curu said that this is very similar to many folk religions, where one can become an 「義子」 (*yìzǐ*, "adopted child") of certain deities. Two such people were encountered in the interviews, both of whom were 「乾女兒」 ("adopted daughters" or "god-daughters") of Mazu.

Tattoo Ju spoke about Mazu the way one spoke about a god-mother. She did not once try to prove Mazu's existence, but only talked about respectful ways to interact with her and how she ought to show reciprocity with the good things she has been given. Looking at the topics of discussion in the interview, Tattoo Ju seemed to assume that the interviewer, like herself, saw the existence of Mazu as something that did not need any discussion. In contrast, how to interact with Mazu as a family member needed more discussion and clarification. Genie was the other god-daughter of Mazu. She too spent most of the interview discussing proper ways to relate to Mazu, which for her was saying hello often instead of only going to Mazu when she had a need. To all of them, faith in a deity was more about treating the deity as an older member of the family.

Relationship of Exchange

Many participants described their "faith" in a deity as a give-and-take relationship of exchange. Fishu explained that whether it is a good deity or bad deity, 「你必須跟祂交換什麼」 ("you have to exchange something"). She defined it as an 「對價交換」 ("exchange of consideration"), a legal term referring to bargaining so that both sides receive something of value. In other words, she was referring to *quid pro quo* and that there was no such thing as a free favor. Like all relationships, there must be reciprocity. She explained that if one does not somehow meet the bargaining criteria acceptably (i.e. return the favor through performing an act of service to the deity), something bad may happen. She mentioned getting into an accident as one possibility of what may happen if one does not complete the exchange with a deity. She then mentioned that even after having been a Christian for a while, with its concept of "free gift" (Rom 3:24), it was difficult for her to stop thinking about the LORD in terms of exchanging *quid pro quo*.

Pei-Pei was asked to explain 「信仰」 ("faith"). She responded by saying, 「我們會希望我們生活過得更好的時候，就會去請求這些神明來幫助我們，對。但是其實對我來說這有一點點交易的味道。」 ("When we want our life to be better, [we] would go to these deities to help us, yes. But actually, for me, this tastes a little transactional."). She continued and explained her own mindset, 「我燒紙錢然後我給你供品然後你滿足我的心願」 ("I burn paper money, then I give you offerings. And then you satisfy my heart's desire."). Pei-Pei later clarified that she thinks this transactional model of treating deities is neither good nor bad, but simply 「台灣人的現況」 ("the reality of the situation for Taiwan people"). Reciprocity is important for folk religion in Taiwan. Pei-Pei used the idea of reciprocity and of transactions to define "faith" itself. To her, "faith" was asking for something and getting something in return.

Pei-Pei's idea of interacting with a deity may not be as extreme as Fishu, but a relationship of exchange is nonetheless present. The main idea is to have a nice relationship with the deity. She explained that during special holidays or the deity's birthday, one can give a special gift, perform a certain ritual, or burn incense, all as a way of keeping a good relationship. Then when a person has a special request, that particular deity is more likely to respond favorably. The deity and the person have a relationship of exchange in which the human offers reverence and material gifts while the deity offers non-material assistance to what the human asks for.

Like Pei-Pei, Genie also treated this relationship of exchange as fundamental to interacting with a deity. She recounted the story about her becoming a goddaughter of Mazu. Genie's mother was told by a spokesperson for Mazu that Genie may be a good candidate for being Mazu's goddaughter. In a simple religious ritual where a sign indicated acceptance or not, she was first rejected by Mazu. Genie's mother told Genie to ask again, but this time telling Mazu all the good things that she would do and the many ways that she would serve Mazu if possible. This second time, the ritual indicated that Mazu responded favorably. Genie told the researcher that she learned an important moral that day. She told him,

> 你要跟神明要什麼之前，你不能只有一昧的索取，……你是要有辦法給予的，對；因為如果你只是一昧的索取，而沒有奉獻，那其實不管是哪一個宗教，不管哪一個神明或者祖先都沒有保護你、庇護你的必要 (Before you beseech something from a deity, you cannot just single-mindedly demand, . . . you have to be able to give, yes. Because if you just single-mindedly demand, but do not offer [something], then it

does not matter what religion, nor what deity, nor what ancestor, they do not have the obligation to protect you, to bless you).

To Genie, the idea of exchange was not just fundamental to how she interacts with her deities. To her, exchange was fundamental to interactions with any deities in any religions. She mentioned Jesus Christ of Christianity a few times throughout the interview, each time applying the same standard to Jesus's followers that she applies to herself as Mazu's goddaughter.

Bài (Small Worship)

So far, we have discussed a few ideas related to *xìn* (faith). But we have not discussed specific words people use in place of *xìn*. The most common word used in place of *xìn* is 「拜」 ("*bài*"). In colloquial language, 拜拜 (*bàibài*) is used to signify the action. As a verb, *bài* refers to worshipping something. The term *bài* used in folk religion and normal conversation is the same term used by Taiwanese Christians to talk about worshipping God: 敬拜 (*jìng bài*). The extra character in the front, *jìng*, means respect or reverence. In Christianity, the verb worship is associated with music and singing praise to God, often with some reverence. A Christian worshipper may not expect anything in return other than an emotional experience (e.g. thankfulness, joy, etc.). The usage of *bài* in Taiwan includes a sense of emotional worship, but also includes a range of other meanings. These other meanings are detailed in this section.

Physical Action

The verb *bài* is often associated with an action, namely 「雙手合十」 ("the clasping of both palms together"). This physical action was specifically explained by Fishu and Ms. Sha. The action is located on visible signs at many temples in Taipei to help first-time visitors know how to properly perform the ritualistic action of *bài*. See figure 10 for one such instructional "sign" at Taipei's famous 行天宮 (Hsing Tian Kong), with instructions available in Chinese, Japanese, English, and Korean. See figure 11 for a paper sign that contained detailed instructions on the five actions for a proper *bài*.

Figure 10. A digital instructional sign on how to
bài and do other important rituals

A Broad Semantic Range

In English, especially among Christian circles, worship can be understood as an emotional form of showing one's devotion to and love of God. In Chinese, *bài* can be understood as any form of interaction with a deity. One participant mentioned that he *bài* every time he sees a temple while walking down the street. Another participant *bài* the Earth God at doorway on the first floor every time she left the apartment. Yet another participant *bài* the deities at Hsing Tian Kong every morning. For some, like Disciple Wong, *bài* lasted for thirty minutes. However, *bài* for most participants lasted no more than five seconds at a time. Due to the loaded meaning in the English word worship, a better translation for *bài* is "small worship."

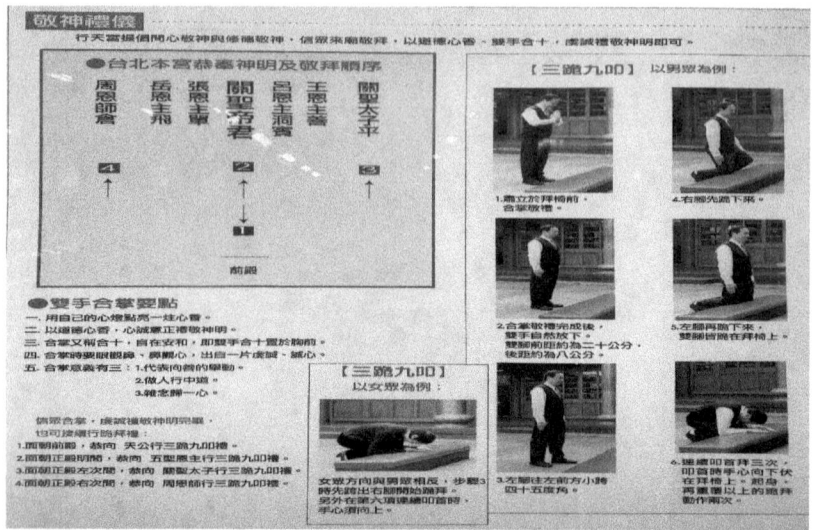

Figure 11. A poster explaining how to conduct proper worship at this temple

For a few of the participants, including Mommy Farong and Company Woman, *bài* happened for five seconds right before leaving the house and right after coming back to the house after a workday was over. For most of the participants, one did not *bài* a deity unless one needed something. When a person *bài* a deity or ancestor or ghost, a request is usually made. This request, if answered favorably, may result in a person returning to a deity to offer thanks. But the word used is often no longer just *bài*, but 「感謝」 (*gǎnxiè*, "offering thanks").[6] Thus, *bài* is usually not associated with thankfulness or joy, but rather with desperation, need, or respect. Throughout the rest of this study, the many ways and contexts these associations are formed in the participants' minds are illustrated.

Worship and Praise

As mentioned earlier, the idea of *bài* includes worship. However, there are possible, intangible benefits associated with *bài*. For example, Fishu mentioned

---

6. This difference in terminology is based more on reality than it is based on the actual meaning of the term *bài*. *Gǎnxiè* was how the participants usually talked about returning to a deity after a request has been answered. Technically, the term *bài* still covers the action of returning to thank the deity. But in the interviews, the participants would very often switch terms automatically when "offering thanks" was the reason for visiting the deity. *Bài* was conspicuously left out of the picture in those cases, which led the researcher to draw this conclusion.

that having food that has been offered to the deities can be a good thing. It is good because the act of having been offered to the deity during *bài* means that the food may now have blessings and protection associated with it. Consuming this food means that the blessings and protection can possibly be transferred onto the person.

When asked to explain *bài*, Mommy Farong started by saying that humility is important. She then explained the many actions associated with *bài* (how to bow down, how the head must touch the floor, etc.). She associated *bài* with *Sādhanā*, which refers to self-improvement in mind and body, encompassing disciplining one's actions, words, diet, and potentially every aspect of life. Mommy Farong *bài* Guanyin because Guanyin has reached a level of *Sādhanā* that almost no one reaches. She continued to praise Guanyin with many positive attributes. For Mommy Farong, *bài* involved praising of a deity's characteristics and is primarily defined by one's action. She saw *bài* as an action that must be combined with 「實際的心靈的……信」 ("actual belief… within the heart and soul"). This religious ritual is efficacious only when all the elements are present.

Xìn and *Bài*

When asked whether the word *xìn* is interchangeable with *bài*, Mommy Farong said that 「相信」 (*xiāngxìn*, "to believe") is the first step, namely that one must first believe before one can worship. However, she did not elaborate on how she understands *xiāngxìn*. Despite the researcher further asking two questions to clarify, she talked about daily rituals (i.e. praying over a special Buddha water). She did not talk about the object of her faith, but rather the actions resulting from her faith. To be more accurate, the interview revealed that Mommy Farong treated *xìn* ("faith") as something that is more about what one does than what one believes in. Believing in something was indeed important as the first step for Mommy Farong, but that was neither the primary focus in her religiosity nor was it how she explained her religion to the researcher.

The two words of *xìn* and *bài* were used interchangeably. Mr. Rich used terms like 「比較喜歡拜」 ("prefer to *bài*") to describe how people choose between deities. Mommy Farong said, 「財神會拜的話應該是……做生意的人會比較多，所以他們當然相信嘛」 ("Those who *bài* [worship] the god of wealth… are business people mostly, so of course they *xiāngxìn* [believe]"). Other participants used the words interchangeably in similar ways, preferring *bài*. *Bài* is something that everyone does, with the reason being unimportant. To *bài* a deity implies at least some amount of intellectual belief. To *xìn* a deity implies having done some amount of worship (*bài*). There were no participants who indicated that they fully believed in a deity's existence or power before they *bài*. This shows that to *xìn* is to *bài*, likewise to *bài* is to *xìn*. The most likely conclusion is that the two terms are conceptually similar to Taiwanese people in Taipei. Judging from the inability or difficulty of most participants to explain to the researcher the difference between the words, the two terms are inseparable to many people.

Mommy Farong said, 「就像我們拜佛一樣，……你要先拜祂、再學祂、再信祂」 ("Like we who *bài* Buddha, ... you must first *bài* Him, then imitate him, then *xìn* him"). It bears noting that consistent with other participants, she did not describe herself as a believer of Buddha. Rather, she described herself as a *bài*-er of Buddha. For Mommy Farong, *bài* was the more foundational of the two terms. On many levels, *bài* encompasses more ideas, including *xìn*. To her, *bài* was the beginning step while *xìn* came later. In Christianity, the typical order is often: believe Jesus, then worship God, then imitate him. For Mommy Farong and many other participants, the typical order was: *bài* [small worship] a deity, then imitate the teachings, then *xìn* [believe] came last.

She explained in the interview that *bài* did not require effort or even her own will. She *bài* Buddha because of a 「深的因緣」 ("deep *yīnyuán* [fateful coincidence]"). She explained that after one has done enough *bài*, one starts to learn about the many deeds of the deity and the deity's characteristics too. This learning naturally leads to imitation. In Mommy Farong's words, 「學了之後當然就深信不疑啦」 ("After imitating, of course, one would believe beyond a shadow of a doubt"). To believe intellectually is thus the last step of the process.

Mommy Farong was asked whether the process can be reversed, that is to believe, then imitate, then worship. She looked confused and said, 「你……你怎麼樣先信？因為我覺得相信這個是你一定要所謂的很多的驗證」 ("You ... How would you first believe? Because I think to believe this, you must [first] have a lot of verification"). To Mommy Farong, to believe without first having an extended time of practicing the religion was unthinkable. The "verification" she was talking about was more experiential; that is, she thought one must first have positive *bài* experiences, then verify how applying the teaching has improved one's life, and only after then is believing possible.

So, in Taiwanese thinking, a deity is someone to be worshipped more than to be believed. One's intellectual consent is secondary to one's actions of devotion to a deity. The many examples from the participants show that the existence of the deities is assumed. Moreover, performing actions of devotion toward an idol is acceptable (and preferred) even if one does not know the name of the idol, as was the case with Hsiang Wu and Smoker Ang.

Mystical Aspect

To some others, *bài* was more mystical. Coe Bei articulated this mystical nature using the idea of the power of positive energy, similar to the positive thinking concept voiced by Mr. Rich. Coe Bei explained the effect of *bài* as a 「磁場」 (*cíchǎng*, "magnetic field") that generates positive energy. The determinant for how much energy gets generated is based on the heart of the person and on the number of people doing the *bài*.

No Allegiance Required

Another aspect of *bài* is its separation from existing allegiances. Perhaps a little like worship, one can *bài* something while retaining allegiance to something else. Tour Guide Man used the example of himself doing *bài* with elders in his family but believed neither the religion of the elders nor the 「信仰」 (*xìnyǎng*, "faith") behind the action of *bài*.

Fishu said that when she thinks of 信仰 (faith), she thinks of behavior. As a Christian with significant experience with folk religion, she contrasted Christian faith and *bài*. She explained the difference like this,

> 拜拜會是，你覺得你有需要的時候，你才去要。……信仰比較是，它跟你的生活是mix在一起的。……但是拜拜感覺……會是一個模式，但它不會是你的生活方式 (*Bàibài* is like, you feel that when you have a need, then you go ask for it … Faith is more like, it mixes together with your life … but *bàibài* feels like … a mode [in your life], not a way of living.

For Fishu, *bài* was temporary and need-based. On the other hand, Christian faith was permanent and life-based. *Bài* did not interfere with how one lives but Christian faith interfered completely with how one lives, making it a "way of living."

In fact, for many, *bài* did not require allegiance to any deity at all. According to Coffee Girl, many people did not even specify a deity that they *bài*. They simply indicate that they sometimes *bài* in their daily lives. It was almost as if the identity of the deity or the total number of deities was inconsequential to the concept of *bài*. All that matters was that a person respects this realm of deities enough to occasionally *bài* at some place to some deity.

Beseech

The idea of 「求」 (*qiú*, "beseech") was mentioned by every single one of the twenty-five participants. The participants used the word in slightly varied ways, but all in the context of describing one's relationship to a deity. The participants used the term to describe their own relationship to their deity or their friend's relationship to another deity. For example, Mommy Farong said, 「我們會求觀音菩薩就是說祂慈悲，祂非常的慈悲」 "we beseech Guanyin because she is compassionate; she is very compassionate." For her, mentioning the reason for beseeching or the object for which she was beseeching was not important. She mentioned other deities like 阿修羅 (Asura) in the context, seemingly indicating that Guanyin was a much better deity to approach if one needed to beseech something. Bookstore Lady pointed out Guanyin's reputation for being compassionate and open to all requests. The main idea here is that if one has a strong request, one often asks a deity to fulfill that request. It is only natural to go to the nicest, most compassionate deity for requests.

Next to *bài*, *qiú* is the most popular word that people used to relate to a deity. Instead of saying "I have faith in Mazu," the participants said things like, "I beseech Mazu to grant safety." 平安 (safety) is the most common issue mentioned in the interviews. But there were some other issues that the participants wanted to address. One did not beseech a deity without an issue, which seems to indicate that "faith" in a deity requires having some issues in this life.

Fishu thought that beseech is a better term than faith to describe one's relationship with a deity. Unlike *bài* or *xìn*, the meaning of *qiú* is directly translatable to "beseech" or to "ask for."[7] When people go to a deity, it usually means that they have something they want to ask for. In other words, many people do not make trips to temples unless there is a specific request that they would like answered. Similarly, many people *bài* not out of reverence or gratitude or love, but out of a desire to ask for something.

In normal usage, the terms *bài* and beseech are often used together or even interchangeably. Fishu used the terms interchangeably a few times even in the same sentence. Pei-Pei and Chi used the terms in direct connection. For example, Chi said that 「台灣很多人拜拜的原因就是為了⋯⋯求，求發財跟求身體健康」 ("many Taiwanese people *bài* because of . . . beseech, to beseech getting rich and having a healthy body"). The concept of beseeching does not always need to be tied to a deity. Without mentioning any deities, House Gongon said that he beseeches for peace for his household. Healthy Chen used the term beseech when talking about interactions with Jesus.[8]

Beseeching was not just a way one related to one's own deity. One can beseech any number of deities simultaneously. Coe Bei did not shy away from asking for various things from any of the deities in Taiwan. She said her primary deity is Buddha but because she believes in all these other deities, she interacts with them too and treats them with 「感恩崇敬」 ("thankfulness and reverence").

The idea of 「求」 ("beseeching") something from a deity is not just derived from the interviews with participants who thought of their own deities this way. Other participants, when describing followers of deities they do not themselves associate with, used this same idea of "beseeching." Curu described Mazu followers this way, so did Tour Guide Man and many others. This means that not only is "beseeching" a common way that people relate to a deity, it is a commonly known way. Instead of "believe" or "faith," the term

---

7. The similarity in meaning is why the English word beseech is used directly. While directly translating *bài* or *xìn* can lead to misinterpretations, there is no such danger with beseech.

8. However, Healthy Chen also thought that beseech may not be the most appropriate term to use to relate to Jesus. He said it is because the term beseech does not carry the idea of mimicking someone's example, which he said he was supposed to do as a Christian. At some points, he defaulted to using the term beseech but then caught himself later and tried to use other words like *xìn*. His flipflopping between the terms might have been a sign of his worldview before his conversion carrying over to what he was being taught to think. This could indicate that he was, at some level, treating Jesus the way he treated folk religion's deities, even though on another level, he knew he was not supposed to. Chapters 6 and 7 analyze this possibility more fully.

"beseeching" may be a much better term to describe people's relationships with their deities. College Hua, a junior in a renowned university in Taipei, went further to say that beseeching is the only relationship people have with the deities.

Beseeching as a Normal Expectation

We have seen that beseeching is a common way Taiwanese treat a deity. This treatment is expected from certain religious organizations in Taiwan. A Buddhist example can be used as a case in point. Special religious festivals draw more crowds because they are seen as days when many requests are granted. Mommy Farong recounted that on the birthday of 釋迦摩尼 (Gautama Buddha), her temple located on the mountaintop was filled with people. She did not mention how many people are normally in this temple, but the idea is the numbers swelled dramatically on those days. In just one day, it attracted over five-hundred tour buses full of people. On normal days, Mrs. Ting said there are over two-hundred tour buses. Assuming the Taiwanese standard charter bus capacity of fifty-six people, five-hundred tour buses translate to 28,000 people arriving on the temple in one day from buses alone. This does not take into account the number of people driving their own cars. Mommy Farong mentioned that the master of the sect (救世師父菩薩, Salvation Master Bodhisattva) is compassionate and grants any requests that day. She noted the multiple people who make requests, ask for peace, and acquire 「大悲咒水」 ("Great Compassion Mantra Water"). Mrs. Ting added 「平安麵」 ("Well-Being Noodles") to the list of things people yearn for.[9]

Mommy Farong believed that the hordes of people were there not to worship or learn from this religion, but just because of their desire to beseech something. She did not see anything wrong with this, treating it as completely normal. She mentioned that everyone has struggles in life, and that Gautama Buddha can help relieve these struggles. Multiple people, including Mrs. Ting and Coe Bei, added that the bodhisattva 觀世音菩薩 (Guanyin, also known as Avalokiteśvara) 「有求必應」 ("answers any request") and desires people to ask for anything.[10]

---

9. These items are seen to provide blessings and protection to the person.

10. The tone Mommy Farong used suggested that relieving the pain of the world is part of the mission of Gautama and by extension Mommy Farong's mission as a devoted follower.

Summary of Words

We have discussed many words used by the interview participants to describe how they treated a deity. We have seen that the ways that Taiwanese people in Taipei express faith can be very varied. The idea of believing in something was present in all these different expressions, but there were many other concepts mixed in, including superstition, familial relationship, and relationship of exchange. Moreover, rather than the word that Christians may expect, *xìn* (faith), it may be better to use the word *bài* or beseech when describing a response to a deity, both of which are much more commonly used in Taiwan. Understanding these words show that one's behavior and daily needs are important aspects of Taiwanese religiosity and the way that Taiwanese people in Taipei conceptualize "faith." To uncover more nuances of Taiwanese religiosity, we now discuss the various ways that the interview participants treated being part of their respective religious systems.

Being Part of a Religious System

We have looked at the general orientation and attitudes people had toward the unseen realm. We have also looked at the different words that people used to express faith in something or to relate to a deity. Now we will examine how people perceived themselves in a religious system. We will examine how the research participants thought about conversion; then examine a few concepts that were prominent in the interviews regarding belonging to a religion.

Conversion

Conversion is a complex term that is very useful to religious studies while at the same time is a little problematic to our discussion. Chapter 6 deals with this topic more thoroughly. For now, we examine a few examples of conversion among the research participants. These few examples are not enough for thorough analysis, but they do help in beginning to paint a picture of

---

By comparison, whether one believes or worships is inconsequential to that mission. Mommy Farong talked about believing and worshipping, but was much less passionate in her tone and spent much less time discussing those two concepts. Mommy Farong and Mrs. Ting said that responding to these requests is enough for them. This suggests that conversion, theological teaching, donations, or continued visits to the temple were not part of the agenda for them, nor for their organization.

the kind of concepts that are active in the Taiwanese mind when thinking about conversion.

Specifically, the participants were asked what, if anything, was different before and after they belonged[11] to certain religious systems. These were self-identified issues, not categories that were given to them. For this reason, this section may feel incomplete to the reader, especially to those versed in religious studies. On the other hand, these participant-chosen categories are useful to show which ideas are important to the participants and which are not, regardless of what the theologian may think. Moreover, this section is noticeably short because useful data on this topic was very rare in the interviews. Instead of removing the section, it was left here to highlight the possibility that the idea of conversion may not be in the minds of many Taiwanese people in Taipei.

Methods to Have Faith

To begin this section on conversion, we first examine how the research participants defined having faith (or believing) in a religion. Talking about popular folk religion deities, Mommy Farong said, 「我不是說不信我也不拜」 ("I would not say I do not believe or do not *bài*"). She meant that despite being a devout Buddhist, she had no problem *bài* deities like Mazu if the occasion arose. To *bài* does not require special knowledge of the deity or personal consent to the deity's power or existence. To *bài* simply requires closing one's palm and showing respect to the deity that one has the *yuánfèn* (fateful coincidence) to cross paths with at that particular moment.

For people like Mommy Farong, "believing" was not a concern that one has when it came to accepting a religion. She mentioned that if one had the *yuánfèn* to get in touch with Jesus, one would naturally believe. True to the concept of *yuánfèn*, it is as if whether one believes or not is not one's choice. *Yuánfèn* dictates one's path in life, including one's religious affiliation.

Mommy Farong said, 「你拜他覺得你信他就會有一定的」 ("When you *bài*, if you believe, it would definitely be so"). For her, the act of believing

---

11. Belong is not a great word to use. However, a word like practice implies too little and other words like believe or convert have their own problems. This section only analyzes the participants who "belonged" sufficiently to call themselves "Buddhist" or call their primary deity "Mazu." Others who did not self-identify similarly (even if they practiced many elements of Buddhism or visited some deity with some regularity) were not analyzed in this section.

could make things possible. This sentiment was echoed by Tattoo Ju, 「那有沒有關聯也都不重要，因為我相信這件事情。……有沒有那個東西的存在也不是一個非常重要的問題」 ("Whether they [faith and theological concerns] are related is not important, because I believe in this thing. . . . Whether this thing even exists is not a very important question"). To her, theological issues were not important. Even the existence of her deity was not a question worth considering. To Tattoo Ju, the act of believing could also make things possible.

Religious Practice

For Mrs. Ting, faith was just one step on the journey. She explained, 「在拜的過程更加的信念之後，然後你又更接近佛法的時候，你又更產生良性，你更要做善事，你要正能量去修」 ("In the process of *bài*, faith increases, then you are closer to dharma, [then] you generate more good, [then] you do more compassionate works, [then] you use the positive energy to do religious practice"). This idea of 「修行」 (*xiūxíng*, *Sādhanā* or "religious practice") was central to Mrs. Ting. Religious practice itself can be the word that summarizes a Buddhist's spiritual journey. The word 修 (*xiū*) literally means "to fix" and the word 行 (*xíng*) literally means behavior or conduct. The concept of *xiūxíng* (religious practice) is understood to mean fixing one's behavior. Bookstore Lady said this includes fixing her own behavior as well her past life's mistakes.

This "religious practice" involves 「身心意」 ("the body, heart, and will"). Mrs. Ting explained 「修的次第」 ("the steps in religious practice") as having all the elements of believing, moral improvement, moral action, and 「發揮那種智慧」 ("utilizing that kind of wisdom"). It is 「不是……剃光頭髮，……是對真的正向東西去做」 ("not . . . shaving one's head, . . . it is doing something positive in life"). In other words, faith is not step one, followed by religious practice as step two. Neither is faith an encompassing concept that includes practice as an expression of faith. Rather, religious practice is the main concept that is used to describe a Buddhist' spiritual journey. Faith, *bài* (small worship), moral issues, and living wisely are all parts of this spiritual journey.

"Religious practice" was the most prominent and defining term for the Buddhist participants. Mrs. Ting herself used the famous Buddhist concept of 「信，願，行」 ("faith, desire, practice") to briefly describe the nuance of the three essential components of a spiritual journey. So, in theory faith is a separate category from practice. However, the result of the interviews indicated that in reality, this line is blurred. Like Mrs. Ting, people treated practice as the main concept. The majority of the discussions (even when asked specifically about faith) were centered on the concept of religious practice.

Intellectual Knowledge

In discussing the method to have faith, it is useful to briefly discuss the idea of intellectual belief. In the interviews, most people did not mention doctrine or many concrete things about the object of belief. Rather, the focus was often on the subjective element of belief, on what a person's "faith" looks like. The previous section on religious practice is a case in point. In order to understand this phenomenon more, the following question was added to the later interviews, 「要理解多少才可以相信？」 ("How much does one have to understand in order to believe?"). Company Woman said she does not understand much doctrine. Coffee Girl went further to say that it is actually impossible to understand the doctrine of most kinds of folk religion. The results matched the existing literature on the topic, namely that the doctrinal component is not that important for folk religion.

This same lack of focus on doctrine was seen in the Buddhist participants too. Mrs. Ting replied to this question first by stuttering a bit, then by saying, 「佛菩薩在對話，就OK啦」 ("Just talk to Bodhisattva Buddha, then it's okay"). She then mentioned doing 「禮佛」 (*lǐfó*, a ritual of worship of, prayer to, and study of Buddha) as something one does every morning and evening as a sign of one's belief. In other words, there were no specific intellectual beliefs that defined one as a Buddhist. Rather, it was a practice (which for Mrs. Ting was daily and for others much less frequent) that defined her as a Buddhist. Her religious identity was not defined by her beliefs but by her behavior. Reading between the lines, it did not seem like intellectual knowledge was unimportant; on the contrary, all practices presumed both believe in and knowledge of some kind of doctrine. The phenomenon seemed to be that intellectual knowledge and acceptance of certain beliefs was assumed by the participants to be normal; thus, it was not mentioned to the researcher, who is himself Taiwanese.

Heart Change

We have looked at having faith in terms of religious practice. We have also seen how participants mostly viewed intellectual knowledge as common ground and thus unnecessary to talk about. Other participants spoke of true faith as having a heart change. Coe Bei defined true faith thus,「真正的信呢其實……是一種經驗，……不是一種求的概念，而是呢你希望你的心就能夠跟佛一樣」("True faith is actually . . .a kind of experience, . . . not a concept of asking for something, but is you wanting your heart to be able to be the same as Buddha's"). This heart change was what true faith was all about for her.

In a similar vein, Shi Gu explained true faith as raising one's spiritual level. This spiritual level can be interpreted in many ways. The two traits she provided were「同理心」("compassion") and「恢復純淨」("restoring of purity"). Later on, she mentioned that someone who is advanced in their religious practice is better at「反省」(*fǎnxǐng*, "self-reflection" or "reflexivity"). Through self-reflection, this religiously advanced person was supposed to be able to continually and progressively understand their own wrong and fix it.

Christians on Conversion

Now that we have examined a few ways that the participants spoke about what having faith in a religious system or deity means, we examine what coming into a religious system looks like. This section focuses on the self-identifying Christian participants. They were asked what differences they saw in themselves before and after "conversion."[12] Specifically, they were asked whether they approached or looked at faith differently. Among the Christians, the resulting data can be split between two main categories.

Object of Faith

Curu said that the biggest difference was that before, she followed her parents to *bài* several deities associated with folk religion, but she「沒有一個真實的信心的對象」("did not have a real object of faith"). After becoming a Christian, Curu said that now she had a real object, someone she could get

---

12. Conversion as a term was never used in the interviews. Rather, more common terms that describe religious change were used. The exact wording used to describe conversion can be found in question 8 in appendix 2. In English, it is, "What is different for you now that you are a [term for converted religion's adherent]?"

to know more and understand more through the Bible. She found out that this Christian deity is reliable, which in turned caused her faith to strengthen. In the past, she said that the lack of a clear object of faith made what she felt less real. She could not seem to clearly articulate what it was about the past deities or the rituals involved that she did not like, only that they were part of folk religion in Taiwan. For Curu, lacking a clear object of faith meant she lacked ownership of her faith.

Emotional Health

After converting to Christianity, Healthy Chen said that the biggest change for him was that he 「情緒好很多」 ("has a much better mood"), meaning that he is more emotionally stable. Anytime he felt a bad mood coming on, he said that he remembers the main points of the Bible and tries to calm down. He could not tell the researcher any specific passages or even the context of the main points of the Bible that he referred to. It seemed that he treats Christianity as a way to help himself become a better person. Conversion for Healthy Chen was thus more akin to maturing emotionally.

An Unclear, Long Process for Everyone Else

The non-Christian participants provided data on conversion that was much more ambiguous. The data on this was very fragmented and most of the participants did not articulate a clear idea of what their own conversion process looked like. In fact, most of them said they did not have a conversion, even if they used to be in one religion but now belonged to another. It was as if the process was so natural that they never really thought about it. Tour Guide Man explained this phenomenon that was noticed in the interviews.

Tour Guide Man talked about believing in the reality of a religion's doctrines as the second to last step before one is considered an adherent of that religion. This was the last step in his five-step process: 「一個很不明確或者說很長的一個步驟就是……透過實證的方法。例如說他在相信這個信仰之後，他可能跟生活當中某些經驗做些結合……［才能確定］他所相信的這件事情是正確的」 ("an unclear, or better yet, a long process is . . . through an evidence-based method. For example, after he believes in the faith, he may combine it with some life experience . . . [to confirm] that what he believes about this thing is correct").

In other words, there is "an unclear" and "long" process before one can become part of a religion. Merely believing in something is not enough to be a part of that religion. In Tour Guide Man's mind, people were not converts until they experienced the religion for a long period of time and confirmed for themselves that the religion is "correct." By the term correct, Tour Guide Man was referring to his "evidence-based method," meaning that the religion needs to have been tested in one's life experience and worked out well.

Coe Bei's example in Buddhism illustrates what this "unclear, long process" may look like for a person. Coe Bei described her conversion to Buddhism as her 「佛緣的開啟」 ("Buddha *yuán* being activated"). After studying abroad (during which she became Christian), she had returned to Taiwan when she was roughly thirty-six years old. It was then that her *yuán* (fateful coincidence) was activated. She explained what she meant by this later. She started by explaining that she was glad that her initial exposure to Buddhism was with the sect she was currently with at the time of the interview. The revered master of her sect was 聖嚴法師 (Master Sheng Yen). He held a PhD and was the head of 法鼓山 (Dharma Drum Mountain), one of the four "mountains" of Taiwanese Buddhism. Coe Bei said that when Master Sheng Yen was alive, his main focus was on 禪 (*chán*, Zen), which was one thing that attracted her initially.

Coe Bei did 禪修 (*chán xiū*, "religious practice of Zen" or simply "meditation") at various locations for varying lengths of time, ranging from three to ten days.[13] At some point in time, perhaps years later, she wanted to start learning about Master Sheng Yen's Buddhism. She read many of his books and came to understand this religion more through them. She ended her story on this subject by talking about how she had been practicing Buddhism for a long time now. She never specified the point in time when she "became" officially Buddhist.

Coe Bei's conversion process started with having *yuán* (fateful coincidence) with a religion, with having been somehow put in contact with it. Then she started practicing some aspect of the religion for many years. Then she started learning the teachings and doctrines of the religion. It is unclear

---

13. She did not specify how many hours she practiced *chán xiū* per day for those day ranges. *Chán xiū* during religious retreats are common in Taiwanese Buddhism, so it is likely that she was referring to going on these retreats.

at which point she stopped being a Christian and became a Buddhist. From the interview, it seems that the exact point of conversion was irrelevant and even non-existent. Based on her whole interview, she would never frame her religious journey in terms of a point of conversion. Instead, she used the term "practicing dharma" as a way to describe her religious journey. Instead of defining her conversion as a point in time when she entered some religious boundary, she defined her conversion as a direction of moving closer toward dharma. To use Paul Hiebert's terms, she used more centered set thinking rather than bounded set thinking.[14]

Utilitarian Perspective of Deities

We have explored how Taiwanese people in Taipei view converting to a religion, namely that many related it with dharma or a similar concept that highlighted behavior and spiritual journeys. Ultimately, these interviews indicated that Taiwanese people in Taipei for the most part do not see themselves as belonging to a religious system. They see religious systems as pathways to enlightenment or methods to attain what they need in life.

This perspective was especially prominent in the interviews. It seems to be more utilitarian; that is, treating religious systems as the means to an end. The view was prominent in all the participants who practiced folk religion regularly. For example, Tattoo Ju saw religion in Taiwan as a 「很功能性的事情」 ("very utilitarian thing"). Police Lady likewise said that she only visits temples to *bài* deities when there is an issue. More than just folk religion adherents, this utilitarian view was visible in the self-identifying Buddhists, Daoists, and even Christians interviewed. For example, Healthy Chen became a Christian because he saw it as the best pathway to be happy and healthy. He could not articulate many doctrines of Christianity nor did he seem to care much about what God might want or how he might help others. The focus, like the folk religion adherents, was on finding the best deity to fulfill his needs. Healthy Chen sought out Jesus Christ, Mommy Farong sought out Guanyin, Coe Bei sought out Buddha, and Tattoo Ju sought out Mazu. The deity was different, but the motivation remained the same.

Perhaps because of this utilitarian view, most participants did not view their religious participation as part of a religion. They viewed their religious

---

14. Hiebert, "Sets and Structures," 217–27.

rituals and temple visits as part of their daily routine. When pushed for clarification, participants often could not think of ideal words to describe this religious part of their life. Tattoo Ju's interview about her interactions with Mazu is one good example:

> 我不會把他稱之為宗教，因為對我來說我沒有真的去信奉哪個特別的宗教。對，然後信仰的話，我也不太確定，因為我也沒有好像真的很像其他人非常虔誠的到可能要甚麼初一、十五要幹嘛，還是那些去符合那些他們的規範阿、禮俗阿等等的。我就是以個人……的方式去進行。……我沒有想過，對我來說就是一個習慣的事情 (I would not call it religion, because to me, I do not really have faith in and serve some special religion. Yes. And as for faith, I am not sure either. Because I am not really like other people, [I am not] so devoted that maybe on the first or the fifteenth of the year [I] have to do something. Nor do I conform to their norms, rituals, and so on. I just use my personal . . . method to go about [interacting with Mazu] . . . I have never thought about [what to call this part of my life]. To me, this [interacting with Mazu] is just a thing I am accustomed to doing.)

For Tattoo Ju, her "folk religion" was not folk religion at all even though devotion to Mazu is classified as such both in Taiwan and abroad. For Tattoo Ju, she interacted with Mazu because it was a part of her upbringing and now was a part of her life. She was so accustomed to it that she has never even thought about it. Understanding what Mazu taught, learning the history of Mazu, visiting the temple every Monday, or participating in some set rituals are all non-essential components to belonging to a religion, at least to the Taiwanese mind. Like Tattoo Ju, for the majority of the interview participants, being part of a religious system was as simple as incorporating certain aspects of this system in one's everyday living. Belonging to a religious system was defined by everyday behaviors and tied together by supernatural threads, linked to one or many deities. Due to its daily applicability, religion was seen as utilitarian at its very core.

Ms. Sha, a psychologist by training, mentioned that she would be surprised if someone *bài* a deity without a special need in the person's life. She said that if a friend said he was going to *bài* a deity, she would wonder, 「他是

不是最近發生什麼事情？」 ("Did something happen to him recently?"). In other words, it would be highly unusual to visit a deity unless something happened in one's everyday life. Ms. Sha herself did not visit deities unless there was a specific need at that moment in her life.

Emotional Health of Healthy Chen

Earlier, Healthy Chen was alluded to briefly. A deeper analysis of his view is helpful to further elaborate the utilitarian nature of religious thinking in Taiwan. Moreover, Healthy Chen's case can show the similarity between a Taiwanese Christian's view of religion and that of a Taiwanese folk religion adherent. Healthy Chen was an engineer who did not mention any Christian family members or relatives. He said that he was baptized about thirteen months before the interview. This meant that he saw himself as being officially Christian for that length of time. Despite being a Christian, Healthy Chen did not know whether he was going to heaven or hell. When asked what it was that he believed about Jesus, he did not mention any historical facts nor did he mention the cross, resurrection, or Jesus being a full God-man in hypostatic union.

Eventually, Healthy Chen was asked what exactly it is he believes about Christianity. He jokingly replied,「信我的心理健康」("[I] believe in my emotional health"). After he was done chuckling, he started explaining what he meant and that what he said was only a half-joke. He explained that he thinks the point of believing in Jesus is to help people be emotionally healthy. He talked about how Jesus had helped him improve his emotions, turning him from an angry, cynical person to someone better. He said Jesus was a role model for him, a 「做人的標準」 ("standard for how to live"). He was asked whether he believes that Jesus died on the cross and then was raised back to life. He said he does not truly believe this, but he does not deny that it could have happened. He defined his own strength of belief as 「勉強相信」 ("barely believing").

Based on what Healthy Chen mentioned and what he did not mention, it seems that he did not become a Christian because he saw the depravity of his sin and thus the need for a savior. He did not become a Christian because he feared dying and going to hell or some other scary, unknown place. In fact, he said he does not think about the afterlife or the previous life (i.e. reincarnation) at all. Healthy Chen did not become a Christian because he saw the truth of Christianity whether in its historicity or its truth claims (which he had little knowledge of). He also did not become a Christian because he thought it provided a better worldview. Rather, Healthy Chen became a Christian because he saw it as the best way to be "emotionally healthy," a phrase that was repeated twenty-four times in the interview.

Healthy Chen was a first-generation Christian who chose Christianity due to the benefits in this life, not the next life. His utilitarian perspective was in many ways like Tattoo Ju's. Both of them treated religion as a means to a specific end. Both of them saw doctrines, rituals, history, and visiting the religious center as non-essential components of religion. Both of them went to their respective deities to attain what they wanted from this life. In other words, this utilitarian perspective seems to be something that most of the interview participants shared, regardless of their religious orientation. Tattoo Ju the Mazu goddaughter, Mommy Farong the Guanyin devotee, and Healthy Chen the new Christian all shared this same utilitarian perspective.

Healthy Chen, as a Christian, was not alone in his understanding of heaven. College Hua could recite certain teachings about the end times but when it came to heaven, he was unsure and seemingly unconcerned. Fishu, despite being a small group leader, was also unsure about what happens to a person after they die. She said that she does believe in a heaven but is unsure how to reconcile that with the multiple stories in Taiwan about roaming ghosts, which she believes as true. She said that she believes that after a person dies, they spend many days in "standby"[15] before they transition to a non-earthly realm. These examples show that heaven as a concept is either not well taught in Taiwanese Christianity or the importance of this life is too ingrained in Taiwanese thinking for heaven to matter very much. It is also possible the answer lies between the two, a possibility that chapter 6 examines more closely.

Part of Life

We have talked about conversion and religion being above all utilitarian for Taiwanese people in Taipei. Now we talk about how religion was part of the participants' lives. For some people, folk religion was such an ingrained part of their daily living that they did not treat it as a religion. For example, Tour Guide Man did not treat folk religion as a distinct entity that one has

---

15. She used English for that word, hence the lack of Chinese in the quotation.

to formally agree to be a part of. It was not something that necessarily required a certain amount of faith or a set kind of ritual. He explained it thus, 「拜拜的形式是我們生活當中的一個部分，一個元素。……拜拜這件事情能夠造成一些生活上、心靈上安定的作用」 ("The ritual of *bài* is a part of our lives, an element of it . . . The act of *bài* can cause a calming effect on [one's] life and emotions").

It seems that the idea of religion being "part of our lives" is a recurring theme. Genie saw her interactions with Mazu as part of her life. When asked what term she would use to describe this interaction, she specifically said that the term 「宗教」 ("religion") does not fit because it lacks the organizational structure and particular rituals that religions like Christianity or Islam have. She preferred the term 「信仰」 (*xìnyǎng*, "faith") because to her, that more closely describes her religious system of thought. To her, it was a loose affiliation with a deity that became more obvious during certain parts of her life. However, she was conscious of this affiliation all the time and tried hard to live up to her position as Mazu's goddaughter. She told the researcher that there is no special doctrine in her religion, but only that we should all try to be good people. When asked to describe her religion, she said, 「是生活的方式、生活的道理」 ("It is a way of life, [a] philosophy of life").

Defining a Devout Person

We have mentioned a few themes that show how Taiwanese people in Taipei define being part of a religious system. We now turn our attention to how Taiwanese people in Taipei define excelling in a religious system. In other words, who is a devout or pious person in a religion? What are the qualities that people look for? The participants were asked to list some traits, actions, or any signs that a 虔誠 (*qiánchéng*, pious or devout) person in their religion would exhibit. This line of questioning was very useful in uncovering how Taiwanese people in Taipei conceptualize religiosity and religious devotion.

For many people, they would not say that they have a religion. Rather, they had a temple (e.g. Hsing Tian Kong) or deity (e.g. Mazu) that they felt the most *yuánfèn* (fateful coincidence) with. The question was phrased differently depending on the person, but the general idea was the same. Words other than "devout" were used, words such as "strong adherent" or "someone you look up to." Sometimes the question was phrased thus, "Describe a good Mazu follower." The idea was to get them to describe what it means to be an invested, deeply connected part of a religious system. The goal was to discover what Taiwanese people in Taipei valued in the area of religious devotion. The following are some of the traits or characteristics listed.

Frequent Religious Action

To Coe Bei, a pious or devout person was someone who *bài* frequently, which she said could be up to 2,000 or 50,000 times a day.[16] She carefully stated that what is in the heart is most important. This means that for Coe Bei, one's inner self is the only accurate indicator of piety. Nevertheless, her response did indicate that *bài* is at least an accepted outward appearance of piety. Many other participants also talked about frequent *bài* as the first obvious sign of devotion before listing others.

For Company Woman, a devout person was her old boss, someone who hired a feng shui master frequently to discover what furniture to move in the office in order to generate more income in the company. Others mentioned in passing the devotion of those serving in the temple. Healthy Chen highlighted the 「廟公」 ("head of the temple") as someone who is particularly devout because he runs the whole temple, presumably daily. These frequent religious actions were accepted by the interview participants as indicating special devotion or piety.

Some participants defined going to a temple two to four times a year is normal behavior. By contrast, if a person goes to a temple more than five times a year, whether it is a Mazu temple or Hsing Tian Kong, this person was considered as more devout than normal. This was different from how most of the Christian participants measured devotion. More than half of the Christian participants said that they visit a church service weekly, which by implication would make them very devout in the eyes of the other participants. Nevertheless, for the non-Christian participants, it seemed that as long as a person went to a temple more than five times a year, this person was considered devout. Police Lady said that her father is "overly"[17] devout

---

16. A single chant of a short phrase or a single bow could be considered one *bài* in this context.

17. She used English for this word, hence the lack of Chinese. She also admitted that her father was consistent in his thinking and behavior. So, in Police Lady's mind, being religiously consistent actually meant being overly devout.

because he visits their holy temple every Tuesday for the special service, making him many times more devout than the average devout person.

"Going to the temple" is a sign of devotion in Taiwan; however, not all religious actions, even performed frequently, make one devout. For example, Genie said that she burns incense at her company every morning when she comes in the office and every evening when she leaves. In addition, she said that her family takes turns making sure that someone does the same for the family altar at home. Despite these frequent religious actions, she did not consider herself devout. At her workplace, she did it because the altar to a certain deity was set up at the entrance. At home, it was a tradition that has been there for a long time. To her, these actions were ordinary. In Genie's view, to be extraordinary, one must go out of one's way to visit a temple and do so frequently. Hsiang Wu, a middle-aged office worker, described pious people as those who look very serious and are focused when they perform religious actions at these temples.

Behavior

Another outward indicator of piety was how a person behaved toward others. Mr. Rich thought that a devout person is someone who lives out the religion in normal life. He used the example of Christianity and said that if Jesus said to be honest or loving, a devout Christian is someone who displays that honesty and love in their life and workplace. He clarified, 「我不可能要求他hundred percent是perfect的，但是……你起碼要比一般人要來的要好，因為你有一個…… mentor在那裡」 ("I cannot expect him to be one hundred percent perfect, but … you should at least be better than the average person, because you have a … mentor there"). He continued to use the idea of a mentor to describe someone who has a relationship with one's deity. It brings out an idea of discipleship, of a mentee following whatever the mentor says as a sign of followership.

Piety is something that is seen in a person's behavior, namely in the conferring of blessing and the showing of compassion. Coe Bei mentioned Mother Teresa as a prime example of piety, calling her a 「大菩薩」 ("big Buddha"). Tattoo Ju stated that she would describe a devout person as someone who lives out their religion by doing good deeds. This idea of being a good person was present in multiple places in numerous interviews, sometimes when complaining about other religions (as Shi Gu did). Fishu and Coffee Girl, talking about a devout Christian, used behavior as the best measure of piety. Disciple Wong also treated behavior as an indicator, but specifically pointed to a person being willing to do difficult, but necessary, deeds that others are not willing to do.

Integrity

Mr. Rich saw 「誠信」 ("integrity") as an important characteristic of pious people. He said that because of the integrity he sees in people, he does not mind going to temples or churches.[18] Lon Le said that when a person's belief matches their behavior, that person is devout. It is especially apparent if the behavior demands much of the person.

Money

Tour Guide Man said that a strong adherent of a religion is someone who 「不管是在心力或財力的奉獻上都有一個很顯著突出的一個角色」 ("excels both in emotional devotion and monetary giving"). He mentioned the example of a Taiwanese mini-celebrity 顏清標 (Ching-Piao Yen), who has given much money to Mazu temples and now heads up the board of a specific temple's foundation, the 大甲鎮瀾宮 (Dajia Jenn Lann Temple).

Like Tour Guide Man, House Gongon also pointed to financial giving. He spoke about the founder of 慈濟基金會 (Buddhist Compassion Relief Tzu Chi Foundation), one of the largest humanitarian organizations in Taiwan. The founder, 證嚴法師 (Master Cheng Yen), is a strong adherent because she has devoted her life to giving resources to the poor and needy. Coe Bei echoed the same idea of financial giving, adding that it is significant because giving money causes those around the person to be happy and blessed. Moreover, the devout person should have great compassion and should not insist on much.

Composure

Bookstore Lady said that a "good Buddhist" is someone who is calm in his or her emotions. This person is always emotionally stable regardless of what he or she encounters in life. She further explained that this means that the person's "religious practice" is at a very high level.

---

18. Interestingly, he preferred churches over temples because he thought that churches are cleaner, namely that they do not have many statuettes.

Relationship with Deity

Smoker Ang described a devout person as any person who stays exclusive to one deity and talks about this deity often. It is especially obvious because exclusivity to one deity is not seen often in Taiwan. For example, Curu said that a devout Christian is someone who 「跟耶穌建立很親密的關係」 ("has built an intimate relationship with Jesus"). This person talks to God and reads the Bible to hear from God. This person prays to God daily and has a relationship built on love. Tattoo Ju, as a folk religion adherent, also strived for a good relationship with her deity. She strived to be close to Mazu because she was Mazu's goddaughter. To her, family greeted one another even when there was nothing to request. She saw it as a normal way of keeping a relationship going.

"Devout" as a Potentially Misleading Term

We have gone through a small list of characteristics that indicate devotion or piety for a person. Not once in the interviews is knowledge mentioned. The characteristics mentioned suggest that for the Taiwanese people in Taipei, their main focus is not on knowledge or orthodoxy, but on action and strength of character. For example, some Buddhist participants answered the questions regarding devotion and piety by talking about the inability to truly measure devotion. Nevertheless, they mentioned certain things that people do, such as time spent in meditation and time spent doing certain things valued by the particular Buddhist sect.

It was initially perplexing to see the lack of clarity in all the participants' responses. It was not until Pei-Pei's response that the situation was clarified. Pei-Pei, though not a Buddhist herself, explained that in Buddhism, she does not hear the word 「虔誠」 (*qiánchéng*, "devout") often. Instead, when people want to talk about a respected person in Buddhism, what is mentioned more are phrases like 「學佛很多年」 ("[The person] has been studying Buddhist dharma for many years") or 「禪修功底很深」 ("Zen practice reflects deep foundation").

Pei-Pei's response indicated that *devotion* may be a misleading term. In other words, a good Buddhist is not praised for being wholly devoted to Buddha nor for doing what Buddha wills nor what the Buddhist scriptures call one to do. Rather, a good Buddhist is praised for spending one's life studying dharma and practicing Zen. The focus seems to be on the subjective element of faith, on how people live out their lives. It may be a sign of Buddhist influence that even among the non-Buddhist participants in the research, behavioral action and strength of character were still on the forefront of defining piety.

Summary of Being Part of a Religious System

We have now examined, from multiple angles, what it means to be part of a religion in Taiwan. We have seen from the participants' view of conversion that religious practice is important and may even be the defining feature of conversion. Moreover, it is largely an "unclear and long process."[19] We have seen that many of the participants had a "utilitarian perspective"[20] of deities and religious systems. The extreme example of Healthy Chen is an illustration of this. We have seen that religion for many participants was just a part of their lives, intertwined with daily living. We have lastly seen from the many participant-given definitions of a "devout person" that devout may be a potentially misleading term. Namely, being in a religious system is about spending time and improving character for Taiwanese people in Taipei. This data has given useful glimpses into how a Taiwanese person views and interacts with religion, deities, and everything in the unseen realm.

Summary of Findings on the Unseen Realm and General Religiosity

We have explored some qualitative data from the interviews conducted in Taiwan. We have looked at the general orientation and attitudes people have toward anything in the unseen realm. This has given us a glimpse into the religious worldview of the Taiwanese person. We have looked at different words that people use to express "faith." This has revealed the semantic categories that people have regarding religion. We have looked at being part of a religious system. This has clarified how Taiwanese people in Taipei relate to religions, how they think of converting to a religion, and what they think the purpose of religion is. In the next chapter, we move on to details about findings related to choosing a deity and issues of "faith."

---

19. Using Tour Guide Man's words.
20. Using Fishu's words.

CHAPTER 5

Findings on Deities, Jesus, and Christianity

In the last chapter, we discussed some of the findings from the field research. In this chapter, we continue discussion about the findings, focusing more on deities. Specifically, we discuss these three categories of data: (1) the concept of choosing a deity, (2) how people interpret the phrase "believe in Jesus for eternal life," and (3) key objections to Christianity. We start the discussion with the first category.

Choosing a Deity

Remember that the ultimate goal of this work is to begin developing a contextual approach to gospel transmission. For this to happen, we need to understand how Taiwanese people in Taipei perceive the gospel. It is also useful to understand how Taiwanese people in Taipei perceive Christianity itself as well as how they perceive "faith" in a deity. In this section, we explore faith in a deity by examining three points of interest: (1) how to have "faith" in a deity, (2) why people choose a particular deity, and (3) assumed belief in multiple deities.

How to Have "Faith" in a Deity

In the interviews, participants explained various ways to have "faith" in a deity. This section shows examples from Christianity, Buddhism, folk religion, and the spirit world. Other, shorter examples are shown to nuance the findings.

Example from Christianity

In the research five people self-identified as Christian. They were asked to tell someone how a person can become Christian, specifically explaining what "faith" refers to. The Christian participants interpreted "faith" in more practical, behavioral, and visible ways. When asked how a person can believe or have faith in God, Curu mentioned that Jesus is the 「信仰的中心」 ("center of faith") and 「生活的中心」 ("center of life"). For Curu, "faith" was tied to the person of Jesus and to the way one's life is lived.

Fishu said that having "faith" in Jesus means accepting him in one's heart and having him 「cover你的生活」 ("cover over your life"). Healthy Chen said that "faith" means imitating Jesus's actions and morality. Coffee Girl explained it as the changing of one's 「價值觀」 ("value system"). College Hua said that in order to have "faith," one must be connected to a church. For all the Christian participants, "faith" was something that had direct effects on one's life. The researcher was expecting more answers that talked about the historicity of Jesus or an explanation of believing in the work on the cross; but no Christians talked about those things.

Example from Buddhism

Buddhist participants were asked how a person can become Buddhist. Mommy Farong referred to the idea of *yuánfèn* (fateful coincidence) as a method. For Mommy Farong, the Buddha that she had the most *yuánfèn* with was the one who was born in 1931 with the family name Chen. This Buddha acts as the head of 九華山 (Jiuhua Mountain), one of the top four most famous "mountains" in Taiwan. These "mountains" refer to the four biggest branches of Buddhism in the country. Mommy Farong talked about this Buddha as the 「救世師父菩薩」 ("Savior of the World Master Buddha") but did not go into detail about a method to become a Buddhist that is more proactive than relying on *yuánfèn*.

To clarify the issue, other Buddhist participants were asked what it meant to have "faith" in Buddha. Mrs. Ting said it meant to follow the 「佛法」 (literally "Buddha dharma"). And what did it mean to follow dharma? She did not point to specifics but simply said, 「我們是拜了佛會是覺得無盡的智慧、無盡的覺悟，覺了宇宙的人事，人生的一切的事故」 ("We who *bài* Buddha would feel infinite wisdom, infinite understanding, understanding the people and events of the universe, the happenings of one's entire life").

Coe Bei also preferred the term *dharma*. Coe Bei saw religion as "understand [sic] of the true essence of life."[1] She did not like the term 「佛教」 (literally "Buddha religion"); more specifically, she explained that "religion" is 「整個世界你的一種basic的……認知」 ("kind of your basic understanding ... of the whole world"). She thought that whatever the word used, the essence is not religion or dharma, it is Buddha. At other parts of the interview, she referred to herself as someone who practices 「佛法」 ("dharma") but she never referred to herself as a 「佛教徒」 ("Buddhist" or literally "Buddha disciple").

Mrs. Ting was careful to point out that she does not even talk about dharma when introducing people to Buddhism, specifically when she introduces them to the Jiuhua Mountain branch of Buddhism. She said that she usually tells her friends to go 祭拜 (*jì bài*, "do ritualistic worship") at Jiuhua Mountain if they have problems with 「病啊或是家裡啊、工作啊，還是什麼結婚啊還生小孩」 ("sickness, family, job search, marriage, or having kids"). After the prayers came true, Mrs. Ting's friends acquired faith, then came into contact with the essentials of dharma.

Mrs. Ting's story shows that even in Buddhism, people approach deities the same way as people do in folk religion, namely that of treating them as powerful entities who can answer prayers and can help with current life situations. "Faith" comes after the power is seen as actually powerful. Only after the power is felt does dharma become sought after.

Example from Folk Religion

The folk religion adherents were asked how they interacted with deities. The interviews contained multiple examples that show what "faith" in a deity may look like. Two interview participants' stories are covered here to illustrate the points with proper depth. The other examples can be found in snippets throughout the rest of the findings.

Deities as Big Uncles and Aunties

When asked about their experiences with deities, many of the participants mentioned Yue Lao. For example, Pei-Pei answered this question immediately by stating her experience seeking out Yue Lao. She mentioned a specific

---

1. She spoke in English for this phrase.

temple housing Yue Lao that is famous in Taiwan.[2] This temple in Taipei, 霞海城隍廟 (Xia-Hai City God Temple), draws numerous people due to its Yue Lao's reputation as being 「靈驗」 (*língyàn*, "efficacious"). Thus, many people seeking a romantic partner visit this temple. Ms. Sha, Pei-Pei, and many others mentioned visiting this temple due to its reputation of being "efficacious." See figure 12 for the temple they mentioned.

Figure 12. The temple that Pei-Pei and Ms. Sha mentioned had long lines

Pei-Pei talked about a series of six to eight steps that she had to carry out in the temple to properly *bài* Yue Lao. She had to mention her name, address, birthday, and some other information for Yue Lao to truly know who she was. When it was time to beseech Yue Lao for a romantic partner, the directions said to be specific about the qualities one is looking for in a partner. Pei-Pei said that she had a little bit of an expectation before visiting the Yue Lao temple, that she would get a romantic partner. As a girl in her twenties, she

---

2. There are multiple temples and multiple statuettes of Yue Lao. Certain temples' Yue Lao have a better reputation than others.

wanted to meet more guys. She said, 「姻緣這件事情好像看緣分，但是緣分我們……我們還可以做什麼」 ("A thing like getting married is kind of dependent on *yuánfèn*, but [except for] *yuánfèn*, we . . . what else can we do")?

She said that a week after praying to Yue Lao, she actually met many guys that were similar to the specific list of qualities she had asked for, proving in her mind the efficacy of this particular Yue Lao temple. She knew that she still had to actively befriend guys and go out on dates; but she knew that Yue Lao can at least help her with the part on *yuánfèn*, on crossing her path with the kind of guys she asked for.

Pei-Pei compared the way Taiwanese deities are perceived to the way the LORD is perceived: 「基督教的神給我一種感覺就是祂就是唯一的真理，然後台灣的民間信仰比較像是……鄰家大叔或大嬸」 ("Christianity's deity gives me a feeling that he is [seen as] the only truth; and then folk religion in Taiwan is more like . . . the neighborhood big uncle or big auntie"). She summarized her conception of deities later: 「就很像我們身邊的人然後只是祂們在另外一個世界」 ("[They] are very much like [normal] people around us, but they are just in another world"). Disciple Wong described the deities similarly but treated them as 「我們的長輩」 ("our [family] elders"). Mountain Pi added that because of the familial aspect, the deities in folk religion are more approachable than Christianity's high God. To Mountain Pi, Christianity was 「這麼嚴肅」 ("so serious").

In other words, the deities common in folk religion in Taiwan are seen as more down to earth. They are big uncles and aunties who help take care of people's everyday problems. To Pei-Pei, Christianity's deity was this distant being that must be acknowledged as the only truth while folk religion in Taiwan provided multiple deities who may not be as powerful, but are closer to home. These deities live in a world parallel to our own, but are otherwise similar to human beings. In this parallel world of deities, the residents hold more power. This power is why it is beneficial for humans to approach these deities.

Pei-Pei thought that the deities' powers are related to how many people have "faith" in them. She explained "faith" in terms of the number of people burning incense to the deity. She repeated the Taiwanese idiom, 「這間廟的香火旺不旺？」 ("Is this temple's incense burning vigorously or not?"). In Taiwan, this saying is a common way of asking whether a temple's deity is powerful, namely by tracking the number of people going there to burn incense. From this idiom, Pei-Pei derived that a deity's power must come from people believing and performing *bài* to the deity. Another interpretation favored by people like Tattoo Ju was that because a deity is powerful, many people recognize this power and flock to them.

The idea of deities can be further complicated due to the Buddhist influence. Pei-Pei, even as a non-Buddhist, said she likes and believes in the idea that 「人人都有可能成為佛」 ("anyone can be a Buddha"). It is an idea popular in Taiwan, one that stresses the divinity in everyday people. For some participants, including Pei-Pei and Coe Bei, deities are simply people who have already advanced to the state of Buddha through religious practice. Genie called this a 「升官」 ("promotion") to godhood. Genie said that deities have ranks too. This means that as deities are promoted in the heavenly ranks, they are retitled and gain more authority, which in turn leads to more worshippers. Again, this supports the idea that deities are in a parallel, higher realm of existence.

"Faith" in a deity seems to be nothing more than approaching the "big uncles and aunties" in this separate realm to ask for help in various things in life that is hard to do on one's own. By virtue of being a big uncle or auntie, the deity would help out the neighborhood "kid" that is in trouble. Disciple Wong added that if there is a close relationship to the big uncle or auntie (in the form of better *yuán* or more frequent *bài* by the person), it makes help more likely. After all, close relatives are more likely to help a person than just any uncle or auntie. Furthermore, many things that seem to be important are irrelevant to Taiwanese like Pei-Pei. The irrelevant things include knowledge of what kind of person the big uncle or auntie is and the truth of what the big uncle or auntie claims. What matters is whether this big uncle or auntie is powerful, efficacious, and willing to help the person out.

Help from Mazu, Earth God, and the LORD

Another notable example is Company Woman. She grew up visiting Mazu temples. For that reason, she went to Mazu temples for most of her needs. This was different from most of the other participants, who went to different deities depending on the issue and the specialty of the deity. Company Woman had gone to Mazu for blessings and protection, peace, and romance. She acknowledged that other deities may be known for various things, but she said that she was more used to Mazu. Due to this closeness, she said that she has gone to Mazu when she feels depressed. She specifically mentioned

2011 as a year she sought Mazu more than before because she had just moved to a different province and broke up with her boyfriend. It seemed like she treats Mazu as an advocate whom she can talk to, complain about life, and help her solve problems.

Despite her closeness to Mazu for most of her life, Company Woman did not shy away from approaching other deities. She mentioned multiple deities throughout the interview. One interesting story was how 土地公 (*Tǔdì Gong*, Earth God) helped her with a rent issue. She mentioned having been evicted from an apartment just five days before she had to fly to Japan. This meant she had five days to find a new place, move, and prepare for her work trip to Japan. She mentioned having been 「很焦慮」 ("very anxious"). She tried hard for three days but found nothing, resulting in her feeling 「非常的沮喪」 ("extremely depressed"). Per a friend's recommendation, she tried praying to the LORD during those three days.

Unfortunately, the LORD did not grant her petition, leaving her 「很挫折」 ("very frustrated"). On that third day, after walking in the rain and on the verge of crying, she called a friend to talk. This other friend recommended that she should find the Earth God temple nearest to her apartment and tell him the entire situation. The friend recommended that she should beseech the Earth God to help resolve everything, even telling him the kind of new apartment that she wanted. She did so that same night. The next morning, for fear that she was unclear in her request, she went again to the Earth God nearest to her to tell him the exact type of apartment she wanted. That same day, she got a call from a landlord to see an apartment. That same evening, she saw the apartment, was able to get it, and did not even have to put down a deposit until a week later.

After she moved, she went to a new Earth God, the one nearest to her new apartment, to talk about her situation. Her friend reminded her that she had to thank the previous Earth God and tell the new Earth God the whole situation so that he can better bless and protect her in this different jurisdiction. The friend said that these two Earth Gods most likely talk to each other, so it is better that she approaches both of them directly to be polite. She promptly did so. Her other friend who asked her to pray to the LORD told her that the LORD must have secretly helped her too, so she should pray to thank the LORD also. She did so as well.

Company Woman said that in this experience, multiple deities helped her. She said that she believes that the LORD has helped her in this experience by teaching her valuable lessons. Earth God has helped her by 「冥冥之中推了［她］一把」 ("imperceptibly giving [her] a push"). She said that her own hard work in looking for places also played a role. She refused to give credit only to Earth God or to herself or to another deity. She thought that she was able to resolve the situation through the combination of all those elements and every deity she turned to.

This story shows that Company Woman has approached multiple deities for one single issue, looking for the deity who could solve her problem. She said she is closest to Mazu, yet she did not shy away from beseeching Earth God or praying to the LORD. To her, "faith" in a deity did not mean that she trusted a deity to be true and all others to be false. It did not mean that she has signed an exclusivity contract with a deity while locking other deities out. It did not mean that deities that are more foreign to her (e.g. the LORD) was someone she was fearful of approaching. To her, "faith" in a deity was like "trying to get help" from a deity. She tried Mazu, Earth God, and the LORD, all concurrently. This shotgun approach seemed to be something she has done more than once.

Example of Spirits

In order to better understand how to have "faith" in a deity, we have looked at examples from Christianity, Buddhism, and folk religion. We now look at an example involving spirits. Bookstore Lady mentioned that when she was little, she did not revere the unseen spirits. However, at the time of the interview, she believed that 「雖然我們肉眼看不到，他事實是存在的」 ("even if our naked eye cannot see [it], it truly exists"). She mentioned 「山靈」 ("mountain spirit"), 「山神」 ("mountain god"), and other ghosts that we cannot see but are 「事實是真的」 ("emphatically true").

Bookstore Lady mentioned that sometimes, when one experiences a case where 「受驚嚇」 (*shòu jīngxià*, "[something] frightened [one's spirit] away]"), one may need the help of a specialist to 「收驚」 (*shōu jīng*, "recover [the spirit] after the fright"). After all, it is believed that one would suffer numerous physical side effects from having one's spirit depart from the body. When seeking for help in *shōu jīng*, people often go to a 「姑婆」 (*gūpó*, literally "auntie") available at many temples, who perform these services for free. The *gūpó* would repeatedly chant a 「咒語」 (*zhòuyǔ*, "spell") to drive out whatever bad influences remain on the person and recover the lost spirit.

These types of information were mentioned by Bookstore Lady, whose grandmother was a *gūpó* at the temple 行天宮 (Hsing Tian Kong) in Taipei. Not just any "auntie" can be a *gūpó*. Despite the service being free and all *gūpós* being volunteers, one needs to have certain verifications before being allowed to perform the service of *shōu jīng*. Bookstore Lady mentioned that the power to perform *shōu jīng* does not reside in the *gūpó* herself, but with the deity that resides at the temple; the *gūpó* only channels that power. See figure 13 for a picture at Hsing Tian Kong of people lining up for two separate *gūpó* to perform *shōu jīng* for people.[3]

Figure 13. People in a zigzag line, waiting for two *gūpós* to perform *shōu jīng* for them

When asked about needing some kind of faith or belief for *shōu jīng* to work, Bookstore Lady repeatedly answered that it does not matter. She said,

---

3. The people in blue were volunteers who directed traffic and made sure people lined up properly. The researcher witnessed several rituals of *shōu jīng*. In some cases, the person would be visibly distressed and looked physically unstable during the ritual. Each ritual of *shōu jīng* lasted only a few minutes.

「你今天如果是一個外國人，洋人他去收驚，他也一樣可以收到」 ("If you are a foreigner, a white person, [and if] he goes [somewhere] to *shōu jīng*, he can also recover"). She added that believing in Jesus may lower the spell's effectiveness, but she said she is just guessing and does not know for sure. According to Bookstore Lady, it did not matter what one believes, it only mattered that a spell may be effective because of the power of the deity. The main idea here is that "faith" in a deity is inconsequential. What matters is the power of the deity, not the "faith" of the human being.

Other Examples

We have now seen examples from four broad categories of religiosity in Taiwan. The following are three shorter examples that do not fit neatly in the categories but nevertheless give good insight into how Taiwanese people in Taipei might have "faith" in a deity.

Do Human's Part, Then Listen to Heaven's Fate

House Gongon explained that when he approaches the deity, he does not have a strong expectation that the deity will consistently grant his requests. He did not always have a specific request either. He said that most of the time, he asks for general prosperity, health for family members, and occasionally romance for his grandchildren. When asked what his emotional attitude was, he replied, 「沒有甚麼期待，我認為我是盡人事嘛！盡我們虔誠的心去拜嘛！其他的就是聽天命嘛！沒有期待」 ("No special expectations. I think I just do the human's part! That is to *bài* with devotion. The rest is to listen to heaven's fate! No expectations"). Genie explained the same concept as 「天助自助者」 ("Heaven helps those who help themselves").

House Gongon further explained that even if we keep beseeching the deities for certain things, but do not put forth our own human effort, it would be for naught. To him, "faith" was when humans play their part and deities play their part. One needs to put those two elements together to truly have all of one's desires fulfilled. Fishu and a few other participants echoed this sentiment as well. When talking about her attitude in seeking Lord Superior Wen Chang's help in tests, Fishu said that she still needed to work hard. However, Lord Superior Wen Chang could help her cover the areas that hard work alone cannot achieve. She mentioned clarity of the brain, questions asked on the tests, and other unknown factors. Genie mentioned that deities tend to help those who are already good and working hard. House Gongon, Fishu, or Genie would not neglect their own parts after beseeching a deity. To them, both should be done in conjunction to each other.

Sincerity
Both Chi and Hsiang Wu believed that 「心誠則靈」 ("If the heart is sincere, it is efficacious"). In other words, it is not so important whether the deities themselves are real or are powerful enough, it is more about the sincerity of the heart. Mr. Rich mentioned the concept of electromagnetic fields generated by brain waves. Mr. Rich's explanation was essentially the same kind of thinking as Chi and Hsiang Wu, namely that efficacy comes from within the person. To them, "faith" was nothing more than sincerely believing. Mr. Rich treated "faith" as no more than 「精神上的安慰」 ("emotional comfort") or more positively as the 「力量的產生」 ("production of power"), effects that can be experienced as long as one is sincere.

Uncertainty over Specifics
Sometimes the participants themselves were not sure about the specifics of a deity. However, they *bài* the deity anyway. For example, Fishu recounted that she has *bài* all kinds of deities, including Mazu, Guan Shengdijun, and the Jade Emperor God.[4] When she used to *bài* the deity, she asked for blessings and protection most of the time. But she said that she often did not know what specific thing to ask for because she did not know what these deities can actually do for her. In other words, Fishu did not know about their main powers.

The relevant thing to note here is that Fishu did not need to know the specifics of the deity, including their main powers, their likes or dislikes, or even the proper way to worship or *bài*. Fishu, back when she was very involved in folk religion, did not think these things were important or relevant details. To her, she saw a deity and she *bài* it. It is likely that she treated the deities the same way Pei-Pei did, like neighborhood big uncles and aunties. She sought help and figured that asking them for help can only be beneficial, not harmful. Police Lady summarized it using a famous proverb, 「寧可信其有，不可信其無」 ("[One should] rather believe there is [something] than believe there is not [anything]").

---

4. She used the term 「玉皇大帝」, which is a common alias for 玉皇上帝 (Jade Emperor God, also known as Shangdi).

Summary of How People Have "Faith" in a Deity

We have examined many examples of how participants described having "faith" in a deity. We have seen from Christian participants that "faith" is often understood along more practical and behavioral ways. We have seen from Buddhism that dharma and wise living are the essence of "faith." We have seen from folk religion that deities are like big uncles and big aunties in the neighborhood. Therefore, for those practicing folk religion, having "faith" in multiple deities is no more than asking for help from multiple uncles and aunties. We have seen from the world of the spirits that power is the most important thing in matters of the supernatural, not so-called "faith." We have also seen a few smaller examples that show the nuances of how Taiwanese people in Taipei conceptualize "faith." In the next section, we explore why people choose a deity.

Why People Choose a Deity

In the interview, there were multiple reasons given for why a participant approached a certain deity. The "how" is important because it reveals the process of approaching a deity. The "why" is important because it reveals the rationale and religious worldview of the person. The data was categorized into the following seven reasons.

Resolving Grievances

Mommy Farong needed to 「解怨釋結」 (*jiě yuàn shì jié*, "resolve grievances and release grudges"). She was in an emotionally difficult time and wanted to feel better. A friend explained that at this mountain temple's branch of Buddhism (九華山), she might be able to "resolve grievances and release grudges," particularly if they are related to her past life. When she was there to *bài* Buddha, that was when she became 「真正的投入」 ("truly devoted"). For her, choosing a deity was due to resolving a grievance in life.

Need a Good Test Score

Fishu went to a deity named 文昌帝君 (*Wénchāng Dìjūn*, Lord Superior Wen Chang) because she needed to get a better score for her college entrance exam. This exam is a big deal for Taiwanese students because it near single-handedly determines what school one can attend. Lord Superior Wen Chang is a common deity that students go to because, having been an academic himself, he is known for helping people get good grades. The special thing about Fishu is that she gave up eating beef for one year as a "sacrifice" that she offered to the deity in exchange for good grades. The reason is that in many of the temples that include a Lord Superior Wen Chang, he is often seen riding on a cow, which made her think that perhaps he would appreciate it if she stopped eating beef. Her test score was revealed about halfway through the one year fasting from beef. She thought about eating beef again at that time but said that she was scared of breaking the promise. She did not say what she was scared of precisely, but indicated that since she made a promise to the deity, she would fast for one year; it was better to keep the promise.

Numerous other participants mentioned having visited this deity too. Pei-Pei's class president took everyone's 准考證 (*zhǔn kǎozhèng*, test admission ticket) to Lord Superior Wen Chang to pray for his blessing to get good test results and hence get into good universities. Tour Guide Man asked many of his family members to *bài* Lord Superior Wen Chang, each of them bringing photocopies of his test admission ticket. He said it was like buying insurance, to improve his chances in any possible way. Police Lady, Ms. Sha, and a handful of other participants had experience with this deity for the same reason.

Perceived Power

Another reason one might "believe" in a deity is due to the deity's perceived power level. Tour Guide Man said that he prefers Guanyin out of all the deities because her 「法力比較高強」 ("power is the greatest"). He mentioned a few other deities that he thinks are worth *bài*. The reason given was that he has heard of their legends in his daily life and knew them by name, presumably indicating that their powers are well-known. Similarly, Fishu has chosen a few other deities because she thought they were more powerful, at least in the area that she needed help in (i.e. seeking Yue Lao for help with love). Disciple Wong chose his temple due to a mixture of *yuán* and perceived power.

Power level is not just a matter of whether the deity has the power to effectuate change. Company Woman chose to go to Mazu and Earth God in her moment of need because she 「感應」 ("sensed") those deities and they responded to her. Shi Gu and Bookstore Lady described the same reason for choosing certain temples over other ones, namely that she could "sense" something spiritual there. The idea is not that they were more sensitive than other people. As the participants put it, they could sense the deities better because they had better *yuán* with these deities. Being able to sense the deities in turn led to the participants more easily experiencing the deity's power.

Bless and Protect

One of the most common concepts mentioned in the interviews was the provision of peace, prosperity, and stability. The term used most often was 「保佑」 ("bless and protect"). Every participant (except the Christian minister) mentioned 「求平安」 ("beseeching for peace and safety") as a reason they approached a deity. Company Woman, Tattoo Ju, and Hsiang Wu specifically mentioned approaching Mazu for peace and safety for themselves.

Sometimes a person may feel nervous if they did not ask for a deity's blessings and protection at the beginning of the year. Company Woman was one such person. She said that she feels like she has to go to a Mazu temple during Chinese New Year in order to *bài* and burn some incense. She has been doing this since she was a child and she felt like her entire year would not be smooth if she did not go through this religious ritual. She expressed her anxiety this way: 「媽祖不會保佑我」 ("Mazu would not bless and protect me"),

Others asked for the same thing for the whole region. House Gongon said that the multiple deities who reside in each temple help 「保佑這個地方。……那所以對這個社會安定是有一點幫助」 ("bless and protect this region. . . . So, it helps a little in the stabilizing of society").

Even atheists seem to value the idea of beseeching for peace, blessings, and protection. Mr. Rich, even though he was an atheist, has the same understanding about "faith." He saw "faith" in Mazu as trusting in Mazu for protection. He said that 「他沒有信媽祖是信什麼東西，而是信媽祖他能夠保佑他」 ("there is nothing [concrete] to believe about Mazu, just that Mazu can bless and protect him [a person]").

Smoker Ang, though not an atheist, had a similar idea. Smoker Ang was not sure about the existence, the power, the specialties, or other details of many deities. He said that he is not even sure whether the rituals he does are effective or not. However, he said that he still visits temples to beseech for blessings and protection for himself and his family.

Same Artery and Vein

Yet others believed not mainly because of a particular reason or need, but because of *yuánfèn*. Remember the full elaboration of the concept in an earlier section. In the context of believing in a deity, when a person has *yuánfèn* with a deity, belief comes eventually. It is related to a deterministic worldview where everything has been decided for a person before a person is even born. When asked about what it means to *bài* Mazu, Shi Gu said that it means 「他是屬於媽祖這個脈絡」 ("He belongs to Mazu's artery and vein"). Shi Gu's explanation was that for any person who belongs to Mazu's artery and vein, this person would follow Mazu and perform all these rituals. Shi Gu used this concept multiple times throughout the interview, sometimes referring to it as a 「線」 ("line") and a few times even as 「一串粽子」 ("a string of rice dumplings"). The idea is that there is a line that ties the person to one original source, a line that is hard to escape from.

It is not entirely up to the person to which artery and vein they would belong. Some might belong to Mazu, others to Buddha, and still others to Jesus. Shi Gu used the phrase 「原先就是屬於」 ("originally already belonged to"), which signifies how this was decided before birth. Shi Gu said later in the interview that she is not a Christian because she is not in the same artery and vein as Christianity. Her religious allegiance was not due to some agreement over theology or preference over rituals. It was determined by the heavens long ago that she belonged somewhere else. She merely followed her fate.

Mommy Farong admitted that when she was a small girl, she wanted to be a nun because of the way they dressed. The reason she ended up not being a nun was because she always participated in different kinds of folk religion festivals with her parents while growing up. This participation in her mind precluded her from following any other path. She explained that ultimately, she became a Buddhist because she was fated to be one. Similarly, Coe Bei described her conversion to Buddhism as her 「佛緣的開啟」 ("Buddha *yuán* being activated"). It has the same idea as a fateful coincidence, of always having belonged to the same artery and vein.

Godchildren

Tattoo Ju was a 「乾女兒」 (*gān nǚ'ér*, "goddaughter") of Mazu. This came to pass because when she was born, Tattoo Ju's mother noticed that she was

「八字輕」 ("eight-character light"). The "eight-character" is related to the 「八卦」 ("eight trigrams") discussed in the chapter on folk religion but is based more on the date and hour of birth. In any case, because her eight-character was considered "light," Tattoo Ju's mother decided that the daughter needed more 「保佑」 ("protection and blessing") in life. The mother sought out Mazu and went through a ceremony to have Tattoo Ju adopted as Mazu's goddaughter.

As Mazu's goddaughter, Tattoo Ju treated Mazu as a family member. She said that she grew up going to this big temple near her house just to greet Mazu. This was still a yearly occurrence when she returned to her parents' home. She said that when she is there, she speaks certain greetings to Mazu and then asks for a blessing for the following year. In Taipei, where she lived at the time of the interview, she still visited Mazu temples, albeit with no set frequency. She said that she is there to 「跟祂問聲好」 ("say hello to her [Mazu]"). She would update Mazu on how things are going and thank Mazu for the protection and blessings Mazu has given her until then. This had become a habit for her, and she would visit even if she did not have specific things to beseech. In her mind, Tattoo Ju did not choose Mazu, she was the one who was chosen as Mazu's goddaughter.

Efficacious

For many people, a deity being 「靈驗」 (*língyàn*, "efficacious") is reason enough to believe in the deity and visit the temple. Pei-Pei went to a certain temple's idol of Yue Lao because of that specific one having a reputation of being efficacious. Likewise, Bookstore Lady, Company Woman, Police Lady, College Hua, Disciple Wong, and Smoker Ang all mentioned that a deity being efficacious was enough to draw either themselves or their friends.

House Gongon and Shi Gu used the same concept on fortune telling, another popular aspect of folk religion in Taiwan. Shi Gu explained it thus, 「聽人家講說『欸這一家很靈啊！』我們……就幾個人約一約就跑去了」 ("[I] heard others say, 'Eh, this one [temple] is very efficacious!' So, we . . . got a few people and went."). If a deity or fortune teller or some other thing is efficacious, the normal response is that the person would go try it out. Questions of doctrine or historicity were never brought up in these participants' responses. The idea is that whether something is efficacious is one of the most important things to consider for the Taiwanese person. For most of the aforementioned participants, it was the only thing to consider. As alluded in the last chapter, this focus on the deity's being efficacious really shows the utilitarian nature of Taiwanese religious thinking.

Other Concerns

There were a few other concerns that did not fit into neat categories. One example worth mentioning is choosing a temple because of their care for the environment. Ms. Sha confessed that she does not know anything substantial about the main deity housed at Hsing Tian Kong. However, she was drawn to the deity because the temple took away incense sticks and other items that are very common in the ritual involved in doing *bài* of deities. The reason was that these items have bad effects on the environment. Coffee Girl and House Gongon also alluded to being impressed by temples that have made these change. These changes do not say anything about the deities themselves, but they nevertheless have drawn adherents.

Assumed Belief in Multiple Deities

We have looked at how and why Taiwanese people in Taipei choose a deity. But as seen in Company Woman's example, sometimes people do not just choose one deity but several deities. This is normal because of the apparently common belief in multiple deities. A more accurate way to phrase this statement is to say that the existence of each deity is assumed unless proven otherwise. This means that Taiwan has a certain level of religious pluralism. Coe Bei for example said that she believes in the existence of almost every deity she encounters. She said, "包括神啊、地基主啊，這些我也都相信啊。包括城隍爺啊，什麼我也都相信啊。而且我覺得這些有很多都是善良的啊。善神祂是要幫大家解決問題的，那我是懷著一種感恩崇敬的心來嗯 (As for God, Earth God, I believe in these. City God too, I believe in whomever. I also think a lot of them are kind. A kind deity wants to help fix problems, so I maintain a thankful, reverent heart)." Coe Bei explained later that this reverent heart is important to 「祈願」 (*qíyuàn*, "beseech for a wish"). Hsiang Wu said that she already believes in the existence of all the deities and spirits, but she just does not have the 「靈性」 ("spirituality") to feel and experience them often. Even an atheist like Lon Le believed that the deities in Taiwan are real and have powers that can affect us. He just preferred to see them as spirits rather than as gods.[5]

The assumed existence of multiple deities means that joining another person's religious ritual is seen as normal and respectful, not as any kind of special commitment. Mr. Rich indicated that he does not mind praying along with other people. He simply 「跟著一起拜」 ("*bài* along") with the person regardless of the deity. He said he has done this with his Buddhist wife on multiple occasions and with two Christian coworkers. When asked how he felt, he answered that he did not feel anything special beyond 「被祝福到」 ("feeling blessed"). He thought going along with the person's religious actions is a sign of respect and that there is no need to reject it.

One example of this pluralism is Company Woman, who self-identified as a Buddhist and very interested in Christianity. She saw herself as on the verge of choosing between religions at the time of the interview. She explained her way forward,

> 這兩個宗教，目前在我生活中，是一個屬於比較balance的狀態。……所以以我自私的想法，我覺得就像買保險，我要佛祖的保佑，但也有上帝的保守，所以雙重保障啊 (These two religions, currently in my life, are in a state of balance . . . So, according to my selfish thinking, I think it is like buying insurance. I want Buddha's protection and blessing, but also Shangdi's [the LORD's] protection and keeping, so a double guarantee).

Company Woman continued by saying that she has a long road ahead of her in life and she does not know what will happen in the future. For Company Woman, she saw nothing wrong with aligning herself with both religions. Shi Gu also aligned herself with two religions, Buddhism and Daoism. Company Woman seemed to think that having multiple deities protecting and blessing her can only be a good thing. In her own words, getting an insurance policy from two deities can only be beneficial.

Tattoo Ju is another, even more extreme example. She believed that all the deities worshipped in Taiwan were real. In addition, all the spirits and ghosts

---

5. This suggests that for some Taiwanese people, being an atheist just means that one does not believe in the existence of gods. The existence of spirits is still accepted.

that people talk about were real too. When asked whether some may be on a higher level or "more real" than others, she replied stating, 「不是耶……我相信全部都存在」 ("No, no . . . I believe they all exist"). When asked for their rationales, many of them stated that the evidence is ubiquitous. For example, House Gongon said that there are often tales of possession by the deities, causing people to do things and utter things that are supernatural. Many looked at the researcher strangely when he asked the question, as if asking for proof or doubting the deities' existences was strange. The participant interviews indicate that most Taiwanese assume deities to be real unless proven otherwise.

Going back to the idea of believing multiple deities, Tattoo Ju's response matched that of many other participants. Most of them revered deities they passed by on the streets. For example, Company Woman said she *bài* deities whenever she sees them. She did not mention a reason but said it as a matter of fact, like something a normal person is supposed to do. House Gongon said he almost always 「磕三個禮」 ("prays three times in politeness") to deities as he passes by them on the street. He said that he does that because he thinks that all these deities truly exist. In fact, at temples where there are multiple deities (which is the norm in Taiwan), House Gongon said that he prays to all of them.

It seems that to "believe" in a deity is not a big deal. One can just as easily believe in Mazu as one can believe in Jesus. This means that "believing in a deity" means very little, suggesting neither religious commitment nor religious change. As Company Woman put it, what is important is not whether a deity exists or whether one believes a deity exists, but whether one is 「link 上」 ("linked up") with a deity or 「感應」 ("senses") a deity. In other words, one must be first linked through *yuán* and then have the deity 「觸動到［他］心靈的深處」 ("touch a deep part of [one's] heart and soul").

"Believing in a deity" may be more appropriately thought of as "choosing a deity." After naming a list of three deities, Genie was asked what deity she would recommend to others. She answered, 「祂沒有所謂的排名……因為祂們三個代表的東西都不太一樣」 ("They do not have a ranking . . . because these three represent different things"). For Genie, no deities were inherently better than another deity to believe in or to worship. She refused to compare the deities because they all serve different purposes. She did mention that some deities may have more power, perhaps like a CEO of a corporation.

However, she said that it is still better to go to deities who control specific realms (e.g. money, childbirth, etc.).

There is another important point of consideration beyond believing in multiple deities' existence. The abilities of the deities often overlap one another. As discussed elsewhere in the work, deities do have specialties that they are known for. For example, Earth God is known for protecting the land, Yue Lao for romance, Lord Superior Wen Chang for academics, and so on.

For adherents who are more loyal, they tend to focus on one deity to solve all their problems. Company Woman for example said she goes to Mazu when she needs blessings and protection, but also when she needs romantic help, the latter of which is usually the specialty of Yue Lao. Likewise, Disciple Wong went to 關聖帝君 (Guan Shengdijun, or Guan Yu) for every single kind of request. They both did this without denying the existence of other deities. Company Woman was loyal because she has been visiting Mazu temples since she was a child and Disciple Wong was loyal because he thought the power of Guan Shengdijun is sufficient. Loyalty means that a person frequents one temple almost exclusively. See figure 14 for the front of Disciple Wong's temple. See figure 15 for the way people worship on a weekday morning. See figure 16 for the same temple in the afternoon. See figure 17 for a volunteer guide explaining the stories and functions of all the deities featured in this temple.

Figure 14. The front of the temple 行天宮 **(Hsing Tian Kong) in Taipei, Taiwan**

Findings on Deities, Jesus, and Christianity

Figure 15. People at the temple doing *bài* while a message was given

Figure 16. One of about six older ladies reciting out loud a religious text

Figure 17. Explanations of the deities' stories happen throughout the day

Issues of loyalty aside, the point here is that Mazu has the same power over romance that Yue Lao has, and Guan Shengdijun has the same power over the world that Guanyin has. Belief in multiple deities does not necessarily mean that people have to go to different deities for different requests. It also does not have a direct correlation to loyalty. The point relevant to this study is that the Taiwanese participants in the research tend to assume that deities are real, even ones they have not heard of. This phenomenon neither translates to exclusivity nor to worshipping multiple deities (though both were recorded in the interviews). This phenomenon translates to an attitude of acceptance (at least on a surface level) of gods, both known and unknown.

In terms of Christian conversion, this sense of religious pluralism comes into play too. Fishu mentioned that before she became a Christian, she always reacted to Christianity thus, 「OK, 有一位另外一個神，就是眾多神明之中，還有另外一個叫做耶穌，但是我不知道祂不熟啦」 ("Okay, there is another deity. Like in the pantheon of deities, there is another one called Jesus. But I do not know him. [I am] just not familiar [with him]"). Police Lady was not a Christian, but she has gone to church, seeing only benefits with visiting multiple holy places from multiple religions.

Religious pluralism can be seen in religious self-identification too. For example, Shi Gu and Genie both defined themselves as 「佛道教」 ("Buddhist-Daoist Religion"). House Gongon did not use the same term but self-identified with both religions as his religious identity. It seems that not only is belief in multiple deities normal in Taiwan, but identification with several religions is also normal.

Loyalty to Deities

We have discussed briefly the fact that, except for people like Disciple Wong, most of the participants did not worship just one deity. However, even Disciple Wong said that he shows respect to other deities when he passes by their idols on the streets. It is useful to explain in more depth the issue of loyalty to deities.

Mommy Farong was one of the more devout people who showed much knowledge and passion in her deity. In her home, she had multiple deities on her altars. In the main altar, she had three statuettes, two of which were different models of the deity she worshipped more (Guanyin bodhisattva) and one of which was 地藏菩薩 (Kṣitigarbha bodhisattva).

Mommy Farong and Mrs. Ting spent most of the time talking about Guanyin, but they both *bài* other deities too. Mommy Farong had an idol of Mazu in her home while Mrs. Ting mentioned that she *bài* 「釋迦牟尼佛、阿彌陀佛、藥師佛」 ("Siddhārtha Gautama, Amitābha, Bhaiṣajyaguru"). She explained that she *bài* many deities, but she "corresponds faster" (「更快相應」) with Guanyin. She mentioned that some of her friends "correspond faster" with other deities, which makes it perfectly reasonable to focus on other deities.

In other words, loyalty to a deity is not dependent on the actuality of the deity's existence (for that is already assumed) nor the veracity of the deity's truth claims (for that is not widely studied). Rather, loyalty to a deity seems to be dependent on whether one can "correspond faster" with a deity, that is, whether one can more easily feel a heart connection to a deity and sense their presence. This connection is felt in how often the deity is seen to have answered a person's prayers and in the miracles that one perceives in one's own life.

Devotion to this deity does not have to be exclusive either. Mrs. Ting saw nothing wrong with other deities being worshipped even though she thought

Guanyin was the best. This same sentiment is reflected in numerous other participants in talking about their own religious devotion. The few participants who knew the researcher was Christian mentioned specifically that there is nothing wrong with worshipping Jesus since the researcher must be more connected to Jesus and have *yuánfèn* with him.

Moreover, one could be mostly loyal to one deity but still seek others out in special occasions. Company Woman, while mostly familiar with Mazu, still sought out Earth God and even the LORD in her time of need. In her home, there was an idol of Guanyin. She said that she *bài* Guanyin most often, twice a day to be exact. However, she preferred to go to Mazu for serious issues. This shows that loyalty to a deity does not mean signing an exclusivity contract with the deity.

Another example that shows that exclusivity is not required is with Lord Superior Wen Chang, who is the famous deity that everyone goes to for good test scores. However, during test time, it is common for students to *bài* several deities. Fishu admitted that even though she had a special feeling about Lord Superior Wen Chang, she asked for help from multiple deities. This was not done secretly but encouraged by her parents. Staying exclusive to a deity was seen as foolish because the more deities are sought out, the more help one might potentially get.

Mountain Analogy

Some people framed belief in multiple deities using analogies. Pei-Pei used the analogy of a mountain to describe belief in deities,

> 每一個廟好像就是一個山頭，然後一個山頭就會聚集起一些人，然後這個山頭他覺得不OK他就……轉移到另外一個山頭去，然後差別是什麼？就是我覺得他……沒有一個核心的思想吧。」 ("Every temple is like a mountain peak. [For example, say that] one mountain peak has a lot of people gathered. And then [if at] this mountain peak, he thinks [something is] not okay, he just . . . transfers to another mountain peak. And then what is the difference? I think he . . . does not have a central thought [regarding a belief system]").

Being part of a religious system is not dependent on loyally staying on one mountain. In fact, it is unusual to even think about a religious system as something that one belongs to. The few devout Christians or Buddhists interviewed talked more about loyalty. But the vast majority of the participants interviewed were just like Pei-Pei, talking about experiences from one temple to another as if they were simply places to visit depending on the situation or one's preference. It was not seen as a disloyal or disingenuous thing to visit one temple one day and another temple the very next day. Taiwanese people in Taipei, who hold much reverence for these deities, do not feel like they are insulting the deities either. In their minds, the deities do not mind or even care when people pray to multiple deities or adhere to multiple religious systems. In fact, Disciple Wong proudly explained the religious system of his own temple as a mixture of Confucianism, Daoism, and Buddhism. Syncretizing multiple religions is a badge of honor to people like Disciple Wong and Pei-Pei.

Summary of "Faith" in a Deity

We have seen in this section the various topics related to choosing a deity. After uncovering all this data, what can we say about what Taiwanese mean when they say they have "faith" in a deity? "Faith" was often explained in behavioral terms and linked to changing one's way of life. "Faith" was not even an important topic because if the neighborhood big uncle and auntie are willing to help and has the power to do so, that was all that a Taiwanese person wanted or needed. The focus was on the efficacy of the object of faith (i.e. how efficacious is the deity in granting one's desire) rather than the strength of the subject of faith (i.e. how strong does one's faith need to be to have one's desires granted).

We have also discussed several reasons for people choosing to engage with a deity. For many, it was about gaining blessings and protection. Others went to certain deities simply because they are efficacious, which is linked closely to the deity's perceived power. The data suggests a utilitarian, pragmatic, and consumerist mindset in the way Taiwanese approach deities and religion. Still others saw it as *yuán* playing out instead of a choice at all. There were other reasons too, including academics, resolving grievances, and being godchildren of the deity.

Lastly, we have seen that the very idea of having to choose one deity is abnormal in Taiwan. There is an assumed belief in multiple deities, namely that they are assumed to be real unless specifically proven otherwise. This means that the religious pluralism in Taiwan is more akin to religious plurality, namely that personally participating in multiple religions is acceptable to the Taiwanese person. Loyalty to just one deity, while not unheard of, is unnecessary.

We have examined what choosing a deity looks like for a Taiwanese person. But this study's goal is to begin developing a contextual approach to gospel transmission. To that end, it is useful to understand how Taiwanese people in Taipei view the gospel and Christianity. This is the very topic for the next two sections.

Interpreting "Believe in Jesus for Eternal Life"

An important research question for this research is, How do Taiwanese people understand Christian beliefs and practices? This was a topic that people freely talked about without the researcher asking them and generated fascinating insights for the research. The topic became so interesting that by the fifth interview, a new question was added into the interview protocol. The question was: "When you hear a person or broadcast say a statement like 'believe in Jesus for eternal life,' how do you react? What do you think it means?" This phrase, based on John 3:16, is seen on billboards, used in evangelism, and spoken on certain television programs. All the participants have heard it several times throughout their lives.

Even though they may be professing Christians, not all Christians have the same understanding of the gospel. Among the interview participants, the Christians did not fully agree on the meaning of the phrase "believe in Jesus for eternal life." Non-Christians had an even more unorthodox understanding of what the phrase means.

This section unpacks the different ways that this phrase was interpreted. We first look at what they thought "believe" means. This helps us figure out the usefulness of one of the most popular words currently used in gospel transmission in Taiwan. Next, we look at what they thought "eternal life" means, which reveals what they thought is the goal of Christianity. Finally, we look at the general reactions they mentioned having when they hear the phrase.

Interpreting "Believe"

The Chinese term used for "believe" in "believe in Jesus Christ for eternal life" is 信 (*xìn*, "faith"). Everyone interpreted the term *xìn* differently. The following are the views expressed in the interviews.

Jesus Is True

Genie, Mazu's goddaughter, said that "believing in Jesus" means Jesus existed. Curu, a Christian minister, said that believing means acknowledging that Jesus died, was buried, then was raised from the dead on the third day. She continued and listed many theological doctrines from the Bible, saying that these are doctrinally true. Other non-Christians were not as detailed. Tour Guide Man said that "believing in Jesus" means that Jesus is real and that we should believe his words to be real as well. There was no mention of what Jesus said nor of the essence of his being. Mountain Pi and Lon Le added that believing must mean thinking that Jesus is real and thus following in his example. Most of the participants who spoke about the intellectual aspect also spoke about the behavioral aspect, and vice versa.

Having a Relationship with Jesus

Fishu and College Hua, both Christians, added to the truth aspect by saying that "believing in Jesus" means having a relationship with Jesus Christ. College Hua said that without an object of faith, there is no faith. Fishu compared it to deities in folk religion, that unlike going to those deities only when one needs something, one should have faith in Jesus every day and 「經營關係」 ("work on the relationship"). She said that without having a relationship, 「你認識跟知道祂，但是你不是信」 ("you know him and know about him, but you do not have faith [in him]"). To have true faith in Jesus, Fishu thought a person must have a relationship. She said that is true faith whereas other forms of faith are no different from the folk religion that she experienced in her past.

Disciple Wong, a non-Christian, mentioned that perhaps believing for Christians meant that people can feel God's miracle or God's compassion. He explained that if there is any extended relationship with any deity, there must exist events that touch a person in a way not commonly experienced, things that indicate the deity is blessing and protecting the person. Any sustained "belief" in a deity must mean that this uncommon effect from the unseen realm is felt and experienced.

Do Good Deeds

Both Police Lady and Pei-Pei understood "faith" as 「行善良之事」 ("doing kind deeds"). Police Lady explained that Christian "faith" likely means suppressing the bad part of our human nature and exalting the divine nature. As a psychologist, she related it to the Freudian superego, namely that "faith" is living up to the ideals passed on to us. She said that we achieve that by doing what Jehovah tells us to do. So, "believing in Jesus Christ for eternal life" was translated in Police Lady's mind as "do good deeds with the help of the Christian deity, then you will have eternal life."

Shi Gu said that "believing" should mean having a peaceful heart and acting out deeds of love. Shi Gu explained, 「你就是要回歸你的那個本心，本心的純淨、清靜，然後一心一意的……發揮你的博愛精神啊」 ("You have to return to your original heart, original purity, serenity. Then, devotedly . . . exude your spirit of love"). She continued for a long time with more explanations of what "believing" looks like. By the time the researcher interviewed Shi Gu, he had much experience with participants not explaining "believing" in terms of intellectual understanding. Despite how much she was pushed to answer abstractly, she never described what "believing" meant as an abstract concept, but only as what it looked like in the life of the person. It seemed that to Shi Gu and many other participants, "believing" was a concept that was inseparable from the behavior or emotional state of the person.

The Christian minister Curu said that she initially came to Jesus Christ because her sister took her to church. Judging from the way she talked about the phrase "believe in Jesus," it had the idea of intellectually believing in the reality of Jesus's resurrection as well as living faithfully as God's children. She said multiple times that those who 「信奉」 (*xìnfèng*, "believe-serve") Jesus can receive eternal life. Her idea of "faith" strongly implied a life of service in addition to believing.[6]

During Chi's time as a Christian, he thought that Christianity as a religion was great. He believed that being Christian turns one into a good person.

---

6. It is unclear whether Curu thought "believing" needed to happen throughout one's entire life or just at one moment. The interview data could possibly support both conclusions.

He nuanced it thus, 「不代表說我拜神把我變成一個好人，變成……好人是自己的修行，自己的靈修」 ("It does not mean that when I *bài* God [the LORD], it turns me into a good person; turning into a . . . good person is my own *Sādhanā*, my own spiritual discipline").

Multiple things must be noted here. First, Chi treated character and personal growth as the main things that Christianity is for. Second, Chi used *bài* to relate to the Christian deity, the same word that people use to indicate visiting deities at temples a few times a year. Third, Chi equated the Buddhist idea of *Sādhanā* (religious practice often including Zen meditation) with the Christian idea of spiritual disciplines.

Chi repeated this same idea many times throughout the interview. At multiple points, he stressed the importance of being a good person, one time talking about using the Bible to 「人品達到一個神話」 ("raise one's character to a legendary level"). *Sādhanā* was mentioned multiple times in relation to his concept of Christianity.

As with Shi Gu, the researcher pushed Chi to explain exactly how to "believe Jesus." His reply was, 「那個非常簡單啊！你要如何相信耶穌很簡單，你只要做個好人就相信」 ("That is very simple! How you can believe in Jesus is simple: You just have to be a good person; that is believing"). His reply had nothing to do with intellectual acceptance of any doctrine, nor did he mention anything about the cross or resurrection. Chi did not say that believing *results in* behavior change, but rather that believing is *achieved through* behavior change.

Religious Practice

House Gongon thought that the term "believe" refers to 「長期修行」 ("long-term religious practice"). He reasoned that in Taiwan, people are exposed to many deities, all of which are real. But a person may choose to go deep into one branch of the faith or find out more about one deity. The only way to go deep is through religious practice, which must be what "believe" means in this Christian phrase. When pushed for clarification, House Gongon said that ultimately *xìn* cannot be defined because each person must define it for themselves.

Others were more specific in their definition of "believe" as religious practice. Company Woman said that she thinks "believe" refers to praying, going to church, doing homework after listening to the pastor, and learning more about the teachings of Christianity. This was interesting because they were not asked what being a Christian means, but specifically asked what the word "believe" (*xìn*) means in the phrase "believe in Jesus for eternal life." To her, "believe" itself encompassed all those actions.

Believing as a Magical Spell to Chant

Smoker Ang mentioned that he believes the phrase "Believe in Jesus for eternal life" refers to a special chant that grants supernatural power. He considered it to be similar in function to the Buddhist chant 「南無阿彌陀佛」 (*Namo Amitābha*, which is a Sanskrit phrase common in Pure Land Buddhism that translates to "Hail Buddha of Infinite Light"). Due to the phrase being Sanskrit, many people, including Smoker Ang, did not know what the phrase even meant but only knew how to chant it.

Mommy Farong explained the significance of the chant with more detail. She treated the phrase *Amitābha* as a kind of blessing that one can say, a phrase that is associated with power. She called the phrase a 佛號 (*Fóhào*, "Buddha's Name Chant"), signifying 「無量的光、無量的壽」 ("immeasurable light, immeasurable life"). Mr. Rich also made reference to the *Fóhào* chant, saying how their ubiquity reminds people to come to Buddha. See figure 18 for a big billboard with the Buddhist *Namo Amitābha* chant found in Taipei. Notice that it does not advertise any sect of Buddhism nor point to any temple. Signs like this usually indicate a chant of goodwill toward the community for purposes of peace and protection. This is likely what Smoker Ang was referring to. This is a more extreme example. Most signs are found on things like stop signs, lampposts, highway exit ramps, and alley walls.

Anthropologists use the term "magic" to refer to the idea of being able to manipulate spiritual forces through mantras and chanting, or amulets.[7] In anthropology's language, "believe in Jesus for eternal life" is a magical chant that provides protection from spiritual forces. Smoker Ang did not think the Christian phrase meant anything just like he did not think the Sanskrit chant meant anything either. For this reason, he did not know the meaning of either of the phrases. Smoker Ang thought that Christians say the chant at places to protect people from the influence of bad spirits. The example he gave was that sometimes at places where multiple car accidents occur, there

---

7. Terwiel, *Monks and Magic*.

may be some malicious influence from the unseen realm. At those places, one would find posters with *Namo Amitābha* (like the one in figure 18) from well-meaning Buddhists and posters with "believe in Jesus for eternal life" from well-meaning Christians. These chants help protect the common folk, like Smoker Ang himself, from these malicious forces. Apart from the fact that the chant works, Smoker Ang did not know and did not care to know what the Christian "chant" meant. This was not the only chant that appeared in the interviews. Police Lady mentioned another chant from another religious system that afforded some sort of protection in her life.

Figure 18. A billboard in red containing the *Namo Amitābha* chant

Interpreting "Eternal Life"

We have just looked at different ways people interpreted "believe." The other term in the phrase had equally interesting interpretations. It was surprising to the researcher that there were so many ways that people genuinely interpreted this term. The following are the views expressed in the interviews.

Living Forever

Mr. Rich understood "eternal life" as meaning that if someone believes in Jesus, that person can 「長生不老」 ("live forever"). The phrase shows up in popular culture frequently and translates literally to "long life, never old." Following the explanation, Mr. Rich said that the phrase must mean something else because he said as an atheist, he rejected the notion that people could live forever. Mountain Pi also understood "eternal life" as meaning the same thing and similarly rejected it immediately due to it being impossible in her view.

Curu said that believing in God leads to eternal life, that it is having a life that never ends. She alluded to heaven once in her explanation, saying a person is there with God for eternity. She also thoroughly explained the concept of the resurrection from the dead, with Jesus as a first fruit. However, the thrust of her argument was not on the next life, but on the idea of 「超越今生的這個有限」 ("surpassing the limits of this life"). Her argument was this: 「將來永遠的榮耀等著你就可以讓你有一個超越的心境來面對現在的人生」 ("the future, eternal glory is waiting for you, which enables you to have a surpassing mentality to face this life").

Curu did not see heaven primarily as a hope for the future (though she said that is part of it). She did not treat hope of heaven in an escapist sort of way. Rather, Curu saw heaven as a hope that enables her to "surpass" the pain and the limits of this life. The focus, like all the other Taiwanese participants, was on this current life instead of the next one.

Curu's focus on this life was not unique to her. Fishu had a similar idea despite being from a different church denomination, having a thirty-year age gap, and working in a completely different career. Fishu was asked what the most important 「信念」 ("belief") of Christianity is. Fishu said that it is having one's life renewed through the saving grace of Jesus Christ. She then said, 「你本來沒有辦法面對的，或是沒有辦法勝過的，但是你可以靠祂救恩，然後依靠祂的大能，死裡復活大能，然後你可以去勝過這些事情」 ("What you used to not be able to face [in this life], or not be able to have victory over, you can lean on his saving grace, rely on his great power, the great resurrection power; then you can have victory over these things").

Fishu also spoke about having a new identity and value in God's eyes. Lastly, she mentioned Sunday worship services, praying, and reading the Bible. She said that all these things help us know how to live. To Fishu, these behavior-oriented, this-life centered things together formed the most important belief of Christianity. True to her understanding, she defined "eternal life" as life from beginning to end. She included life on this earth and life after death as both aspects of eternal life. Even though she saw life in the new heavens and new earth as part of this eternal life, she treated her current life as already being part of Jesus's promise of eternal life.

College Hua phrased the this-world aspect of eternal life thus, 「我覺得永生，最重要的關鍵的一件事情，是讓祂跟我現在有什麼關係，為什麼我現在要來經營我的永生？」 ("I think for eternal life, the most crucial aspect is: What is its relationship to me right now? Why do I have to work on my eternal life now?"). What was most crucial to College Hua was not the fact that he can live forever, but eternity's relationship to his present, day-to-day living.

Completeness

Coe Bei thought that eternal life refers to completeness, a sense of perfection or a state of fullness and blessedness. To Coe Bei, what Jesus offers is 「圓滿的智慧、圓滿的無我、圓滿的大我」 ("complete wisdom, complete selflessness, complete confidence"). She also said that the church has twisted Jesus's teachings, perhaps unintentionally due to the low level of education many of them had. This completeness that Jesus offers is the true message. She would render the phrase "believe in Jesus for eternal life" to mean "believe in Jesus to have a more complete life, complete in every conceivable way." She continued by saying that Jesus is in fact a Buddha, meaning a type of person who has reached complete wisdom and is here to help others do the same. Incidentally, she rejected the claim that Jesus is the creator of the world.

Peace in One's Heart

Mr. Rich thought that "eternal life" refers to having peace in one's heart. Moreover, whatever situation the person may face, the person can face it peacefully. Healthy Chen also treated eternal life as an outlook in life. Even though he self-identified as a Christian, Healthy Chen did not think "eternal life" referred to living forever. Ironically, before becoming a Christian, he thought "eternal life" meant living forever. Now that he was a Christian, he thought that eternal life referred to 「精神上的永生」 ("eternity on an emotional level"). To him, eternal life referred to not being scared of death, being satisfied in life, and having great emotional health. Hsiang Wu likewise described eternal life as having peace in one's heart and having good health. Again, we see how eternal life for some participants was more about how one lives this life instead of living forever in the next life.

Detachment of the Soul

Tour Guide Man thought the phrase referred to 「靈魂上的超脫」 ("detachment of the soul") after judgment day and having that soul exist forever. There was no mention of heaven or hell, nor of the condition of the determined destination. He saw the whole phrase as something to 「吸引信眾或是去歸依其他教徒的一種作法」 ("attract the believing public or a method to absorb other religion's followers"). By the way he talked about it, he treated it as a neutral propaganda that did not require deep analysis.

General Reactions to the Phrase

We have finished covering how the participants interpreted the phrase "believe in Jesus for eternal life." This section examines how the participants reacted to the phrase. Because the participants were not told anything about the researcher's Christian identity, there were some candid responses. This helped reveal how well this phrase may be received in Taiwan. The following are the things that the participants thought about and how they felt when they hear this popular evangelistic phrase.

No Reaction

Some people do not think much about the statement. We have already seen this in Tour Guide Man, Disciple Wong, Mountain Pi, and a few others. Chi said that when he hears the phrase, all he thinks about is that the person who uttered it has a religion. He would be willing to go to church or pray during a meal, but he said he would not believe in this religion. Chi did not even care about reflecting on what the statement meant, as if it was just a badge signifying that one is Christian. College Hua and Hsiang Wu likewise said that they never saw how this phrase was applicable to them. Likewise, Smoker Ang saw the phrase as just a magical spell to chant for Christians, which was his reason for having never thought about the meaning or significance of the phrase.

Findings on Deities, Jesus, and Christianity

Christian Expressions of Love

When asked about the major difference between Christianity and her religion, Bookstore Lady said that Christians tend to verbally express love more. She herself has encountered this a few times and has been moved. She said that Buddhists do not usually verbally express love as frequently, but they do physically express love through other felt ways. She said that Buddhists tend to silently express their love and compassion. By implication, she seemed to be saying that while a Christian would often eloquently say "I love you," a Buddhist would often dedicatedly do acts of compassion for a people or community.

Stupid

Some participants were more direct in their response. Tattoo Ju thought the following of Christians,「我就會覺得......就是有點笨嗎？......因為......你沒有真正的去好好的思考，然後就有一點盲目的去相信這一套說的東西。......神明們應該不會希望人們是盲目的崇拜他的」("I think . . . it is a little stupid? . . . Because . . . you do not really think carefully, and just blindly believe what they say. . . . The deities would not want people to blindly worship them").

Others may not have shown as strong a reaction, but they still had largely negative reactions. Company Woman for example said that whenever she used to hear this phrase, she would roll her eyes. She said that she has since toned down her reaction. Pei-Pei, Lon Le, and many others also thought this phrase is stupid, unimportant, or irrelevant. This was by far the most common reaction that people had to this evangelistic phrase.

Summary of Interpretations

Combining what the participants thought about "believe" and what they thought about "eternal life," it seems that many Taiwanese people in Taipei understand "believe in Jesus Christ for eternal life" to mean something it is not meant to mean. Most participants saw "believe" to mean some kind of behavior change, whether it was doing good deeds or religious practice. There was no "believing" without an action, perhaps a lifelong one, accompanying it. Most people interpreted "eternal life" as meaning anything except living forever. One may either have completeness, peace in one's heart, or detachment of the soul. Some people said that they simply did not know. There was a decidedly this-worldly aspect to most participants' understandings of eternal life.

Furthermore, the people's general reactions to the phrase reveal that regardless of how the listener may outwardly react at the moment, there are many negative reactions in the recipient's mind. Some of those negative reactions are detailed in the next section.

Key Objections to Christianity

This section lists some key objections that people had to Christianity as a whole, to the way proselytizing is done, and to the claims of Christianity.

Evangelism Tactic

Many of the participants did not like Christianity due to the way someone shared the gospel with them. Pei-Pei's example illustrates the point most vividly. She mentioned someone approaching her while she was waiting for a pedestrian traffic light in Taipei. This person did some kind of evangelism and ended it by asking her to read a prayer of repentance. When she agreed, they started talking about original sin and how she has lacked in filial piety to her parents. She explained in the interview, a little upset and without censoring, that her mental reaction at the time was 「什麼我不孝啊什麼我對不起我父母啊，然後我就滿頭問號就是 What the f***?」 ("[The person said] something like I was lacking in filial piety and like I have done wrong to my parents, then my head was filled with question marks, like 'What the f***?'").

She did not explain how she reacted to the street evangelizing person. She indicated that she prayed the prayer the person wanted her to pray and they went their separate ways. It is likely that he left feeling encouraged that someone was willing to pray to repent and trust in Jesus Christ. All the while, she left feeling disgusted by the evangelistic approach and has since then harbored a resentment toward Christianity, a resentment she colorfully shared with the researcher at multiple points of the interview.

Lack of Unity

Mr. Rich said, 「我就問我的……基督教的朋友，『你們基督教都沒有辦法統一，我為什麼要信？』」 ("I would ask my … Christian friends, 'Your Christian religion cannot even unite, why would I believe?'"). For Mr.

Rich, the fact that there were many denominations was a reason for not believing. The objection was not about the creed, historical accuracy, theological soundness, or any attribute related to the object of belief. Rather, the objection was to the supposed failed witness of the global Christian body shown in the existence of many denominations. Mr. Rich in particular did not like how one denomination can disagree so vehemently with another one about song choice during Christmas. At least for Mr. Rich, the behavior of Christians was more important than the beliefs of Christianity. It was unclear if Mr. Rich would use this same metric to measure all religions.

At the end of the interview, Mr. Rich asked a poignant question, 「為什麼基督教還有那麼多的不同的派系？那他們詮釋同樣一本聖經、同樣的上帝、同樣的耶穌，為什麼又有不同的詮釋？對我無神論者我覺得這個部分能說服我比神蹟發生在我身上可能對我來講我覺得更重要。」 ("Why does Christianity have so many denominations? They interpret the same Bible, the same God, the same Jesus, why a different interpretation [on life] then? For me as an atheist, I think this might be more important for convincing me than if a miracle happened in my life").

Narrow and Exclusive

Some people thought that Christianity is too narrow. Coe Bei thought that not only is the church 「非常狹隘」 ("very narrow"), but it is very unlike Christ himself. She thought that the spirit of Christ has been twisted to something manmade. She even said that she believes in Jesus offering eternal life, but she is against the way of the church. She repeatedly affirmed that these are nice people; but when it comes to certain issues (she mentions homosexuality and the political elections),[8] these Christians are narrow and stubborn. Pei-Pei voiced the same concern by saying that Christianity 「太強調正確性了」 ("emphasizes correctness too much").

Genie also took issue with Christianity's exclusivity, but explained it differently. Genie did not think it was good for someone to force her to change her religion. Moreover, she thought that Christianity is 「不太有邏輯」 ("not really logical"). She said that the religion is illogical from a scientific standpoint (though she did not explain why). From her full explanation, it seemed that her problem was not really with Christianity's logic, but with its

---

8. This interview happened just a few days before the presidential election in Taiwan.

exclusivity. She took issue with Christianity's 「優越主義」 ("superiorism"). She said she took issue with any religion that claims its path is the only path that leads to the destination. To her, claiming that only one path leads to the destination was illogical due to it clearly being wrong. She said that no other deities in Taiwan are so unaccepting of other paths. Ms. Sha went further to say that Christianity's 「偶像崇拜」 ("idol worship") is too exclusive, that folk religion in Taiwan is much more accepting and less extreme.

Bad Morals of Christians

Chi said that he had been a Christian for a few years in his life. At the time of the interview, he was not a Christian anymore because he saw that the Christians around him were not trying to become better people. On the other hand, he saw that his non-Christian friends and family had better morals. He said that this disappointment was one of the main things that led him to stop calling himself a Christian. At another point of the interview, Chi summarized his concern: 「所以為什麼,……他接受了耶穌之後,他還是那麼爛一個人?」 ("So why, . . . after he accepted Jesus, is he still that horrible a person?"). This goes back to the idea of belief being inextricably linked to behavior in Taiwanese religious thinking. Chi could not comprehend how one can believe in Christianity but have no or little change in behavior. His conclusion was that the religion must be faulty.

Religious Wars

Shi Gu was confused why 「西方那麼多宗教戰爭」 ("[there are] so many religious wars in the West"). She said that she knows Christianity teaches about love. With so much love, she could not comprehend why people would still wage war. In fact, she pushed the researcher for an answer during the interview. Unfortunately, she could not be obliged with an answer.

Strict Requirements

Tour Guide Man mentioned that in Christianity, there is only one deity that is accepted. For folk religion in Taiwan, 「規定沒有這麼嚴格」 ("regulations are not so strict"). He explained that in Christianity, one may be required to go to church or follow many rules. One rule he did not like was regarding Christianity's stance against pre-marital sex. He said that rules and regulations are not so important for folk religion in Taiwan. He said that 「宗教已經是

我們生活當中的一部分」("religion is already a part of our lives"), meaning that religion should be enriching and supporting one's daily living instead of regulating and restricting one's life. He seemed to think that Taiwanese people in Taipei are already religious, that religiosity is not measured by outward forms of devotion or adherence to creeds. Rather, religiosity is measured by constant, daily interaction (in the mind and in temples) with the pantheon of deities available in Taiwan.

Judgmental

Some participants were unhappy with how judgmental Christianity seems to be. Mr. Rich thought that Christianity critiques other religions too much. He specifically mentioned examples of Christianity critiquing Buddhism. He said that instead of talking about other religions' faults, Christianity should talk about its own merits.

Tattoo Ju was more concerned with Christianity being judgmental on a socio-political level. In the context of Taiwan's relatively recent legalization of homosexual marriages,[9] Tattoo Ju was upset and even annoyed at Taiwanese Christians' responses. She said that it is wrong to ask society to accept the standards of Christianity. She said that these standards and rules need to only apply to Christians, not those outside the religion. She compared it with 「台灣的信仰」 ("faith in Taiwan"), where this broadening of standards does not occur. She said, 「他們不會去拿甚麼哪個神明說了甚麼的話去套在別人身上。但是基督教跟天主教就非常明顯會有這個現象」 ("They would not take what so-and-so deity says and apply it to other people. But this phenomenon is very obviously visible with Christianity and Catholicism").

Christianity's perception by the interview participants was that it is a religion with many judgmental people. The arguments sound like this: Christianity espouses standards and moral codes that they think are good; however, they are not necessarily good. Even if they were good, they should not be applied to non-Christians. The act of having done so throughout decades of Christian work in Taiwan has left a bitter taste in many Taiwanese's mouths. The fact that, according to Tattoo Ju, none of the folk religion adherents in Taiwan do this to others exacerbates the issue. Whether this is done

---

9. Same-sex marriage became legal in Taiwan on 24 May 2019, making Taiwan the first country in Asia to legalize it.

rightfully or wrongfully, whether this has a positive or negative impact on society, and whether Christianity has good or bad moral codes are important, but different issues. The issue here is public perception. Christianity is perceived to judge others too much. By extension, Christians are perceived as judgmental, sullying an evangelizing person's interaction with a non-Christian before the interaction has even begun.

Summary of Findings on Deities, Jesus, and Christianity

We have looked at the issues involved with choosing a deity in Taiwan. This has shown how and why people have "faith" along with the strong brand of religious pluralism in Taiwan. We have looked at how people interpreted and reacted to the phrase "believe in Jesus for eternal life." This has revealed that people do not interpret this evangelistic phrase the way that some may think. Lastly, we have looked at key objections to Christianity. These have revealed the negative public perception that Christianity needs to overcome to be more attractive to the general public.

We are now ready to begin developing a contextual approach to gospel transmission that accounts for all these myriad issues in Taiwan. This is the main topic for the next chapter.

CHAPTER 6

Key Issues in the Taiwanese Context

In the last two chapters, the findings of the qualitative research were presented. Now that there is a better understanding of the local attitudes and lived realities, it is time to draw some implications. The goal of this chapter is to develop a contextual approach to gospel transmission in Taiwan. The issue is not about how to preach the gospel in its entirety, but rather how to frame initial gospel conversations (with the content limited by time) with non-Christians.

Imagine that a Christian and a non-Christian engage in a conversation. If the Christian starts by saying, "You are going to hell if you do not trust in Jesus,"[1] the conversation is likely to have no positive effect for either party. Many Christians can fully acknowledge the truthfulness of the statement. Using statements like this to start conversations is an example of "too much, too soon." This statement is an extreme example of street witnessing. It must be acknowledged that most Christians who engage in evangelistic work do not use statements like this. But the question remains: If the above statement is too extreme, then what would be some productive ways to start the conversation and what would be unproductive? Would it be okay to exult the LORD, dismiss ancestral veneration, disrespect a Taiwanese deity, or tell

---

1. This researcher has personally engaged in conversations with some of those people. These people are surprisingly nice when they drop the persona of an angry evangelist. One person outside a university's football stadium told the researcher that he embraced this tactic of saying "You are going to hell" in order to stir up the status quo and get conversations going around campus by other Christians. Their tone when talking with the researcher was completely different from their tone when shouting the phrases.

people they are going to hell? At what point does an initial conversation cross the line into the realm of "too much, too soon"?

There are multiple aspects of Christianity and multiple aspects to the gospel, which we have caught a glimpse of in the previous chapter. In any given conversation, it is impossible to share every single aspect of Christianity and of the gospel. Thus, in a first conversation with a non-Christian, a decision must be made about what to focus on.

This chapter unpacks some of the key, conceptual issues in the Taiwanese context that were uncovered in the qualitative research on the perspective of gospel transmission. The goal here is to help decide what to lead with in a gospel conversation. The chapter focuses on identifying "landmines" – what not to do – such as entrenched worldviews and cultural customs that are better left untouched in the first conversation. The positive, "what to do," aspects are discussed in the next chapter.

This work does not advocate for avoiding hard topics with a person in order to convert them without giving all the information. What is advocated for is choosing the order and timing of addressing these hard topics. Certain things must be communicated clearly before a person makes a salvific step of faith toward Jesus. Nevertheless, based on some of the issues uncovered in the Taiwanese context, it seems that some of those hard topics should be communicated in the second, third, or tenth conversation.

This chapter lists only certain essential issues that have surfaced as a direct result of the qualitative research. The issues are divided into three main categories: (1) issues with worldview, (2) issues with religious boundary crossing, and (3) issues with religious pluralism. This information helps the evangelizing person understand the world of the non-Christian Taiwanese and the way that the gospel might be understood or misunderstood by them.

Issues with Worldview

The first main category we address is the broadest, namely that of the Taiwanese people's worldview. Five main issues surfaced from the qualitative research: (1) *Yuánfèn* and fatalism, (2) this life versus the next life, (3) ancestors, (4) truth claims, and (5) the main ways that Taiwanese people relate to deities and the unseen realm. We now discuss each issue in turn.

Yuánfèn and Fatalism

Taiwanese people in Taipei seem to retain a certain level of fatalism due to the concept of *yuánfèn*. *Yuánfèn* was mentioned by every single participant. In many of the interviews, the participants mentioned *yuánfèn* when they talked about which deity they have interacted with. Shi Gu did not believe in Christianity because she was not in the same 「脈絡」 (*màiluò*, "artery and vein") as LORD. Many people who adhere to a religion adhere not because of some convincing argument or belief; rather, they adhere because of this fatalistic worldview where one's fate has already been determined from one's birth. For example, Bookstore Lady said that only by having *yuánfèn* with a deity can a person "enter into his kingdom, be protected and blessed by him."

Moreover, the section on fortune telling highlighted that many Taiwanese people in Taipei believe that fate can be changed. In fact, the reason that many people visit fortune tellers is to determine one's fate and have the fortune teller advise on how one might go about changing it. This means that even though one's fate has already been determined at birth, it does not mean that one resigns oneself to a negative life.

廖昆田 [Kun-Tien Liao] speaks into this issue in his book titled 《民俗與信仰》 (*Folklore and Faith*).[2] Liao is a renowned scholar of folk religion and a Christian pastor. Liao speaks about the relationship of fatalism and folk religion thus,

> 中國傳統社會……受民間信仰之價值觀影響很深，已將禍福凶吉標準化，甚至絕對化，造成一般民眾以功利主義為價值取向 (Traditional Chinese society . . . is deeply influenced by the value system of folk religion. It has standardized the idea of having one's disasters or luck fatalistically foretold by the stars. In fact, it may even have absolutized it. This has led to the people taking utilitarianism as their value system).[3]

Liao has linked utilitarianism (also uncovered in the interviews) with fatalism. Liao thinks that the root cause for a utilitarian perspective is a fatalistic value system dictated by concepts like *yuánfèn*. Liao does not think the concept is bad in and of itself. However, Liao thinks that this value system does not

---

2. Liao 廖, *Mínsú Yǔ Xìnyǎng* 民俗與信仰.
3. Liao 廖, 20.

improve the morality of society nor does it promote the value or sanctity of human life. Moreover, instead of improving oneself, this value system leads to people trying to fix their surroundings. They do this by consulting fortune tellers and asking how to change their fates, like many of the research participants attested to doing. None of them reported anything resembling personal improvement because of it. True to Liao's analysis, they simply figured out some way to change their own fate without improving society.

Liao says that the surest way to transform a life is through changing this fatalistic worldview. Liao believes that we should have a different 「命運觀」 ("concept of fate").[4] Liao thinks that Jesus has given us abundant life, life that gives us a 「革新的人生觀」 ("revolutionary outlook on life").[5] In Liao's interpretation, nothing can determine the fate of people like Paul because the grace of God has the power to change the eight trigrams.[6] What Liao advocates for is a new value system, one that is based not on utilitarianism, but on a new outlook on life. This outlook does not resign itself to fate, but to a God full of grace, truth, and power.

Beyond the arguments put forth by Liao, it is important to note the way that Liao makes his arguments. At many places in his book, Liao quotes sayings from Confucius, the logic of the eight trigrams, the deterministic forces of the heavens (*Tien*), and different ways that folk religion functions in society. He explained the contrast of 鬼月 (the ghost month) and Jesus's grace,[7] the relationship between the Chinese opera and the gospel,[8] the line between ancestral veneration and honoring one's parents,[9] and the concept of fengshui and wisdom.[10] All these arguments related cultural icons rooted in folk religion to gospel answers rooted in the Bible. More than just answering the question of *yuánfèn* and fatalism, Liao's methodology shows us a way to answer the many questions surrounding folk religion in Taiwan.

---

4. Liao 廖, 20.
5. Liao 廖, 20.
6. Liao 廖, 16.
7. Liao 廖, 35–49.
8. Liao 廖, 117–31.
9. Liao 廖, 131–43.
10. Liao 廖, 185–203.

This Life Versus the Next Life

While *yuánfèn* is an important concept mentioned explicitly by every participant, there are some concepts that are just as important despite not being mentioned explicitly. One such concept is on the Taiwanese people's greater focus on this life and lesser focus on the afterlife. Robert Solomon notices this same trend in another Chinese society and gives two suggestions for gospel transmission in that religiously pluralistic context: "finding culturally appropriate methods" and "avoiding a superficial vision of faith."[11] He mentions the widespread growth and appeal of Buddhism in his context of Singapore, which answers more of this life's questions. This presumably means that Christianity answers less of this life's questions. Solomon shares a Buddhist's response to Christianity, "I find your gospel too simplistic. In Buddhism there is a more elegant and well-developed psychology that explains what goes on within us. Why should I give that up to embrace your faith?"[12]

Solomon notes that many traditional approaches to Christian gospel transmission in Asia focus on the next life, on heaven and hell.[13] McKnight comments on the same focus on the afterlife in North America and Europe.[14] Namely, those approaches frame the gospel primarily as the way to be in heaven for the next life. Solomon's experience shows that this focus on the afterlife does not resonate with a culture that tends to focus on this life. Recall from the research findings that Buddhists in Taiwan see Buddhism as answering questions in this life. The focus of Buddhism in Taiwan is likewise linked to 修行 (religious practice), which deals with how a person improves this life.

Among the participants, for those who believed in reincarnation, even the past life was not as important. Mommy Farong, Coe Bei, Shi Gu, and many others thought that the past life is important insofar as it affects this one. For most participants, neither the past life nor the next life was as important as this current life.

In terms of the next life, heaven was either not important or was downplayed in the participants' conceptions. Most said that it is unnecessary to define heaven, hell, reincarnation, or whatever comes next. Tattoo Ju went so

---

11. Solomon, "Making Disciples in Singapore," 106.
12. Solomon, 106–7.
13. Solomon, 107.
14. McKnight, *King Jesus Gospel*, 70.

far as to say, 「不管它有沒有，對我來說都不是重要的事。……我還是會做……好的事情」 ("Whether [heaven, hell, or reincarnation] exists, it is not an important issue for me . . . I will still do . . . good things"). Even Christian ministers like Curu, who had an orthodox understanding of heaven, saw the next life as a hope that enables her to 「有一個超越的心境來面對現在的人生」 ("have a surpassing mentality to face this life"). Fishu thought that the main belief of Christianity is to have "great resurrection power" to have victory in this life. Both Curu and Fishu believed that Jesus Christ died on the cross and was raised from the dead. They both understood that one can enter heaven by believing in Jesus. Nevertheless, the focus of the work on the cross was not on the next life; instead, they emphasized the effect of the cross on this current life. For Fishu, Jesus's promise of eternal life applied to this current life as well as the next. Likewise, Coffee Girl was not sure what kind of people went to heaven. College Hua similarly felt that the most crucial element of eternal life is how it relates to this present life.

House Gongon specifically said that believing in Mazu is for 「現世的這些事情而已，不是為了來世」 ("the events in this life, not for the next life"). Company Woman, when talking about Christianity as an insurance policy, treated it as something to insure her current life, not the next life. Healthy Chen said, 「與其去想未來你死掉會去哪裡，還不如好好現在活著」 ("Instead of thinking about where you go when you die in the future, it is better to live well right now"). An interesting thing about Healthy Chen was that he self-identified as a Christian. The concept of heaven and hell is traditionally a defining, or at least an important, topic for Christians. Nevertheless, Healthy Chen did not know whether he was going to heaven or hell, neither believed nor denied reincarnation, and specifically said that he does not think about the afterlife. He was an adult, first-generation Christian who "converted" for the perceived benefits in this life, not the next.

Most people even interpreted "believe in Jesus for eternal life" as meaning that if one believes in Jesus, their current life would improve. Mr. Rich and Healthy Chen, among others, said that eternal life refers to one's emotional health in this life. They both rejected the notion that one could live forever. It is more surprising considering that Healthy Chen identified as a Christian. It could be that the Taiwanese worldview's focus on this life is so strong that even after "converting" to Christianity, some people still treat the current life as much more important than the next one, to the extent that the next life's existence is denied.

The interviews from Buddhists, folk religion adherents, and even Christians indicate strongly that Taiwanese people in Taipei do not care much for speculation or discourse on the past life or on the next life. Those lives may exist and may even be important, but they are important only insofar as they help us live this current life in this current world. The gospel, if it is to appeal to Taiwanese people in Taipei, must be presented with a strong this-life, this-world component.

Ancestors

Yet another key gospel transmission consideration in the Taiwanese context relates to ancestors. If we have learned anything from talking to the participants, it is that Jesus cannot be portrayed as antagonistic to the concept of 孝 (*xiào*, filial piety). If somehow following Jesus means that both the living and dead ancestors would be disrespected (as some participants have understood), the gospel cannot take root in Taiwan due to the inextricable nature of *xiào* from the collective culture and individual psyche. Proverbs like 「飲水思源」 ("When drinking water, think of the source") and 「慎終追遠」 ("carefully attend to the funeral rites [of parents] and follow [in ancestral veneration] to the distant future") were mentioned by eight participants directly, while the same concept of honoring one's ancestors was mentioned by all twenty-five participants. A contextual approach to gospel transmission that disregards ancestors would not have wide-reaching appeal. Moreover, a theology that disregards honoring one's ancestors disregards the Scriptural mandate both in the Old Testament (Exod 20:12; Lev 19:3; Deut 5:16) as well as the New Testament (Matt 15:4; Mark 7:10; Eph 6:2).

Taiwan is a society infused with Confucian values, one that treats filial piety as a critical indicator of overall morality, and has many religious rituals associated with honoring one's ancestors. Bookstore Lady mentioned many rituals associated with ancestral veneration. Shi Gu mentioned her fear of even leaving a crack on a tombstone. Chi, despite being a staunch atheist who denied the supernatural, refused to say that ancestors had zero supernatural impact on his life. Coffee Girl, despite being in her late thirties, mentioned that she waited three years to become a Christian because that was how long it took for her parents to agree to her new religion. Disregarding the subject of ancestors at best leaves a gaping hole in the theology of the new Christian and at worst makes the listener pretend to pray a prayer of repentance only to think in her mind like Pei-Pei did, "What the f***?"

A good contextual approach to gospel transmission for Taiwan needs to include ancestors in the presentation of the gospel, whether as direct gospel implications or at the very least as sidenotes. In a generally non-confrontational society like Taiwan, people most likely would not ask many questions during a person-to-person gospel presentation.[15] But seeing as how filial piety came up so often in the interviews, it is not a stretch to imagine that many would internally wonder about what they should do with their ancestors and what the gospel says on that topic. This is not just an issue to grapple with after a recipient makes a personal response to the gospel. This is an issue to address before any response to the gospel should be made. In some cases, a person might feel that they cannot become a Christian because it would not be good filial piety. Those who make a positive response may end up like the researcher, with a grandmother who said that she lost a grandson because he refuses to *bài* his ancestors.[16] Sometimes, embracing the gospel is costly. This cost of discipleship should absolutely be shared with the non-Christian; the existence of Luke 14:26 cannot be ignored or concealed. However, a more robust discussion and theology of ancestors would mitigate the negative effects more.

Even with the ancient Israelites, ancestors were treated with reverence and respect. The Israelites worshipped the LORD because he was the God of their ancestors, of Abraham, Isaac, and Israel (1 Chron 29:18–20). Solomon admonished his people to follow the LORD's commands and decrees because the LORD was the one who gave them to their ancestors (1 Kgs 8:58). Even in the New Testament, we see Timothy saying, "I thank God whom I serve, as did my ancestors" (2 Tim 1:3). One does not stray from the religion of one's ancestors or the deity whom they served; to do so would be a grave sin

---

15. This characterization is based on general observations in Taiwan. It is easily verifiable upon direct contact with the people of Taiwan.

16. The implication is that if the researcher refuses to *bài* his ancestors now, when it is the grandmother's turn to pass to the afterlife, he will not *bài* her either. This means that she will suffer in the afterlife due to lack of attention, paper money, etc. Therefore, she has lost a grandson. It must be mentioned that the researcher's relationship with his grandmother is much better now due to many factors.

in the eyes of the Israelites. This is very similar to how Taiwanese people in Taipei show reverence to their ancestors, making religious change difficult.

In a culture that values filial piety so much, if a person becomes a first-generation Christian, that person now has the task of leading the rest of their family members to Christ. The success this person has with siblings and cousins can be widely varied and depend on many variables. The research shows that one variable is definitely filial piety. A Taiwanese contextual approach to gospel transmission has to address what filial piety looks like for deceased ancestors, as well as how one can disagree with and refuse to do many religious rituals while showing the utmost reverence and respect for one's parents and elders.

One possible way is to transform existing ancestral veneration rituals and co-opt them for Christian purposes. Liao writes about the way that Christianity could take a concept (e.g. offering sacrifices and *bài* ancestors placed on a shrine at home) and adapt the concept in a way that honors God (e.g. turning the whole home into a shrine, a place where the whole family worships God).[17]

Dealing with ancestral veneration in Chinese societies is not a new concept. Over the years, much English literature has dealt with the issue.[18] Chinese discourse on the topic is even more common, especially on a popular level, for example in sermons and seminars.[19] However, few (if any) of them tie the issue directly to one's initial exposure to the gospel. In other words, these works of literature address how new Christians can successfully win over their family to Christ and how to deal with ancestral veneration.[20] But the literature does not usually address the many people who do not become Christians in the first place partly because of not dealing with the issue of ancestors.

Some interviews (like the one with Pei-Pei) showed that this very issue of filial piety can be the biggest stumbling block for a person. Qualitative research like this study is a beginning point that can enable future scholarship to better explore this topic. It is important to help the 5.8 percent of Taiwanese

---

17. Liao 廖, *Mínsú Yǔ Xìnyǎng* 民俗與信仰, 131–39.

18. Bolton, "Taiwan's Ancestor Cult"; Halporn, *Gods, Ghosts and Ancestors*; Nadeau and Chang, "Gods, Ghosts, and Ancestors"; Scott, *For Gods, Ghosts and Ancestors*.

19. Liao 廖, *Mínsú Yǔ Xìnyǎng* 民俗與信仰; Chuang 莊, *Christian Perspective*, 說禪論道 — 基督教與儒、釋、道之對話.

20. Liao 廖, *Mínsú Yǔ Xìnyǎng* 民俗與信仰 accomplishes these tasks especially well.

Christians grapple (figuratively) with ancestors and living parents. It is even more important to figure out why the other 94.2 percent are not responding favorably to the gospel yet. Is there something wrong with the way the gospel is presented? Does the contextual approach to gospel transmission need to be revisited? Do family and ancestors need to be addressed in more detail in gospel presentations? As one issue among many, would removing this stumbling block at least help the task of Taiwanese evangelization? The answer is a resounding yes for all four questions.

Truth Claims

For many participants, the truthfulness of a religion is not the most important question to consider in joining a religion. This was especially exemplified by Tattoo Ju, who said, 「因為我相信這件事情，……有沒有那個東西的存在也不是一個非常重要的問題」 ("Because I believe in this thing, . . . whether this thing even exists is not a very important question"). Mommy Farong also said how the act of believing can make things possible.

These interviews show that in Taiwan, fighting for the veracity of truth claims may not be the best approach. The qualitative research shows that, generally speaking, Taiwanese people in Taipei are fixated on pragmatism, namely anything and everything to help them get through life. If a deity works, they flock to that deity. Mrs. Ting's tour bus example showed how many people would flock to a deity that could help them in life. In the Taiwanese mind, whether something "works" is much more important than whether something is "true." M.-H. Lin explains this phenomenon thus: "Folk customs demonstrate a group's lifestyle, reflect a group's value system. . . . Furthermore, it does not matter if it is true or false, logical or not, the populace will abide by it."[21]

What then should the Christian do in the process of gospel transmission? Should they ignore all the truth claims of Christianity in favor of Simon the Sorcerer's approach? Should they turn everyone into "rice Christians" because that works? Or should they double down on truth claims as one of Christianity's advantages? A full answer is difficult to give in just one chapter. However, five things must be considered. The first three points uphold the importance and even the usefulness of making truth claims in gospel transmission in Taiwan. The last two points do not negate this argument, but

---

21. Lin 林, *Dà Miào Chéng* 大廟埕, 248.

nuance it and tailor it to make gospel transmission more convincing and less time-consuming. The call is not to abandon truth-seeking as a concept nor to remove it from Christian discourse with non-Christians, but to make it secondary in an initial gospel presentation.

First, in strategizing about gospel transmission, the Christian evangelizing person must not treat pragmatism as the most important issue. For in doing so, they would present Christianity as no different from folk religion in Taiwan. There are essential cores of Christianity that are founded on the authenticity and historicity of true events. These cores must not be compromised in search of a more "pragmatic" way to "get people saved." Pragmatism is important, just not the most important issue.

Second, there is a rich, millennia-long history of Christian theologizing by ancient Israelites, Roman Jews, African bishops, European monks, tenured professors, Chinese house churches, and many more groups of people. While this may not be important to some people, it may be an attraction point for people looking for truth. Sharing the gospel with those who have never heard it must always include the essentials of this gospel. The points included in this chapter are not meant to remove certain aspects of the gospel, but to highlight those more culturally relevant to Taiwan.

Third, Jesus must not be treated as just another deity that the person turns to for fulfillment of some desire. Whoever spoke to Healthy Chen may have neglected this point because that was all Heathy Chen talked about, namely how Jesus can help him be healthy and successful. Truth claims may not be important to the Taiwanese, but unless one shares a little bit about the truth claims of Christianity, many more Healthy Chens may be part of the Christian landscape in Taiwan.

Fourth, if the non-Christian does not care about truth claims, why spend so much time focusing on them? Discourse on truth may be important to some segments of the population, but based on the interviews, that is a small segment. From the findings the key issue to address is not whether Jesus is true, but rather what problems people have and which deity can address them most efficaciously. The focus should be on things that people care about: money (as shown when they *bài* the God of Wealth), family (ancestors), love (Yue Lao), etc. But the Christian must dig deeper, beyond the surface issues of health and wealth and into the many other things that people care about in life. Whatever the Christian discovers should be addressed first, whether it is self-confidence, longing for approval, or loneliness. The idea is that addressing truth claims is not the best use of time in initial gospel presentations.

Jesus can in some cases make people well and bless people with financial prosperity. Jesus can heal old family wounds and give someone true love. Even if these are not the core of the Christian gospel, these are certainly the most relevant and the biggest points of interest; thus, these may well be the entry points for the non-Christian listener in Taiwan. Jesus can certainly hold his own as compared to any of the deities in Taiwan. However, Christian evangelizing people would do well to recognize how Jesus can compete on the terms of Taiwanese culture (i.e. pragmatism), and not necessarily the terms with which they feel the most resonance (i.e. truth, getting into heaven, etc.). Jesus can win in either competition but why not remove obstacles if possible?

Fifth, the Christian evangelizing person should remember to present the gospel as something that "works." If Tattoo Ju's perspective is found in other Taiwanese people in Taipei (and the interviews indicate so), then showing how well the gospel works may actually enhance gospel transmission. The evangelizing person does not have to spend as much time proving that Jesus existed because that is unimportant to people like Tattoo Ju. The evangelizing person does not need to argue abstractly about the spiritual laws of this world or about substitutionary atonement. The evangelizing person may do those things, but only as an addition to the core of the message. The core is that turning to Jesus simply works. It works in this life as well as the next. Jesus called people to simply come to him (Matt 11:28); perhaps Taiwanese gospel transmission efforts would do well to repeat this call more often. Another demonstration of the fact that turning to Jesus works is power evangelism, which includes things like healings, exorcisms, power encounters, etc. The idea is not to present an exhaustive list of things to do in an initial gospel encounter, but to suggest a contextual approach to gospel transmission that downplays (without erasing) truth claims and highlights Taiwanese concerns.

Relating to Deities and the Unseen Realm

The findings in the previous chapters showed how Taiwanese people in Taipei felt about fortune telling. The resulting data showed that many participants believed that fortune telling works, while only a few did not. Among those who believed it works, there were a few who continually engaged in it. Bookstore Lady and Mrs. Ting were two people who especially praised the accuracy of certain fortune tellers. Nevertheless, they both said that they stopped seeking them out because they did not see a need to rely on fortune telling in their current circumstances.

This scenario could be explained by saying that both Mrs. Ting and Bookstore Lady stopped believing in the accuracy of fortune telling. We could, on the other hand, say that these two people stopped relying on fortune telling despite believing in its accuracy. The former statement explains the abandonment of fortune telling through a change in belief, while the latter statement explains it through a change in situation. To illustrate, if we were trying to recruit more clients for fortune tellers, we would tailor our strategy to our understanding of the underlying cause of the situation. In the former situation, where the issue is people having stopped believing, we would try to reinforce belief. In the latter situation, where the issue is people having stopped relying on it, we would focus our efforts on reliance.

Applying the illustration to our development of a contextual approach to gospel transmission, what are some explanations for the situation in Taiwan where relatively few people are turning to Christianity? One explanation is that many people do not believe the truth claims of the Bible or the power of Jesus to save. Another explanation is that many people do not see the need to rely on the teachings of the Bible or the power of Jesus. The former explanation frames the problem as one of belief and of knowledge. This logically leads to the solution as better teaching or more fervent explanation of this belief and knowledge. The latter explanation frames the problem as one of reliance (i.e. usefulness in the person's present life) and of lacking in demonstrations of power. The latter explanation logically leads to the solution as showing the utility and supremacy of the LORD in the midst of many other deities who claim to offer great results also.

Issues with Religious Boundary Crossing

The second main category is what it means to cross a boundary from one religious system into another. The idea of crossing a religious boundary means that there is some form of change, whether social, theological, or otherwise. People do change religious allegiance occasionally but the markers of this change as well as how people treat the necessity of making a change may look different in Taiwan. The following are a few concepts that surfaced based on the qualitative data.

What Needs to Change

The interview findings show that Taiwanese people in Taipei are mostly apathetic about the afterlife and ignorant of the concept of sin. In Taiwan, there are really no criteria for "getting in" to a religion, but only for "staying in." One can enter the doors of a temple anytime, as Mommy Farong proudly declared.

In the findings we discussed the fact that virtually all the participants described their religious identity using behavior instead of beliefs. This was the same for those classified as folk religion adherents as well as Buddhists. For example, Mrs. Ting answered the question of "How much does one have to understand in order to believe?" by talking about behavior and daily rituals. No mention at all was made of any doctrine. The lack of information was even more obvious for folk religion adherents. Most Mazu followers, even those who were "adopted godchildren" like Tattoo Ju or Genie, did not know of any specific set of beliefs one should uphold. Instead, they promised to Mazu that they would try to be good people in this world.

In the discussion on "Defining a Devout Person" in chapter 4, frequent religious action, behavior, integrity, money, and relationship with the deity were the most important factors. In fact, devotion to a deity is a potentially misleading term because the important point is not how devoted someone is to Buddha, but how much compassion one shows to the world. Again, we see Taiwanese religiosity focusing primarily on behavior.

The Buddhist examples highlighted that dharma was an important concept to them. But what is dharma? The English equivalent for Christianity is likely theology. However, there are key differences. Mrs. Ting explained dharma as things that she abstains from, a good management of wealth, infinite wisdom and understanding, and a few ways of morality. Dharma seems to be a way that one ought to live one's life. There was very little mention in the interview about the characteristics of Buddha. The parts that did relate to the character of the deity are not related to dharma. This was the case throughout all the interviews with all the participants.

Herein lies a key difference between the Buddhist dharma and Christian theology. Christian theology deals with all things relating to God and humanity, but has its foundation in the truths about God, soteriology, hamartiology,

Christology, and areas of study about God's attributes. The Buddhist dharma focuses on truths about morality, wealth, suffering, and other areas of wise living.

These foundational differences (or at least foci) have big impacts on the cultures in which we find them. In Taiwan, Buddhists tend to focus on wise living. To them, wise living is the end goal of a religion. If a deity is seen as powerful through prayer or exposure, then the person may start having faith in the deity, which looks like living wisely under the instructions of the master. There is no boundary that one crosses that coincides with one's efficacious or salvific faith in Buddha. The Buddhist view of faith seems to be focused on following the dharma in one's daily life. In that sense, anyone who even minimally tries to follow the dharma can be considered a Buddhist (i.e. House Gongon).

In a culture that prioritizes behavior to define religious identity, it is much more straightforward to share initially about gospel identity using behavior. This is not to say that beliefs are never shared, only that the initial encounters and explanations ought to be behavior oriented. Moreover, this focus on behavior is more akin to how Yong views Christian conversion, namely "as a lifelong path toward being made into the image of Jesus," a path that is "unfinished" and includes elements of religiosity (i.e. beliefs) and religious life (i.e. behavior and praxis).[22] In Yong's view, we should all view praxis so that "praxis becomes just as, if not more, important than beliefs (doctrines) and that precisely because pneumatology calls attention to divine activity rather than divine being. This complements the classical understanding wherein 'praxis' was secondary to 'doctrine' in defining a religious tradition."[23]

Elevating the importance of behavior in religion results in a theology of religion that pays more respect to folk religion in Taiwan, where behavior is already elevated above doctrine. It results in a contextual approach to gospel transmission that helps Taiwanese people understand the gospel in a framework that Taiwanese people in Taipei are more familiar with and more ready to act on.

---

22. Yong, "P(New)Matological Paradigm," 178.
23. Yong, 178.

Conversion as a Problematic Term

In the previous discussion, we have alluded to the concept of conversion as one way to describe religious change. Conversion is well researched in the field of religious studies.[24] Space does not permit us to discuss in full detail all aspects of conversion: the importance of history in religious conversion, the sociology of conversion, the psychology of conversion, and many others.[25] All these topics, except for brief mentions, are unfortunately left out. What we discuss here more fully is religious change in the context of folk religion in Taiwan and its conceptual comparison with conversion.[26]

To make a comparison, we must first give a simple definition of what we mean by the term conversion. Rodney Stark and Roger Finke define conversion broadly as "shifts across religious traditions," like changing one's religious affiliation from Buddhist to Muslim.[27] Within Christianity, it is often understood as people transitioning from being a non-Christian to being a Christian. There are important theological concepts that some theologians say are inseparable from the process of conversion, like repentance, the indwelling of the Holy Spirit, discipleship, and more. For the limited purposes of this study, we define a traditional understanding of conversion thus: leaving an old religion (or no religion) and establishing allegiance to a new one through a series of theological, sociological, and psychological changes. This definition implies exclusive religious identity. With this definition in mind, we now discuss the usefulness of the term conversion in the context of folk religion in Taiwan.

Problems in the Context of Folk Religion

Conversion as a term and as an approach may be problematic in the context of folk religion in Taiwan. Conversion as a term does not have a direct Chinese translation. The idea of 皈依 (*guīyī*) is the closest term to conversion; however, it is used only theologically in Buddhism and practiced rarely. The word 宗教 (*zōngjiào*, religion) did not enter into Chinese vocabulary until

---

24. Rambo, *Understanding Religious Conversion*; Robbins, "Anthropology," 633–52; Rambo and Farhadian, *Oxford Handbook*.

25. Baer, "History and Religious Conversion," 25–47.; Yang and Abel, "Sociology of Religious Conversion," 140–63; Paloutzian, "Psychology of Religious Conversion," 209–39.

26. Fan and Chen, "'Conversion,'" 556–77.

27. Stark and Finke, *Acts of Faith*, 114.

the early twentieth century.²⁸ The term conversion was another added term during this time. Unlike *zōngjiào*, which has come into more common usage, no term for conversion has become common in Mandarin Chinese. In normal conversation, it is more common to hear Coe Bei's description of herself as someone who practices 「佛法」 ("the [Buddhist] dharma"). Coe Bei's mentioned her past experience as a Christian, but no word was used to signify religious change except that she practiced something else at the time of the interview.²⁹

As a term, conversion is foreign to Taiwan. As an approach, it is foreign as well. Notice that in the research findings, the section on conversion was noticeably short and fragmented. It seems that Taiwanese people in Taipei in general just do not think about this topic as much. 范麗珠 (Lizhu Fan) and 陳納 (Na Chen) argue that "conversion" is inadequate for folk religion in China as well. Fan and Chen write that conversion "is a problematic term when used in the study of Chinese indigenous religious practices and beliefs."³⁰ They believe that the expression of religiosity in Chinese society "creates modes of self-fulfillment and meaning that transcend the traditional, constricted understandings of conversion."³¹

What Fan and Chen are referring to is the idea of imposing an artificial restriction on the person, insisting they must belong to religions delineated with clear boundaries and only to one at a time. As a term, conversion implies that one has stopped being a member/adherent of a religion and transitioned to become a member/adherent of another religion. This conceptualization is at odds with the mindset of the vast majority of the research participants. Company Woman sought out the deities Mazu, Earth God, and the LORD for help with one problem. Mommy Farong had multiple deities from Buddhism and folk religion at home; she had no problem doing *bài* to them daily. Conversion does not fit the Taiwanese context well, namely the

---

28. Fan and Chen, "'Conversion,'" 558.
29. Therefore, "religious change" may be a neutral enough phrase to describe Taiwanese religious experiences. However, this would be an English word to describe a Taiwanese phenomenon. One phrase used in Mandarin Chinese is, 「我換了宗教」 ("I changed religion"). But this phrase is not used often.
30. Fan and Chen, "'Conversion,'" 557.
31. Fan and Chen, 557.

assumed belief in multiple deities and the accepted norm of worshipping any or all of them.

The goal of this work is not to describe religious change, but to figure out why religious change is not happening as much as some Christians would want. This goal requires describing the whole spectrum of religious thinking in Taiwan, especially of people who see conversion as a foreign concept. It requires describing how people treat deities, what "being religious" means, the significance of diffused religion,[32] and how "faith" is used in everyday language, to name just a few aspects missing from some current approaches. This study is advocating for a better term, one that does not carry centuries of sociological and theological baggage. This work is advocating for a better approach, one that takes into account the fluidity of adhering to religions. Instead of strategizing about people leaving folk religion and joining Christianity, it might be more helpful to strategize about getting people to incorporate more of the gospel into their daily, religiously plural lives. To put more practically, instead of stopping people from doing *bài* to Guan Shengdijun at Hsing Tian Kong, it might be more helpful to get people to start beseeching Jesus at churches. The strategy does not focus on a person having an exclusive religious identity, but rather proposes, as an entry point, a person incorporating the LORD into the pantheon of deities that he or she already *bài* and beseeches.

Can the LORD remain as just one God in a pantheon of deities? Does the person need to make a choice one day between Christianity and everything else? There is only one God and he is the Lord. Therefore, the person cannot keep the LORD as just one deity in a pantheon of deities. The person absolutely must make a choice one day and exclusively turn to Jesus. The approach proposed here simply argues that this "one day" should be much farther in the future than some Christians may think.

This study argues neither that conversion as a term be thrown out nor that it is somehow contrary to the gospel. Rather, one should use a different term to talk about Taiwanese religious change and one should use a modified conceptual approach to be more effective in transmitting the gospel to Taiwanese people in Taipei. If Fan and Chen are correct in their analysis, conversion as a term is too foreign to cultures accustomed to folk religion.

---

32. Yang, *Religion in Chinese Society*.

Problems as Seen in the Interview Participants

Remember that 「修行」 (*xiūxíng*, *Sādhanā* or "religious practice") was an important concept that the Buddhist participants used to describe their religiosity (when talking about their journey, their allegiance, or their daily lives). Non-Buddhist participants also used religious practice to describe their spiritual journey. It is significant that "practice," not "faith," was the word used to describe a Buddhist's life and religious belonging. First, it indicates an attitude that focuses on behavior more so than belief. It is true that belief is a part of the process of behavior change, but belief was not focused on as much as behavior in the participants' own descriptions of their religious change as well as in their explanations of what their religion focused on. Recall the open-ended way Mrs. Ting talked about the thousands of people in the tour buses and the utilitarian way many other participants talked about deities. Conversion for these participants was less about changing one's thinking and more about changing one's behavior. Both are eventually changed, as Mrs. Ting was careful to point out; so, it is not a matter of one being more important than the other. However, the starting place is different.

Second, the fact that "practice" is used to describe the Buddhist life means that when one stops religious practice, one stops being a Buddhist. This is a simple and logical concept, one that Mrs. Ting herself explained matter-of-factly. However, for Christians whose theological traditions emphasize that "salvation cannot be lost," this may be a foreign concept. It comes back to how one defines a "true believer" in a religious system. If a "true believer" is someone who has at one time proclaimed belief in a religious system, then one can never stop being a "believer." If a "true believer" is someone who needs to continually believe, then the moment one stops believing, one stops being a "believer." Now, if a "true believer" is someone who needs to continually do "religious practice," then the moment one stops practicing, one stops being a "believer."

One may start to see the problem with using the word believer. This is one reason this study uses the word adherent. The word believer favors religious systems, like Christianity, that traditionally has put a high emphasis on intellectual belief. Words like adherent, or even disciple do not favor intellectual belief as much and may even lean the other way. This change of wording affects a change in gospel transmission tactics and emphases.

Remember that for Tour Guide Man, believing in a religion's teachings and doctrines is only the second to last step before "true conversion." The last step is experiencing the religion during an "unclear and long process" in which one keeps testing the religion in one's life. To contextualize to Christianity, one does not become a baby Christian after "believing in Jesus," rather one becomes a "tester of Christianity" for a period of time after believing in Jesus.[33] Then, after the test has been satisfactory, one finally becomes a Christian. The testing period, where one experiences the religion and tests out how it "combines" with one's life, is essential to the conversion process. At least, this is how the participants framed it, which means that this process is what others like him would be comfortable experiencing if they were to "become Christian."

Remember that Coe Bei described her beginning into Buddhism as "Buddha *yuán* being activated." She did religious practice of Zen, then practiced increasingly more and more aspects of the religion. She did not describe herself as having ever converted in the sense that she left one religion and became another. Rather, she said that she has been "practicing dharma." In that sense, even though she would call herself a Buddhist if someone asked, she used other descriptors for her religious identity. To her, Buddhism was a lifelong journey and practice that was best discussed with terms other than "conversion" (i.e. religious practice of Buddhism).

There are a few takeaways here. First, her religious journey was very much based on fuzzy set thinking or centered set thinking; her idea of religion was definitely not a bounded set.[34] That is, there were no boundary markers signifying that she had crossed over from her old religion (which was Christianity) to her new one. She simply ended her conversion story by stating that she has been studying dharma for twenty to thirty years now and highly recommended the researcher did the same. There was no official ceremony either, only a progressive deepening of her following the dharma. Buddha was the center point of her centered set view of religion. She herself said in multiple occasions that modes and methods do not matter, only the end goal, which is Buddha, matters.

---

33. At some point in time, regeneration occurs in the person to allow him or her to take these steps and become a child of God. Regeneration, along with other steps in the *Ordo salutis*, (order of salvation), are important theologically but irrelevant in the minds of Taiwanese non-Christians.

34. Hiebert, "Sets and Structures"; Keller, *Center Church*.

Second, Coe Bei practiced a religion before she considered herself truly a part of it. It was only after having practiced Zen with Dharma Drum Mountain that she wanted to start learning about Master Sheng Yen's Buddhism. She did not have a Eureka moment, a blinding light on a road, a solemn prayer, or any such experience, at least not that she explained. At the beginning of her interview, she matter-of-factly stated that she was a Buddhist. But despite much probing, she did not explain at what point she became one. She did not seem to care whether she had an experience to mark some kind of conversion.

This was doubly important because she said that she used to be a Christian but is not one anymore. There might have been moments in time when she held onto multiple religious identities before settling on being exclusively Buddhist, but at some point in time she must have ceased being Christian and started becoming Buddhist. The fact that she did not know or seemed to care about that moment is very telling about the fluidity with which people like Coe Bei experience religious change. For her, being part of a religious system started with a change in behavior (i.e. practicing dharma) instead of learning its beliefs (i.e. teachings from Master Sheng Yen). This approach to proselytizing worked very well for Coe Bei. Perhaps it might work well for Christian evangelizing people also.

Transformation as an Alternative Term

Thus far, this section has been problematizing the term conversion and its conceptual connotations. An alternative has not been provided to describe crossing a religious boundary. The problem is not that conversion as a term is outdated nor that its socio-psychological aspects are irrelevant. Conversion is a useful term in many other contexts. The problem is that conversion is often associated with too many other concepts that do not fit the religious thinking of Taiwanese people in Taipei. This association has the possibility of confusing or misleading the Christian evangelizing person to seek a response that is too foreign to the Taiwanese person. The solution is not to discard terms like conversion, but to focus on words and concepts that are less foreign in Taiwan. In fact, an easy change would be to highlight conversion as a process more than conversion as a moment, an approach that is already being done in many circles.

However, a better term has surfaced from the interview data from the Christian participants. It seems transformation is the term that is used most often to describe a person changing religious allegiance or behavior. It took significant probing to get the Christian participants to point to a moment when they became officially Christians. That moment was always indicated as their baptism.[35] Despite being able to speak about conversion and the moment of salvation, all the Christian participants also spoke on their lifelong processes of transformation during this line of questioning.

When speaking about transformation, they spoke about changes they have felt since encountering Christianity for the first time. Healthy Chen spoke about his anger issues going away slowly as he understood Christianity more, with his baptism happening much further down the road, which was just one moment during his process of transformation. Company Woman spoke about her reading the Bible and praying to God despite not being a Christian, saying that her mind was still not made up. However, she explained that Christianity had already transformed and influenced her more than her family's religion. For its ability to transform, Company Woman spoke about how attractive the religion was to her. The participants who described religious change did not seem to care about their past or current religious identity, only that they had presently been transformed. The important issue for them was not whether their identities had been changed, but whether their lives had been changed.

A contextual approach to gospel transmission in Taiwan must speak to the transformation of the person as one of the more prominent features.[36] This approach understands that people like Company Woman may be experiencing transformation before praying a "special prayer" and that this process is part of transmitting the gospel to her. This approach understands that people like College Hua view his own 「改變」 ("transformation") as the most important feature of Christianity.[37] This approach understands that a long time before certain theological concepts are developed (i.e. heaven and

---

35. Fishu for example had prayed a prayer to trust Jesus Christ as Lord and savior. But she neither participated in communion nor did she call herself a Christian until she was baptized. It was not clear how long it took between her praying "the prayer" and her getting baptized, but the timeframe seemed to be fairly short. For many Christian participants, including Healthy Chen, they responded to the question of "How long have you been a Christian?" with the statement "I was baptized in [year number]." Again, the idea is that baptism indicated their official beginning as a Christian.

36. Note that prominence does not necessarily equal importance.

37. College Hua used "transformation" the most out of all the participants – thirteen times in one short segment. As he told it, College Hua did not convert; rather, he said that he decided to become more committed to Christ after finding more about this deity.

hell), a person could already be far along enough to be baptized (i.e. Healthy Chen). This approach understands that when most Taiwanese folk religion adherents hear the phrase "believe in Jesus for eternal life," they interpret the word "believe" as some form of transformation of behavior occurring throughout one's entire life. This approach understands that the diffused, inclusive nature of folk religion makes exclusivist understandings of conversion too "constricted" to the average Taiwanese person.[38]

Speaking about gospel transmission without transformation does not fit the journey of Taiwanese Christians nor of most folk religion adherents. A contextual approach to gospel transmission in Taiwan must understand that critical moments may exist and may even need to be highlighted at times. However, spiritual and personal formation is not only normal discourse for the average Taiwanese, but this way of thinking is also a key selling point of Buddhism in Taiwan.[39] If leveraged wisely, Christianity's ability to transform people can be a very attractive selling point for Taiwanese people in Taipei. To make this change in terminology is to pay attention to what Yang and Abel call "the macro level" of conversion, that of understanding the "social and cultural contextual factors."[40]

The thrust of this entire section was not to redefine the term conversion. The goal was to show how certain discourse on conversion does not fit the religious thinking of folk religion in Taiwan and Chinese religiosity in general.[41] The bigger thrust of this study is to use terms that Taiwanese people in Taipei use, and to put at the forefront ideas that are most common for them.

Issues with Religious Pluralism

The third main category deals with religious pluralism. We have seen in the research findings that religious pluralism is a cultural norm in Taiwan. This is one of the most important issues to take into account when transmitting the

---

38. Fan and Chen "'Conversion,'" 572 go further to say, "Understanding the resurgence or revitalization of religions/spirituality around the world may be constricted if the term 'conversion' (especially as it has been used in Western Christianity) is deployed."

39. Recall the discussions in the findings chapter about religious practice and Zen in Taiwanese Buddhism.

40. Yang and Abel, "Sociology of Religious Conversion," 141.

41. Fan and Chen, "'Conversion.'"

gospel. Some important questions regarding pluralism are unfortunately left out, including the question of salvation within folk religion and special revelation within other religious traditions. This section unpacks this idea of pluralism as seen in the interviews and how it might affect gospel transmission.

Pluralism as a Concept

Peter Berger defines pluralism as "a social situation in which people with different ethnicities, worldviews, and moralities live together peacefully and interact with each other amicably."[42] In a response in the same book, Fenggang Yang nuances pluralism by speaking of individual and social pluralism. Furthermore, F. Yang adds two more terms that other sociologists use, plurality and pluralization. F. Yang defines plurality as "the degree of religious heterogeneity within a society" and pluralization as "the term for the process of increasing plurality in a society."[43] Putting the three terms together, F. Yang writes, "The three terms – plurality, pluralism, and pluralization – point to the degree, the arrangement, and the process of plural religions in a society, respectively."[44]

In Taiwan, religious pluralization has been around for many decades. Therefore, the "peaceful" and "amicable" type of pluralism that P. Berger describes has been around for many decades. This has created a culture that, in F. Yang's words, does the following: "accepting, affirming, and equally protecting the presence of plural religions in a society" and "creating favorable social and cultural conditions for the presence of plural religions."[45]

If Taiwan were to institute a dominant religion, it would be folk religion.[46] It is ironic because folk religion in Taiwan itself involves a plurality of deities and their temples existing in harmony. Among the religions embedded in the culture, Buddhism is the most widely accepted. Christianity does not dominate the hearts or minds of the Taiwanese people in Taipei as a whole in the same way that Buddhism does. One cannot effectively transmit the gospel without understanding this pluralism more fully.

---

42. Berger, *Many Altars of Modernity*, 1.
43. Berger, 136.
44. Berger, 136–37.
45. Berger, 137.
46. Pew Research Center, "Religious Composition by Country, 2010–2050."

Singapore, as a Chinese society in the diaspora, shares certain similarities with Taiwan that bears significance in this research.[47] Religious pluralism is a key similarity. Robert Solomon writes about the religious pluralism that he experienced in Singapore. He offers three suggestions on the work of gospel transmission in this religiously plural context.[48] One of the suggestions is that Christians practice "religious sensitivity." In Singapore, other faiths complain about the "aggressive forms of Christian evangelism."[49] In an incident that happened "recently," Solomon shares that a Christian couple sent Christian tracts to Muslims that belittled Islam; as a result, they were taken to court for sedition.[50] Therefore, Solomon admonishes people to be "preaching Christ instead of running down other people's religion."[51]

This same admonition should be taken in Taiwan, where religious pluralism is the norm and Christianity is a minority religion. Considering everything we have learned, "running down" folk religion's beliefs and practices is not the best way to bring someone to Jesus Christ. It may work for some people, but it has the potential downside of repelling more people than it attracts. The danger of this practice is a nationwide Christian witness that is diminished. Without a more comprehensive study, the reality of this danger cannot be proven conclusively. However, if the multiple negative comments from several research participants is any indication (e.g. Tattoo Ju, Pei-Pei), this danger is likely already manifesting.

Perhaps due to this perceived danger, there were some Christians (e.g. College Hua) who said things like, 「並不是一定說你信了耶穌之後，就會進入永生，或者是你不信耶穌，就一定會進入到地獄。它是沒有那麼黑白分明的」 ("It is not definite that once you believe in Jesus, you would enter into eternal life, or that if you do not believe in Jesus, you would enter hell. It is not that black and white"). It seems that pluralism as a concept is so entwined with Taiwanese religious thinking that even Taiwanese Christians are more hesitant to proclaim doctrines that stress exclusivity.

---

47. For example, one of Singapore's official four national languages is Mandarin Chinese, which shows the impact of Chinese thinking. Another similarity is that many Singaporeans either look or are Han Chinese.

48. Solomon, "Making Disciples in Singapore," 105–6.

49. Solomon, 105.

50. Solomon, 105.

51. Solomon, 105.

Pluralism as a Lived Reality

Depending on the type of problem faced, a Taiwanese person may go to Earth God, Lord Superior Wen Chang, or any number of deities. Moreover, the famous temple Hsing Tian Kong in Taipei does not just house one deity. People who visit the temple are specifically instructed to be sure to *bài* each deity. Taiwanese are expected to accept all deities and participate in certain rituals. Those who refuse to participate would face varying levels of ostracism depending on their social circle.

Many of the research participants mentioned going to different deities depending on what they were looking for. Beseeching was one of the most popular terms that people used to describe their relationship and interactions with various deities. This is a fitting example of the religious pluralism that characterizes Taiwan's religious landscape. The question many Taiwanese people in Taipei seem to ask is, "Now that I have this issue, whom do I go to for efficacious resolution?"

Fishu's experience in folk religion, filtered through her lens as a recently baptized Christian, gives some insight to answering this question. She said,

> 可是如果是以前民間信仰，我會不知道我要誰，我只能說，我求平安，但是我不知道我找誰，就是好像如果祂們是限定的話，限定的一些項目。……你找不到你要找哪一位神明。對，可是我覺得上帝是你不管什麼，祂全知全能，所以你不管什麼，你都可以找 (But in [my] past folk religion, I would not know whom I want. I could only say, "I beseech peace." But I do not know whom to beseech from. It is as if they [the deities] are limited, limited to certain categories [of power] . . . You cannot find out which deity you need to ask. Yes, but I think with Shangdi [the LORD], it does not matter. He is omniscient and omnipotent; so, it does not matter [what you need], you can ask Shangdi).

In her past, Fishu went to Lord Superior Wen Chang and fasted from beef for a year to get her desire fulfilled. She had gone to several other deities for other issues in her life too. Shi Gu, Police Lady, and most of the other participants mentioned going to different deities for different needs as well. This is what

Tattoo Ju called a "utilitarian" approach to deities and what Yao and Zhao considered a "functional" way of Chinese religiosity.[52]

So, when Taiwanese people in Taipei have an issue, whom do they go to for efficacious resolution? If Fishu's experience is any indication, pointing people to the "omniscient and omnipotent" God of Christianity may be a good solution. Taiwanese people in Taipei need to know and experience that if a person has God, that person has a one stop solution. One does not need to travel to Taichung for the famous Mazu temple there, or to Dharma Drum Mountain for holy water. One needs to only turn to one deity for efficacious resolution on any matter.

Recall from chapter 2 that there is a deity that is known as being more powerful than every other deity. This deity is named Shangdi. It is no wonder that Matteo Ricci used the term Shangdi to translate the LORD in the Bible, a "strange name" indeed.[53] A good contextual approach to gospel transmission should capitalize on this translation to tell Taiwanese people in Taipei that Shangdi is bigger than every other deity they know, a God above all other gods. College Hua already understood this, saying that Shangdi can solve every problem, not just over one realm of nature.

It is true that these "other gods" are not real gods. However, unless the plausibility structure for religious pluralism in Taiwan shifts, it is not helpful to denounce the existence of these other gods. As a Christian, Fishu said that whatever these deities are, they still have power and authority to affect things in this world. Many non-Christian participants also recognized the deities' power. The research revealed that "perceived power" was one of the things that drew people to select deities.

In order to speak to the religiously pluralistic Taiwanese, it may be more helpful to speak like Moses did in Deuteronomy 4:7 (ESV): "For what great nation is there that has a god so near to it as the LORD our God is to us, whenever we call upon him?" Moses's admonition was phrased as if the other gods were real. Of course, Moses later in the same chapter denounced the other deities as "gods of wood and stone" (Deut 4:28). However, it is interesting that his initial admonition understood a context of religious pluralism

---

52. Yao and Zhao, *Chinese Religion*, 149.

53. Kim, *Strange Names of God*.

and addressed people with that assumption. In that context, Moses framed the LORD as better than other gods.

Taiwan does not have "a god so near to it as the LORD our God is to us." It may seem foolish to put the LORD in competition with the many other deities in Taiwan. However, if Moses's example is some indication, if Fishu's story serves as an example, and if perceived power really is an important point, then comparing the LORD to Taiwanese deities may be a very helpful way to evangelize to Taiwanese people in Taipei. A contextual approach to gospel transmission takes into account the context of religious pluralism, choosing to fight some battles (i.e. the LORD is the strongest there is and therefore all you need) and neglecting to fight others (i.e. the LORD is the only God). Other battles may be fought and won, but they are secondary. Focusing on fighting just the necessary battles may be key to winning the war for souls in Taiwan.

Exclusive religious identity is rare. Many participants self-identified as both Buddhist and Daoist. In the interviews, they talked about their experiences with multiple deities in folk religion. We cannot here definitively settle the debate over whether Christianity allows multiple religious identities, which is affirmed by some and denied by others.[54] What is important for this study is not whether having multiple religious identities is theologically possible, but that this pluralistic landscape is the lived reality of Taiwanese people in Taipei.

Shi Gu explained the religious landscape in Taiwan thus, 「就是兄弟登山啦！各自登山，各自努力，阿到最後的話就萬流歸宗啦！」 ("It's like brothers climbing mountains! Each climbs his or her own mountain, each works hard on his or her own. At the end, ten thousand streams converge in one place"). Shi Gu showed the level of religious pluralism that is manifested in the minds of some Taiwanese people in Taipei. Namely, all religions may represent different mountain peaks or different river streams, but all those streams ultimately converge in one place. That is why she did not look down on any other religion nor did she like it when other people did so.

Her religious pluralism was particularly noticeable when asked how she reacts to the phrase, "Believe in Jesus for eternal life." She replied immediately, 「我相信啊！信耶穌，得永生」 ("I believe! Believe Jesus, get eternal life").

---

54. Ruether, "Religious Identity," 29–40.

When pressed for clarification, she replied, 「難道信別的沒有永生嗎？」 ("Do not tell me believing in other [religions] does not result in eternal life?"). Shi Gu thought that all the different religions converge to eternal life, which is explained differently for Buddhism, Christianity, Daoism, and particular beliefs in folk religion. Shi Gu identified as a Buddhist and a Daoist while still "believing" in Jesus. The belief she was talking about is agreeing that Jesus as a deity is real and has some kind of power. This assumption that deities are real was found in almost all the participants and seem to be the accepted worldview in Taiwan.

Shi Gu was not alone in her sentiment, House Gongon also had a strong sense of pluralism. When asked what deity he would most recommend to other people, he said that he would not recommend any deity. His reasoning was this, 「不會推薦，因為我認為他如果相信這一尊神明，而且一直相信他的話就不要去擾動人家的這個信仰。……他如果很虔誠的信他的話，其實都會靈的啦」 ("[I] would not recommend [any deities]. Because I think if he believes in a deity, and continues to believe him, one should not disturb this person's faith . . . If he truly believes him [the deity], it would be efficacious"). Trying to convert someone was seen as a negative act that House Gongon described multiple times as 「殘忍」 ("cruel"). Like Shi Gu, House Gongon believed that all paths could lead to enlightenment; by trying to convert someone, an evangelizing person is 「擾亂」 ("disturbing") and potentially 「毀掉」 ("destroying") the person's path. Healthy Chen did not use such strong words, but nevertheless respected everyone's beliefs and refused to rebut any aspect of other religions.

Due to this religious pluralism, it is unusual to find people who only worship one deity. Some of the Christian participants in the interview were exceptions to this. But every other participant mentioned having had experiences with multiple deities. For example, Tattoo Ju, despite being a goddaughter of Mazu, said that she would *bài* all the deities in a temple when she visits them. Mrs. Ting, despite her devotion to Guanyin, had other deities in her house. Chi, despite his staunch atheism, did not want to disrespect the deities too much. Shi Gu, despite her calling herself Buddhist and Daoist, revered a variety of deities. Staying exclusive to one deity was the exception, not the norm.

Denying the existence of certain deities can be seen as disrespectful. Conversely, worshipping just an unknown deity can be dangerous too and thus looked down on. Police Lady said that if a person *bài* any unknown deity on the street, one might accidentally *bài* a 「陰廟」 ("yin temple"), which results in the involvement of malicious ghosts and spirits. It seems that the correct approach to deities is to *bài* whenever one visits known temples and avoid unknown shrines. This pluralistic reality in Taiwan is important to remember for any religious work in the country.

Power as the Special Factor

Deities are assumed real until proven otherwise. The worldview of the participants assumed the existence of multiple deities, all dedicated to different realms of existence. One deity may be in charge of the land (Earth God), another education (Lord Superior Wen Chang), another romance (Yue Lao), another compassion (Guanyin), and many others in charge of varying subjects. Recall from the interview findings that Fishu used to see Jesus thus: "Like in the pantheon of deities, there is another one called Jesus. But I do not know him." In other words, there is no need to prove that Jesus is real. That was not an important point in Fishu's own path to Christianity. Coe Bei said, "I think a lot of them [deities] are kind." She specifically mentioned elsewhere that Jesus is kind. Yet, she saw no need to explore Christianity further.

In addition to being assumed real, deities also do not demand exclusive allegiance. From Company Woman's example being loyal to a deity does not mean signing an exclusivity contract. It is normal and expected for Taiwanese to approach multiple deities for significant problems. Deities do not even demand strong belief. They are simply powerful beings who may choose to help a human's cause. It is the human's job to impress the deity either through strong devotion, monetary giving at a temple, regular visits to the deity's statue (could be in multiple locations), care of the deity's place of residence, or even one genuine *bài*.

Remember that Bookstore Lady said that if one needed to *shōu jīng* (recover the spirit after the fright), one just needed to visit the temple and see the *gūpó* who performs the ritual. She specifically said that even a "white person" who believes in Jesus can recover their spirit through the spells performed by the *gūpó*. This shows that for many Taiwanese people in Taipei, the important thing about deities is not whether one needs to provide absolute allegiance or whether one needs to be assured of the deities' existences. Rather, what is most important is that there are spells or other rituals that are demonstrably effective. A temple's popularity and online chatroom reviews would testify to which temples and deities are effective.

The logic for those this view of deities is that discovering a deity's power and effectiveness is much more important than understanding a deity's religion and teaching. To put more boldly, whether a deity can accomplish the task that needs to be done is much more important than whether a deity is real.

Evangelizing to Taiwanese people in Taipei therefore does not require much proving of the historicity of Jesus or demonstrating the ethics of Christianity. What matters is whether the Christian deity has the power to help them with their need, whether this same deity has the will to do so, and what ritual to perform to make it happen. It is not surprising then to find out that Smoker Ang thought that "believe in Jesus Christ for eternal life" was a 「咒語」 (zhòuyǔ, "spell") that Christians chant for blessings and protection.

Pluralism in the New Testament Times

We have highlighted a few issues due to the context of pluralism in Taiwan. To give some insight on what the Bible has to say on the topic, it is useful to understand the pluralism in biblical times. Specifically, we look at the New Testament pluralistic context along with an example of Jesus's response to it.

N. T. Wright and Michael Bird highlight many aspects of the cultural context of the first-century Roman world in their book, *The New Testament in Its World*.[55] If a centurion needed help to win a battle, he would give an offering to Mars, the Roman god of war, or Ares, the Greek counterpart. If a lady of an estate wanted wisdom, she would sacrifice to Minerva, the Roman goddess of wisdom, or Athena, the Greek counterpart. The idea is that a pantheon of gods existed in the Roman world during the Second Temple period. A person did not just go to one deity for their needs; rather, depending on the need, different deities were consulted. After all, it was commonly assumed that different deities looked after different areas of life and likewise held power in different areas.

To make it more convenient for people, temples often housed multiple deities. The Capitoline Hill in Rome had a temple to Jupiter, Minerva, and

---

55. Wright and Bird, *New Testament in Its World*, 150–63.

Juno. Augustus built a temple to Apollo, Latona, and Diana.[56] A plurality of deities was part of the daily, lived reality of the ancient Roman world. In fact, anyone who insisted on worshipping just one deity at the expense of others was looked down on and sometimes panned as an atheist. This was the situation in 217 BC, when the Egyptian king Ptolemy Philopater was requiring the Jews living in Alexandria to sacrifice to Dionysus and even be branded with an ivy-leaf symbol (3 Macc 2:29). The Jews who refused were called "hostile and greatly opposed to his government" and bore "no ordinary reproach to them[selves]" (3 Macc 3:7).

When Jesus ministered in this religious context, what did he do? The gospels did not record Jesus condemning the Greek deities Ares, Athena, Apollo, or any of the Roman counterparts that were popular in the land. This may be because Jesus's ministry was mainly to the Jewish people, who were strict monotheists. This may also be because Jesus thought this was a battle not worth fighting. The pericope with the Roman centurion and the sick servant (Matt 8:5–13, Luke 7:1–10) can be used to examine Jesus's response.

It seems that the centurion had already shown some sympathy to the Jews, evidenced by the praise given to him for his financial contribution in building synagogues.[57] The centurion spoke of himself as "a man set under authority" (Luke 7:7) and spoke of Jesus as having the power to affect change with just one command. The Bible does not say whether this centurion was monotheistic or polytheistic. While it is possible for this centurion to be a monotheist, the cultural context makes it more likely that he sought help from a pantheon of deities because he was most likely Roman.[58] Moreover, being an officer under Herod Antipas meant that it was risky to seek out Jesus.[59]

Commentaries point out that the incredible thing about this pericope is that of all the people to show such faith in Jesus, it would be a man of war, a "heathen," a Gentile, and a participant of the imperial cult by virtue of his occupation.[60] The scriptural context further suggests that the centurion might have viewed Jesus as especially powerful and authoritative, which explains

---

56. Wright and Bird, 146.
57. Stein, *Luke*, 219.
58. Wright and Bird, *New Testament in Its World*; Edwards, *Luke*.
59. Edwards, *Luke*, 210.
60. Stein, *Luke*; Hauerwas, *Matthew*; Edwards, *Luke*.

why he asked Jesus for help and did not want Jesus to even "come under [his] roof" (Luke 7:6).[61] When Jesus responded to the centurion, he did not speak of the soldier's belief in the power of deities. Jesus's first response was that "he marveled at him" (Luke 7:9). Jesus's second response was to turn to the crowd and praise the centurion's faith against the lack thereof in Israel (Matt 8:10–12). Jesus's third response was to send the centurion away with the confirmation that the healing is already done (Matt 8:13).

If the commentators are correct, the imperial cult and the Greek/Roman deities were likely part of the centurion's life in some shape or form. Jesus did not even mention the centurion's pantheon of false deities nor did he ask the centurion to exclusively believe in and worship the LORD. There was no comparison of himself to the pantheon of deities. Jesus praised the centurion, presumably for the centurion's belief in Jesus's great power and willingness to help. Some commentators extrapolate further to say that the centurion was praised for recognizing that Jesus really was the son of God.[62]

It is true that Jesus elsewhere spoke of the exclusivity in "the way, and the truth, and the life" (John 14:6). It is true that Jesus also taught doctrines on multiple subjects, including the end times (Mark 13:3–37). However, many of those teachings were to Jews. The gentile interactions were fewer; we have just examined one. At least in this initial gospel encounter with a gentile centurion, Jesus praised him and responded favorably to what he was beseeching.

If people were sick, he healed them. If they were hungry, he fed them. If they were demon-possessed, he drove the demons out. Based on this centurion, Jesus's gospel transmission approach to the pluralistic Gentiles was not on how much truer he was than the myriad of other deities in first-century Palestine. Jesus demonstrated that he had the power to do what they were beseeching and the willingness to do it. In this Greek culture that assumed many deities were real, Jesus's approach showed his superiority without directly insulting the other deities. This tactic is obvious in Jesus's interaction

---

61. Some have suggested that the Greek word παῖς (*pais*, servant) indicates that the centurion's "servant" was really a young, boy lover because otherwise δοῦλος (*doulos*, servant/slave) would be used. Jennings and Liew, "Mistaken Identities," 467–94. It is then argued that the centurion was embarrassed of Jesus's visit. This work rejects this argument and adopts Edwards' understanding of *pais* as simply indicating this was a particularly endearing servant to the centurion (*Luke*, 209).

62. Stein, *Luke*; Hauerwas, *Matthew*.

with Gentiles unfamiliar with Judaism but is missing in many gospel presentations to the Taiwanese unfamiliar with Christianity.

Interreligious Dialogue

Sometimes, bold proclamation of the gospel can be seen as one-way harangues that gives no space for the other side to respond. This was at least how Pei-Pei felt in her encounter with an evangelizing person. Dialogue seems to be a missing piece in many encounters Christian evangelizing people have with non-Christians. There has been a plethora of debates regarding the role of interreligious dialogue. We do not have the time to get into the more extreme views of John Hick in his accepting of the truth of non-Christian religions.[63] 遠藤 周作 [Shusaku Endo] is another person who espoused a more pluralistic view of Jesus, seeing him as one of many ways that can lead to the "Real." There are also the works of the Hindus Swami Vivekananda and Sarvepalli Radhakrishnan, both of whom have been highly influential in the debate.

For our purposes, we forego the bulk of the debate and analyze a more evangelical view. John Stott talks about the different perspectives people have on dialogue, ranging from those who think it is essential to humility to those who think it betrays Christian essentials.[64] He cites people like William Henry Temple Gairdner, Karl Rahner, E. Stanley Jones, Kenneth Cragg, and David Sheppard, just to list a few notable ones. Ultimately, Stott thinks that a true Christian dialogue with a non-Christian must have four marks: authenticity, humility, integrity, and sensitivity. Stott defines dialogue as "mutual listening in order to understand one another."[65]

Harold Netland, in the book *Dissonant Voices: Religious Pluralism and the Question of Truth*, outlines three main categories of religious pluralism: exclusivism, inclusivism, and pluralism.[66] Exclusivists limit truth and salvation to Christianity alone. Inclusivists maintain the superiority of Jesus Christ but allows the possibility for salvation through other religions. Pluralists hold

---

63. Hick, *Christian Theology*.
64. Stott and Wright, *Christian Mission*, 96–119.
65. Stott and Wright, 111.
66. Netland, *Dissonant Voices*, 9–10.

all religions as more or less equal and that God has revealed himself in many ways through many cultures.

In a later work, *Encountering Religious Pluralism*, Netland nuances the categories more. In some ways, Netland explains that in reality, it is difficult to place people in those three categories exactly, when lines are so often blurred.[67] In the even more recent work *Handbook of Religion*, Netland explains his position more clearly,

> While this taxonomy can be helpful, it tends to be simplistic and reductionistic (Netland 2008). For example, the three categories are usually defined in terms of the question of salvation (must one be an explicit Christian in order to be saved?). But the many issues and positions involved in this debate are sufficiently complex that they cannot be reduced to just three categories. Moreover, there are many other significant questions apart from the issue of salvation that need to be addressed in the theology of religions.[68]

Hick might be a pluralist while Stott might be an exclusivist. However, the reality in Taiwan points to a mixing of categories between exclusivism, inclusivism, and pluralism. On the one hand, some people like Mommy Farong showed strong loyalty to her Guanyin. On the other hand, people like Company Woman had no problem aligning herself with both Jesus and Mazu. Still others like Police Lady saw all the deities as somewhat equal.

Dialogue with Taiwanese people in Taipei does not have a standard format nor is there an easy guidebook to follow. However, the qualitative data does show that exclusivist views are rarer. The findings chapter demonstrated that many people found exclusive claims to be arrogant and repulsive. Even semi-exclusivists like Mommy Farong showed proper respect to a range of deities beside Guanyin. Perhaps Netland's point about there being "many other questions apart from the issue of salvation" is important to bear in mind when considering gospel transmission in the context of folk religion in Taiwan.

Amos Yong is helpful in pointing out a way forward that does not require complete alignment with an exclusivist, inclusivist, or pluralist view. Yong

---

67. Netland, *Encountering Religious Pluralism*.
68. Netland, "Christian Theology," 21.

sees the current framework for theology of religions as something that forces people to either preserve the centrality of Christ or preserve the understanding of religions on "their" terms.[69] Yong instead argues for a more "pneumatological theology of religions" as a better framework to use in discussing the issue of religious pluralism. Yong believes that this framework enhances interfaith dialogue, helps in discussions of conversion, and even breeds what he calls "cross-religious fertilization."[70]

Yong thinks that taking this pneumatological approach in theology and missiology allows people from different religions to come together and have better dialogue. This kind of dialogue "does not mean uncritically accepting the testimony of the other as true, but rather making an honest intersubjective effort to understand the other's doctrines from the other's perspective."[71] It means breaking open the boundaries and entering into their lived realities and in the process "crossing-over into the other's perspective, worldview, and even way of life in some sense."[72] He explains this as a kind of phenomenological "conversion" (as opposed to a "Christian conversion"). Even though it is unpredictable and there is always a risk, Yong's idea of conversion "will not contradict or compromise our commitment to Christ. What may happen is that the Christian perspective of Christ will be deepened or transformed."[73]

Yong is included in this discussion for his positive view of other religions and this view's usefulness in the Taiwanese context. But this does not translate to an endorsement of his view of the Spirit's work in other religions nor of his views of salvation within the confines of other religions. The discussion is limited solely to Yong's idea of dialogue. This idea of dialogue is beneficial for evangelizing in the Taiwanese context for the following reasons.

First, it does not violate the integrity of the many existing folk religion deities. Most of the Taiwanese deities are assumed to be real. The religious thinking and practices of the Taiwanese "other" is respected and preserved even as the Christian evangelizing person proclaims the LORD. The evangelizing person should "cross over" into the boundaries of the Taiwanese folk

---

69. Yong, "P(New)Matological Paradigm."
70. Yong, 181–89.
71. Yong, 181.
72. Yong, 182.
73. Yong, 183.

religion adherent. In there, they intersubjectively understand and empathize with this religious other. Just as it is done in critical contextualization, elements of this religious other are critically examined. The evangelizing person may then find that many deities are in fact no more than wooden idols. The evangelizing person may also find that there is much beauty in how ancestral veneration brings extended families together.

Through this process of empathic, critical examination after "crossing-over," folk religion in Taiwan, which is inextricably linked to Taiwanese culture, is neither mocked nor demonized. Instead, folk religion in Taiwan is understood and appreciated, after which it is compared to Christianity. This approach avoids the sometimes imperialistic and colonial attitudes that some missionaries carry and that Yong criticizes. However, one must be careful to discern how much "crossing-over" is too much. One must discern certain ways of participation that stay true to Christianity (e.g. visiting a temple and standing respectfully before an idol of a deity) and certain ways of participation that may go too far (e.g. seeking a *gūpó* to recover one's spirit).

Second, this kind of dialogue allows for the possibility of better contextualization through what Yong calls "cross-fertilization." Yong suggests that "Christian theological reflection will be transformed if we engage not just Plato, Aristotle, and their traditions, as we have done for almost two millennia, but also the Buddha, Master Kong, and Shankara, among other perspectives, in the world religious context of the twenty-first century."[74] Yong stresses that the Holy Spirit is crucial in this process to ensure that what happens is authentic, God-honoring contextualization instead of syncretism. Yong asks the question of where the Holy Spirit is active in the religious traditions or practices of a certain religion. Finding this intersection allows the Christian evangelizing person to find the point of contact with the non-Christian. An example of where the Spirit is active is in the ways that the ancestor is honored in life and even after death. An example where the Spirit is not active is in the ways that people pray to ancestors and half-expect supernatural blessings and protection. The difficulty of interreligious dialogue is often with going too far into the thinking and practices of the "other." It is impossible to list everything that is acceptable and everything that is not. The evangelizing person must practice discernment and be led by the Spirit every step of the way.

---

74. Yong, 184.

Third, Yong's idea of dialogue sidesteps discussions of exclusivism, inclusivism, or pluralism. Instead of soteriology being the defining question (as Netland warns against), the Taiwanese person is allowed to form the categories. Instead of focusing on whether a certain path leads to salvation, the evangelizing person focuses on the most important religious category for the Taiwanese and brings the gospel into that category.[75]

Yong's idea of interreligious dialogue is not just conceptual. It has already been adopted by some Taiwanese theologians. One example is 莊祖鯤 [Tsukung Chuang]. After receiving a PhD in chemical engineering at Northwestern University and having a fifteen-year career in that field, Tsukung Chuang studied for another PhD in intercultural studies at Trinity Evangelical Divinity School. He has since traveled around the world, speaking especially to Chinese scholars on the topic of interreligious studies. In his book 《說禪論道 — 基督教與儒、釋、道之對話》 (*Christian Perspective of Zen and Dao*), Tsukung Chuang brings together multiple concepts from Buddhism into conversation with doctrines from Christianity.[76] He compares the worldview of the religiously plural Taiwan with the worldview of monotheistic Christianity.[77] He speaks about famous philosophers like 孔子 [Confucius], 老子 [Lao-tzu] and 莊子 [Chuang-tzu].[78]

Tsukung Chuang's understanding of the intricate philosophies of these religious fields indicates a deep study of each religion, a fact that he himself attested to at a few points throughout the book. For example, he analyzed the way that Lao-tzu philosophized about Dao, the way that Chuang-tzu explained Dao, and the way that Confucius extrapolated from Dao a set of morality that Chinese societies still follow today. He then explained how this Dao sees its fullest expression in John 1:1, "In the beginning was [Dao]."[79] Tsukung Chuang argues that in Jesus Christ, we see the fullness of what these ancient Chinese philosophers were talking about. Tsukung Chuang praises the wisdom of the ancient philosophers' treatises on Dao but adds the following, 「他們關於『道』對人類罪性及困境的解決之道，卻語

---

75. These categories are explored more fully in the next section.
76. Chuang 莊, *Christian Perspective*, 說禪論道 — 基督教與儒、釋、道之對話, 15–80.
77. Chuang 莊, 81–100, 111–26.
78. Chuang 莊, 101–10, 127–76.
79. For the same Greek word Λόγος (*Logos*), English translations use "the Word" and Chinese translations use 道 (Dao).

焉不詳或默然不語」 ("About 'Dao' and its solution to human sinfulness or struggles, they [the philosophers] either made allusions but were not clear or remained completely silent on the topic.").[80]

Tsukung Chuang argues that Jesus and Christianity fill this gap that is left by the philosophers; namely that in the Bible, these solutions are presented in full. For the most part, he does not argue against Chinese philosophy nor against religious systems. He explained why he takes this approach in the preface of the book, namely that he refuses to denounce Chinese religiosity or philosophy. He wrote the whole book as a way to "start conversations." One could add that more than starting conversations, Tsukung Chuang has already preached the gospel.

Summary of Key Issues

We have just finished discussing some key issues in the Taiwanese context. The first category about worldview helps the evangelizing person contextualize the gospel by understanding the culture better and thus transmitting the gospel more effectively. Understanding how deities are treated helps with understanding how the LORD might be presently viewed. This should help the evangelizing person both to speak with more sensitivity and to correct the non-Christian on how the biblical God should be viewed. The second category about religious boundary crossing helps the evangelizing person convince the non-Christian what it means to embrace the gospel and Christianity. Namely, the terms and concepts used should be that of life transformation, not only theological conversion. The third category of religious pluralism should encourage the evangelizing person to be extremely sensitive to the pluralism that is a big part of Taiwanese religious thinking.

---

80. Chuang 莊, *Christian Perspective*, 說禪論道 — 基督教與儒、釋、道之對話, 161.

CHAPTER 7

Gospel Transmission in Taipei

In the last chapter, concepts and issues were tackled, resulting in a long list of "what not to do" in gospel transmission. This chapter deals with the positive side of "what to do" in gospel encounters and general strategizing. In this chapter, we are not talking about the gospel in its entirety. We are talking about the gospel as initially presented to the non-Christian.[1] Moreover, this work makes no claims to an exhaustive or comprehensive gospel presentation. This chapter presents only a cross section of examples of how some of the issues mentioned previously can be applied in actual gospel presentations.

One positive way of transmitting the gospel is by comparing the LORD's love with a Taiwanese folk deity's love. God is portrayed as loving, even to the point of dying on the cross to save mere humans. Mazu is portrayed as loving as well. Mazu sacrificed herself in order to save mere fishermen. Similarly, Guanyin gave up the position of a Buddha and living an eternity in the heavenly realms so that she could watch over people on earth forever. Many of the deities in Taiwan are revered precisely because of their great love for people. What sets the LORD apart from these other deities? What are some points that may be added in an existing gospel presentation? What are frameworks or strategies for contextually effective and theologically accurate ways of transmitting the gospel in Taipei, Taiwan? These are the concerns

---

1. Sometimes the Christian evangelizing person only has fifteen minutes to verbally make this initial gospel presentation. Sometimes the evangelizing person has a whole day to incarnationally display gospel truths as a gospel witness. The point is that this chapter focuses on initial gospel encounters with people unacquainted with Christianity. Many of the themes may not apply to people who already know about the cross nor to people who already have a positive view of Christianity.

addressed in this chapter. Specifically, the concerns are divided up into two categories. They are aspects of the gospel that need particular attention in order to be more salient in light of (1) local attitudes, including ways of thinking about the self, deities, and the world; and (2) lived reality, including ways that people live out their lives and the connectedness of folk religion through it all. Each area addressed includes theoretical formulations as well as at least one concrete gospel practice.

The Gospel in Light of Local Attitudes

First, we look at how the gospel is perceived in light of local attitudes. Chapters 4 and 5 have revealed many attitudes that Taiwanese people in Taipei have toward both folk religion and Christianity. In this chapter, we address what the evangelizing person ought to do in light of those attitudes. This first section of the chapter addresses four areas that need attention: (1) the place of action in the presentation of the gospel, (2) how the gospel addresses the idea of being a sinned-against person, (3) the gospel's answer to a "relationship of exchange" between deities and humans common in folk religion, and (4) how the gospel relates to deities and ancestors.

The Gospel in Action

盧龍光 [Lung-Kwong Lo] is a reverend and former professor based in Hong Kong. Talking about evangelistic practice, Lo writes that Christians in Chinese societies have been seen "as imperialist invaders, colonists, capitalists, preachers, educators, medical doctors, social workers, and activists."[2] Lo argues that as a result of what Chinese people have seen as well as their own proclivities, Chinese evangelistic practices are highly communal and pragmatic. Lo writes, "The Chinese are pragmatic people; they prefer actions rather than empty words. They prefer to see words-in-action . . . Thus, for evangelistic practice to have integrity among the Chinese, it must be 'infleshed' – the Word must be manifested by disciples of Jesus through 'service-in-action' as well as proclamation."[3]

---

2. Lo 盧, "Making Disciples in China," 80.
3. Lo 盧, 80–81.

Lo has a very positive view of the strength of the discipling spirit found naturally in Chinese Christians. He praises their embrace of "costly discipleship" while at the same time lamenting the "cheap grace" of "Western Christianity."[4] He does not back up this claim with anything other than personal observation and historical anecdotes. Whether his claim about discipleship is true or false does not affect the point. Lo's description of the action-oriented Chinese person aligns with the data found in this study's interviews.

The pragmatism is seen in how *bài* is used to show one's allegiance rather than so-called "empty words." Even then, allegiance may be too strong a term. The data showed that action is what people look for, whether it is going to a temple, burning incense, or offering sacrifices. These actions are seen as "having integrity" among other Taiwanese people in Taipei. Lo's admonition is that Christian actions must likewise be outward and visible for it to have a significant enough evangelistic effect. Lo believes that Chinese people are already more naturally inclined to do so, which explains the rapid rise of Christianity despite persecution.[5] For gospel transmission to have any effect, actions must be seen in addition to words. It is useful to listen to the admonition of 1 John 3:18 (NLT), "Dear children, let's not merely say that we love each other; let us show the truth by our actions."

So, what could the evangelizing person do? Like Lo's admonition, "'service-in-action' as well as proclamation" must be done.[6] Recall that Company Woman mentioned that she was looking for a new apartment. Her friend advised that she pray to the LORD, which was good. But she could have gone further and tracked down apartments for rent (or at least could have made an honest, visible attempt). Such service-in-action would have shown the love of Christians for their neighbors as well as shown that prayer works.

More broadly speaking, think of Mommy Farong's branch of Buddhism and the way that it served the community through bringing them on tour buses and serving them "Well-Being Noodles" in addition to general blessings. Through such service-in-action, this branch of Buddhism likely left a good impression on millions of Taiwanese, attracted thousands of people to its temple, and even convinced hundreds of them to follow dharma more

---

4. Lo 盧, 82.
5. Lo 盧, 77–78.
6. Lo 盧, 80–81.

closely. The word likely is added because we cannot measure the exact impact nor how many "became Buddhists" as a result of what they did. However, the impact these services have on the plausibility structure about Buddhism's compassion is undebatable. Christians can use services like these to form the plausibility structure about Christianity's love as well.

One church that is already doing something similar is 台北靈糧堂 [Bread of Life Christian Church in Taipei]. They sell bento boxes (boxed meals) for a much lower price than what they cost on the market. For older people who require it, they also deliver the bento boxes for free. This researcher spoke to a number of people who appreciated this service greatly. One man in his eighties was against Christianity for most of his life but has since changed his attitude about the religion and has even attended church a few times. There were probably a number of factors for this change, but this service-in-action was likely one of them. This man may not have become a Christian, but his plausibility structure was changed, which is the main goal of the gospel in action.

The Gospel for the Sinned-Against

Raymond Fung, based in Hong Kong, presented a paper in 1979 at a workshop sponsored by the World Council of Churches (WCC) Commission on World Mission and Evangelism. This paper was later collected in *Asian Christian Theology*, a collection of essays highlighting theologizing in the Asian context. Fung's main contribution was the idea of highlighting both the sinner and the sinned-against as important in transmitting the gospel. Fung writes, "If evangelism seeks to speak to the very depth of a person through the proclamation of the gospel, evangelism must recognize and deal with the fact that a person is an object of sin as well as a subject of sin."[7]

Fung explains what he means through what the gospel addresses, "To the sinner in the person, the gospel says: 'Know your sinfulness. Bow in humility before God, and receive forgiveness.' To the sinned-against in the same person, the gospel says: 'Know that you have value. Stand in defiance against the forces which deprive you of it, and receive strength.'"[8] Fung laments what

---

7. Fung, "Evangelism Today," 200.
8. Fung, 201.

he saw as a "very shallow understanding of sin" and how it is hindering the spread of the gospel in his context.[9]

Fung shares about a friend who was a factory worker who finally attended church with him after many invitations.[10] Incidentally, the sermon at church was about sin. After the sermon, the factory worker agreed that he was a sinner. However, he was upset that the sermon mentioned nothing about exploitation in the factories, unfair wages, and forced overtime, all issues that the factory worker deemed as proof that he was sinned against.

In some ways, this focus on the sinned-against draws parallels with parts of the liberation theology of Gustavo Gutiérrez.[11] However, Fung's admonition is not to frame the gospel as primarily about the poor nor is it to reframe the gospel as good news for the sinned-against. Rather, Fung wants to bring attention to an oft-ignored aspect of the gospel. In doing so, he wants evangelistic activities of today (which he views as often "devoid of compassion") to "recover compassion" and perceive people as not just sinners in need of God but also as sinned-against people in need of affection.[12]

Gospel presentations that do not deal with the aspect of people as the sinned-against do not address a fundamental cry among the "sinned-against." Speaking sociologically, Fung says that these are most often people in the lower class.[13] The problem is not just missing an important aspect of the gospel. The problem is that when we evangelize "devoid of compassion," we do not see the people as God does. Fung cites multiple instances of Jesus seeing the people and having compassion.[14] Fung then argues that we must do as Jesus did, to be so close to the people that we cannot help but feel their plight. Fung is describing an incarnational approach to our evangelizing. Fung explains that when we are evangelizing incarnationally, it "enables the non-believer to examine Christianity from within rather than from without. It invites people to look at Jesus as 'you' rather than 'him.' This is how faith in Jesus Christ becomes possible."[15]

---

9. Fung, 201.
10. Fung, 201–2.
11. Gutiérrez, *Theology of Liberation*.
12. Fung, "Evangelism Today," 203.
13. Fung, 202.
14. Fung, 203–4.
15. Fung, 205.

Fung's insight into the sinned-against and compassion shares many similarities with the troubles that Taiwan's gospel transmission efforts have as well. Looking at just the interviews, there were multiple Buddhists who shared about their successful attempts at drawing people to their religion. The many ways these Buddhists talked about their religion, specifically about newcomers, indicated that they are here to help people with their earthly struggles instead of getting people to believe in anything. Based on the results (e.g. Mrs. Ting and her temple getting five-hundred busloads of people in one day), this approach resonates with Taiwanese people in Taipei. It is no coincidence that the biggest religious organization in Taiwan collected NTD$6,770,470,147 (USD$230,278,700) in donations in 2019 alone.[16] Seeing as how there are only twenty-four million people in Taiwan, the fact that 46 percent of the donations were from Taiwanese people alone is a testament to the public appeal of this organization.

"Tzu chi" is literally translated as "compassion relief." The religious aspect of this non-profit humanitarian organization is unmistakable from the name and from the founder. Tzu Chi attracts many followers to come seeking relief as well as to offer donations. The people who do visit are invited, like Fung said, to examine the religion "from within rather than from without." Mrs. Ting shared that they may come with their problems but can leave with peace in the form of noodles or amulets. Her experience told her that after enough exposure, people are inevitably drawn to the religion.

This same method of drawing adherents is the same for many folk religions. Pei-Pei did not know about the details of a temple but went because it was famous for helping people find love. Tour Guide Man sought help from Lord Superior Wen Chang despite knowing few things about him. Shi Gu consulted fortune tellers because of how it could help her with her problems.

The common thread is that when people examined a religion from within, they came to either believe in it or at least kept going back to it. This basic truth should not be too alien to many readers. What may be alien is how Buddhist organizations and folk religions treated this truth as both the strategy and end goal of their evangelistic efforts whereas many evangelical Christians

---

16. Taiwan Buddhist Tzu Chi Foundation [佛教慈濟慈善事業基金會], "2019 Annual Report [2019 年度報告書]" (Hualien, Taiwan, 2019), http://tw.tzuchi.org/financial/2019financial/.

treat it as a strategy at best (i.e. pre-evangelism). The Buddhist participants in the interview were happy that other people's present lives were improved; so, they dedicated tremendous amounts of resources to helping people meet felt needs in their daily lives. The folk religion adherents and the atheists in the interview were also focused on their present lives. It is no surprise that the evangelistic messages interpreted by these participants were all focused on the present life. They saw the Christian message of "eternal life" either as "stupid," "simplistic," "annoying," or interpreted it naturalistically. None of the participants saw any value to the proclamation of eternal life because they were too busy living as the sinned-against in the present life.

After the recorded interview, Chi mentioned many aspects of his troubled, sinned-against life. He spoke of problems with his elders, the unfaithfulness of his wife, and the difficulty of making ends meet. He did not directly say that these issues were the main reason that the gospel did not appeal to him. However, the implication was that he was too emotionally tired as a sinned-against person to turn to any deity for help unless that deity offered actual relief from the situation in his present life.[17]

What can be done for people like Chi? The solution is not to take away the eternal hope that can be found in Jesus nor the reality of an eternal dwelling place prepared for those who abide in Christ. The solution must be an addition, not a replacement. The Christian evangelistic message needs to speak more to the "sinned-against." This is especially good advice in Taiwan, where many other religious organizations are responding to the fact that the present life makes up the bulk of people's concerns. No wonder so many of the participants in Taiwan think so little of Christianity and its evangelistic message. The gospel proclaimed to the Taiwanese people in Taipei must touch on their present lives before it has hope of touching their eternal lives. This is not a ranking in terms of importance, but in terms of order.

For example, a gospel presentation that focuses on the sinned-against aspect would offer comfort to people like Chi. It might be helpful to focus on the Beatitudes (Matt 5:2–11) that Jesus shared in the Sermon on the Mount. For Chi, he might especially like to hear "Blessed are those who mourn, for they shall be comforted" (Matt 5:4). One might also share the words of Jesus

---

17. Recall that Chi said he was a Christian but now calls himself an atheist. Unlike most of the other participants, Chi said that he does not beseech anything from local deities.

in Matthew 11:28–29 (ESV), "Come to me, all who labor and are heavy laden, and I will give you rest. Take my yoke upon you, and learn from me, for I am gentle and lowly in heart, and you will find rest for your souls." The apostle Paul also has words for the sinned-against, "Blessed be the God and Father of our Lord Jesus Christ, the Father of mercies and God of all comfort, who comforts us in all our affliction, so that we may be able to comfort those who are in any affliction" (2 Cor 1:3–4a). Paul starts with empathy but turns the attention toward others. What Taiwanese people like Chi need to hear are words that show empathy and sympathy. After comfort has been received, people like Chi can then be refocused toward helping others in society, creating a cycle of healing for the sinned-against.

It may seem like these words do not deal with one's own sinfulness; it is because that is the second step. Fung shares that in his ten years of evangelizing industrial factory workers in Hong Kong, he came to see that "when the gospel addresses itself to the sinned-againstness of a person, that person will also allow the gospel to deal with his own sinfulness. Or, from the perspective of that person, awareness of his sinned-againstness comes first, followed by awareness of his sinfulness."[18] Done in this order, a person may not always accept sin in response to the gospel presentation. However, Fung's experience and this study's interviews show that this order fits the narrative of Chinese culture better. More generally speaking, this order fits the narrative of the sinned-against in society as a whole.

Fung is not talking about making sure that the gospel addresses a person's present life in a sermon preached to mainly Christians on a Sunday morning. He is talking about the gospel as initially shared with a family, friend, coworker, or even stranger on the street. Of course, the gospel can easily touch on the sinned-against in a sermon. But the sinned-against aspect is often left out in the initial presentation to make room for the sinner aspect. In Taiwan, where people accept their sinned-againstness readily and seek many deities to rectify their situation, the gospel would have much greater resonance with the people if the sinned-against aspect is presented more fully. True, it is ultimately the Holy Spirit, not resonance, who leads people to the Lord. However, it is the job of evangelizing people and missiologists to help, not hinder, the Spirit's work.

---

18. Fung, "Evangelism Today," 206.

The Gospel's Answer to a Relationship of Exchange

Fishu mentioned the idea of an "exchange of consideration" with a deity. She further defined the relationship as something that may potentially bring calamity to the person unless the exchange criteria were met. Mommy Farong, Bookstore Lady, and Pei-Pei all mentioned a similar concept, with varying degrees of severity for not meeting the exchange criteria. This is how many Taiwanese steeped in folk religion are trained to think in their interactions and relationships with a deity. The interview with Genie indicated that some Taiwanese apply this relationship of exchange to any deity in any religion. For Taiwanese people in Taipei, reciprocity is assumed and expected.

For the Taiwanese, the recipient of the LORD's grace has a responsibility to do something in return. The interviews with the Christians Curu, Fishu, Coffee Girl, College Hua, and others showed that "giving back" to Jesus was a natural response to the gospel. A relationship of exchange may not be as beef-depriving as Fishu's experience, but the Christian participants all showed an understanding that some action is required. Some of them (e.g. Curu) articulated clearly the "free" nature of the gift but still stressed the importance of reciprocity.

This idea of reciprocity appears often in the Old Testament. There is mention of the vow offering (Lev 7:16; Num 30:1–16; Deut 23:21–23). This refers to vows that Israelites make, asking God to grant them certain favors in exchange for something. This "something" is often an animal sacrifice, as seen in Deuteronomy. But in some cases, they could be as serious as offering one's daughter as seen with Jephthah in Judges 11:30–40 or dedicating one's son as seen with Hannah in 1 Samuel 1:10–28. This does not mean that God requires things in exchange, only that he allows a format which bears more than a passing resemblance to exchanges seen in folk religion in Taiwan.

Taiwanese people in Taipei can relate to this practice from ancient Israel. In Taiwan, the relationship of exchange is one of the most salient ways to describe one's relationship with a deity. The fact that there are some parallels to the Old Testament creates common ground with the Taiwanese person. The Old Testament contains freewill offerings, sin offerings, and a multitude of other ways to relate to God. The New Testament, with the work of Jesus Christ as the "once for all" sacrifice (Heb 10:10), points to yet another aspect of relating to God. So, the vow offering may be established as common ground with the Taiwanese person, while the Christ sacrifice is a way to point the

Taiwanese to another way to relate to deities. This approach does not dismiss the Taiwanese religious tradition of returning favors to deities, but builds on it and incorporates the God of the Bible into it.

This idea of reciprocity is also picked up by numerous scholars writing on what the Bible teaches about human's responsibility and God's grace. Matthew Bates argues that "allegiance is the best macro-term available to us that can describe what God requires from us for eternal salvation."[19] To that end, he suggests the term "fidelity" as a translation for *pistis* that should be used more often. This is in line with N. T. Wright's assertion that "faithfulness" is a more dominant theme in Paul's own usage of *pistis*.[20] It is also in line with David Gustafson's explanation of *fiducia*, "the personal element of trust, reliance, or allegiance."[21]

This same idea is what Nijay Gupta calls "obeying faith," which is one of three categories of faith that can be translated as faithfulness, loyalty, or allegiance.[22] Gupta sees it functioning as "a social virtue" and "relational commitment."[23] In *Paul and the Gift*, John Barclay provides a nuanced view of what God did and what God in turn expects of us in response. Barclay looks at definitions of gift and the customs of gift giving in antiquity, coming to the conclusion that a reciprocal response or a gift return is expected in gift giving for normal and "divine gifts," even despite the "incongruity" of grace.[24]

What Bates, N. T. Wright, Gustafson, Gupta, and Barclay show is that reciprocity in some form is expected with the LORD. This reciprocity is present in folk religion deities' relationships to Taiwanese people in Taipei as well. This common ground allows the Christian evangelizing person to teach the non-Christian how to interact with the LORD without throwing out every past conception of deities. After all, Barclay's description about gift giving in antiquity is similar to how Taiwanese people in Taipei view gift giving.

While there are many similarities, a relationship with the LORD is still different from a relationship with Taiwanese deities. With the gospel, the exchange is not burning incense to receive blessings and protection (e.g.

---

19. Bates, *Salvation by Allegiance*, 5.
20. Wright, *Paul*.
21. Gustafson, *Gospel Witness*, 130.
22. Gupta, *Paul and the Language of Faith*, 178.
23. Gupta, 178.
24. Barclay, *Paul and the Gift*, 24–50.

Pei-Pei's example). Rather, the exchange is giving the LORD simple faith and earnest faithfulness to receive adoption as sons and daughters of God (Eph 1:5). The exchange is not that we spend a year repaying a deity's kindness for helping us in our exam (e.g. Fishu's story). Rather, the great exchange is that "for our sake he made him to be sin who knew no sin, so that in him we might become the righteousness of God" (2 Cor 5:21).

The gospel teaches that we do not have to do anything to earn our salvation. It teaches that after God grants certain favors (e.g. prayer requests), we do not have to give something back to God for fear of some retribution (e.g. Fishu's old fear). Whatever the Christian gives back to God should not be out of fear, but out of love and thankfulness.

To be sure, there are many Taiwanese who do not seem to fear deities. They do not return to the deity to give thanks after a favor is granted (e.g. Tour Guide Man). There are others who see their deity as so compassionate that thankfulness, not fear, is the default response (e.g. Mommy Farong). Though these rare cases exist, the other interviews show that many more other Taiwanese do have this lingering fear of deities, one that must be addressed in an effective contextual approach to gospel transmission. Taiwanese must not just learn about what the *euangel* (gospel) is, but also about theology proper. Taiwanese must learn about the character of the kind of God who would exchange heaven for earth, angels for fishermen, and righteousness for sin.

One gospel practice that can arise out of this is to show the Taiwanese how to interact with the LORD. In this researcher's experience, gifts are not to be accepted hastily because reciprocity is expected, whether it is a return gift, a future favor, or something else. Taiwanese people in Taipei are already expecting a relationship of exchange with deities. Thus, it would help gospel transmission efforts if people were shown what a proper reciprocal response is instead of letting them guess and wrongly assume that the LORD's expectations are the same as the other deities.

The Christian evangelizing person can capitalize on Taiwanese people's proclivity to do something for the LORD in return for his grace. The evangelizing person can show the non-Christian that they do not need to stop eating beef, pray every day, or promise to be a good person. Rather, the non-Christian can be taught what the LORD requires. Whether it is Micah 6:8 or Matthew 22:37, this is a great opportunity to disciple this non-Christian to do what the Bible teaches.

College Hua's church in Taipei, 新生命小組教會 [New Life Church], is one example of how this suggestion works out in a church setting. College Hua spoke of how fast people in the church are moved into positions of leadership. Even though he had only been a Christian for two years, he was already being pressured into being a small group leader. He also mentioned numerous behaviors he has been told to change or ways he was told to evangelize on his campus. Fishu, in the same church, also mentioned that a leader has been very vocal and even aggressive in telling Fishu to do certain things that the Bible teaches. Fishu said that her non-Christian mother was concerned that the church was too involved in her personal life. Despite all this, College Hua and Fishu both spoke positively about the church and were happy with the fast rate that they were growing in their faith. Their explanations in the interviews indicated that they both understood the exchange that happened through Jesus's work on the cross. Their examples show that New Life Church was able to use this understanding to speed up their discipleship.[25] This gospel practice, if adopted widely, can help church multiplication efforts throughout the island.

The Gospel in Conversation with Deities and Ancestors

Taiwanese people in Taipei are afraid of gods and ghosts. Ghosts give benefits in terms of helping people know things (e.g. if the boss will give someone a promotion, the secret life of someone else, etc.). Deities can give all kinds of benefits, as seen in the previous chapters. Ancestors are known to offer benefits as well. When they give people benefits, it is something that was sought after. As seen through the findings, many Taiwanese people in Taipei worry that if one stops offering incense to the ancestors or do some act that indicates disrespect (e.g. leaving a crack on a tombstone), something bad might happen. The gospel in Taiwan must address the issue of ghosts, gods, and ancestors. A Pastor named 葉明翰 (Ming-Han Yeh, also known as John Marcos Yeh) provides some answers.

---

25. The argument here is not that only Taiwanese people return the favor to God by being active in Christian ministry. All Christians everywhere do this. The argument is that Taiwanese people are able to be pushed into more ministry responsibilities earlier than one may think because they are already inclined to return favors to deities. Instead of waiting until they are fully trained, it may be better to let them immediately work for the LORD because they are already looking for ways to do so.

In the course of the fieldwork in Taiwan, the researcher was introduced to Yeh. He was a famous fortune teller turned pastor. He was a missionary in Brazil for eighteen years before returning to Taiwan in 2015. He has since given multiple seminars and teachings on Christian responses to folk religion in Taiwan. He passed away in April 2020, just 2 months after the fieldwork ended in Taiwan. He was a prolific speaker who appeared on several conferences and talk shows; some of those teachings are still shown on GoodTV, the biggest Christian TV station in Taiwan. The following reflections on folk religion are from one such GoodTV seminar that aired.

In the show, the host Z. Liu asked Yeh about the different ways Taiwanese pastors ought to deal with folk religion.[26] One method Yeh mentioned was that he regularly did what he called a 「聖別禮拜」 ("Holy Farewell Service"). In this service, the deities that a Christian used to *bài* were forced to take a step back from authority in the person's life and the gods were then put under the authority of the 「萬神之神」 ("God above all gods").

As for ancestors, a method Yeh mentioned was 「認祖歸宗」 (*rèn zǔ guī zōng*). It is a play on words meaning that one acknowledges the ancestors;[27] then one puts the ancestor under the first "Ancestor," the Lord himself. For the elderly person, this is safer because one is guaranteed a caretaker in the afterlife. When one entrusts caretaking to one's descendants (the normal custom in Taiwan involving ancestral veneration), one has to rely on one's children and the children's children. If during one generation, the child stops venerating, it could be problematic. However, if one entrusts one's soul to Jesus, one's afterlife is not dependent on one's descendants anymore, but on Jesus himself. Yeh called this 「福音扎根在我們的習俗」 ("rooting the gospel in our customs and traditions").

In addition to issues of ancestral veneration, Yeh also gave practical ways for how one should share the gospel with family steeped in folk religion (specifically ancestral veneration but not exclusively). He was against common methods that usually entail telling the family that these things are idols, wrong, and only superstition. He explained that this would not work because

---

26. "Jīdūjiào Sǐ Méi Rén Bài?! Qīngmíng Sǎomù de Xìnyǎng Wèntí ~mínsú Guóbǎo Lái Jiědá 基督教死沒人拜?!清明掃墓的信仰問題～民俗國寶來解答," *Jīntiān Bù Jiǎnglǐ* 今天不講理 (Taipei, Taiwan: GOOD TV, 2 April 2020).

27. 認祖 (*rèn zǔ*, acknowledge the ancestors) sounds like 認主 (*rèn zhǔ*, acknowledge the Lord).

a child should never scold a parent; this is seen as a big negative in filial piety. Instead, one should work on completely changing one's own life. For example, a stubborn person ought to become easy-going and an angry person ought to become peaceful. One's life becomes the testimony for the parents. When the parent sees the change and asks how or why this is happening, the reply should be, "Jesus changed me."

A common misconception among Taiwanese Christians is that folk religion, including the gods, temples, ancestor rites, and even ideas of filial piety, is a worldly phenomenon that ought to be discarded when one becomes a Christian. Yeh reminded people that this is merely culture, the same as any culture around the world. This is something that has its root in God's original intent but has been perverted through time. It is more effective to bring people back to the roots of culture instead of demonizing the current culture. An example given is that instead of saying that burning incense is evil, one should acknowledge that the Old Testament has examples of burning incense (Exod 25, 30), albeit to the LORD. Because burning incense is rooted in the respect for one's ancestors, they should be commended for this respect (even though the religious expression of this respect may be theologically problematic). Yeh was careful to say that the gospel conversation may begin with commendation, but one should always end with explaining how Jesus's work on the cross has made practices like burning incense unnecessary.

Yeh's admonishments are examples of self-theologizing that is very useful in this context. His words come from years of experience practicing folk religion, as well as years of evangelizing to those practitioners. These gospel practices, if done correctly, are ways to bring the gospel into the Taiwanese people's attitudes toward ancestors and deities, making the LORD superior without directly attacking Taiwanese culture.

The Gospel in Light of the Lived Reality

We have just explored four different areas relating to local attitudes toward deities, the world, the supernatural, and religion in general. In this second section, we address the Taiwanese lived reality, especially the concerns and problems people have as they live out their daily lives. While the first section deals with thinking, this second section deals with living. Here, we look at various areas that have surfaced in the course of the qualitative interviews, including: (1) the importance of a relationship network, (2) how Taiwanese people live in the so-called "excluded middle," and (3) a gospel in daily life.

The Gospel through a Relationship Network

Curu shared that if not for her 「關係網路」 ("relationship network"), she would not have become a Christian. What she meant by this was that she had a friend who introduced Curu to a new way of living. More importantly for Curu, she said she found a new way to express her filial piety. She was in a network of people who were able to transport her to a new environment, an environment where people showed her new ways to fulfill her duties as a child and reinterpret the traditions that she grew up with. The example she gave was that she learned that she does not have to *bài* her ancestors to fulfill her filial piety.

Being in a new environment was important for Curu because she lived with parents who were deeply involved in folk religion and a grandmother who was a 「乩童」 (*jī tóng*, "spiritual medium," literally a "divining child"). Moreover, she lived next to a big temple in a rural area. As M.-H. Lin detailed, temples are centers of culture where many festivities take place, religious or otherwise.[28] Curu herself mentioned the influence of these temples when she was a child. She talked about 「歌仔戲」 ("Taiwanese operas") and 「布袋戲」 ("puppet shows") that made these temples fun. She reminisced about 「中元節」 ("Zhongyuan Jie" or "Hungry Ghost Festival") where every family brought a cooked dish to *bài* together. She said that these events brought the whole village together with 「廟那個為中心」 ("that temple as the center").

House Gongon also made references to his childhood village's temple and all its fun accompanying festivities. He said when he was young, he did not really think about the significance of the religious rituals happening with the festivities. He said that he joined in the festivities and the rituals because they were 「好玩」 ("fun"). House Gongon did not treat the religious elements as fake nor did he completely believe in them as true. He saw the temple as a place where people can congregate and socialize. This matches what M.-H. Lin says about temples being a microcosm of Taiwanese culture and the central

---

28. Lin 林, *Dà Miào Chéng* 大廟埕.

expression of culture for a region. The point was that the temple was the center of the village's culture and this was the environment that he grew up in.

Being in an environment like that, Curu repeatedly stressed the difficulty of coming to any deity other than the ones the village is already associated with. It is even more difficult if the deity has an exclusive claim that denies the power or existence of all other deities. In her own example, she said she was lucky. Curu said that it is possible for others to be brought out of that environment in order to more easily come to Christ. However, she said that she does not know how to reach the entire village. She had seasoned Christian ministers working in her church network in the context of these villages and they were still struggling to have substantial fruit in their ministries.

What Curu was talking about with her "relationship network" is similar to what P. Berger is talking about with his "plausibility structure." More accurately, Curu's relationship network is a specific application of a plausibility structure. For people steeped in folk religion, what they need are new relationship networks that teach new ways of associating with filial piety, the abundance of deities, and the proliferation of temples. In addition, the relationship networks must prepare the new Christian (or seeker) for possible rejection by family members. This means that answers to common misunderstandings should be prepared as well.

Many gospel practices could be possible in light of this. What Taiwan's rural areas need is a new plausibility structure where turning to an exclusive deity like Jesus Christ is not as unimaginable as before. At the very least, it would be easier if new Christians or seekers did not have to face such drastic social ostracism to follow Christ. More than just a plausibility structure, if Christianity is to take root in rural Taiwan, a cultural replacement for the temple must be established. Instead of watching puppet shows at the temple and having a communal meal in the courtyard, the church needs to normalize doing the same things on the church grounds. An abundance of community events could be a first step in building trust among the community. Alternatively, the church could seek opportunities to perform in the temple courtyards.

Does this apply to urban areas as well? Having a culture centered on the church may not be as important because even temples are not seen as cultural centers among many urban dwellers. But even in urban areas, most people flock to the major temples (e.g. Hsing Tian Kong) during major holidays, not to churches. Healthy Chen (who lived in urban Taipei at the time of the interview) said that he became a Christian due to his relationship network at his workplace. One of the managers organized a weekly lunch with a pastor at the office, making Christian topics normal parts of the office conversation. Another worker in the office was Buddhist, but said that her perception of Christianity has vastly improved since working at the company. She was influenced so much that she said that Christianity currently has more influence in her life than Buddhism.[29] For both of these office workers, their environments have made them more amiable to Christianity. Christianity has become normal and even preferable to their original religious systems.

Company Woman used to be more antagonistic to Christianity, to the point where she would roll her eyes whenever she heard the phrase "believe in Jesus Christ for eternal life." Because of her relationship network at work in urban Taipei, she had reconsidered Christianity to the point that she self-identified as a "seeker" at the time of the interview. She said she is 「非常的感動」 ("very moved") by the testimony of her boss and other Christians at her workplace. She mentioned things like staying strong amid near bankruptcy of the company, aiding poor children in faraway regions, and financial giving to strangers.

One reason a cultural shift has not occurred may partly be because the Mid-Autumn Festival, Hungry Ghost Festival, and many other important holidays and cultural artefacts are based on stories that have deep roots in folk religion. Perhaps Christianity can start celebrating these holidays and put distinct Christian elements in them (e.g. have lantern making contests at church on Mid-Autumn Festival and celebrate God's creation of the moon). If transforming a holiday is not easily done (as is likely the case), perhaps new celebrations and new holidays can somehow endear themselves to the Taiwanese public. The task of thinking up exactly how this can be done is not easy, nor is it a simple endeavor. This kind of task requires at a minimum a dedicated monograph that includes strategizing, implementation, evaluation, and long-term analysis. For now, it is already a big step if more Christians in positions of power do what this office manager did. If it is difficult to change

---

29. Company Woman stated that she approves of about 70 percent of what Christianity teaches. She said that what she approves of has deeply influenced her.

the plausibility structure of all of Taiwan, one can at least attempt to do so for one's office building.

The Gospel for the Middle Realm

Recall from chapter 2 Hiebert's concept of the excluded middle (with his discontent over it) and C. K. Yang's concept of diffused religion. C. K. Yang argues that China is characterized by diffused religion rather than institutional religion.[30] The primary thing about C. K. Yang's concept of diffused religion is that it is something that pervades society as it intrudes into the secular space in a way that institutional religion, with its established religious space, cannot or at least often does not. Diffused religion is defined by a variance of creeds due to its diffuse nature, with its adherents being able to navigate multiple religious spaces. That is why Chinese folk religion, which inherently combines multiple religious practices and beliefs, can and should be characterized as a diffused religion.

This diffuse effect and penetration into the secular sphere means that instead of disenchanting the world,[31] modernity has a vastly different effect on Chinese religiosity and modernity. The secular for the Chinese is defined by an absence of institutional religion. What something like folk religion does is make sure that secular institutions (and all social groups) are "imbued with a rich folklore of a supernatural character. The social environment as a whole had a sacred atmosphere which inspired the feeling that the gods and spirits, as well as man, participated in molding the established ways of life in the traditional world."[32]

Chinese folk religion thus overcomes the problem of the "flaw of the excluded middle" by focusing its attention on the so-called "excluded middle" – on ghosts, spirits, local deities, and ancestors – which is not at all excluded in the Taiwanese reality. Taiwanese religiosity is building an ethical system – kinship values are tied with ancestral rites and career progress is tied to the favor of the gods. One may describe so-called primitive societies and their versions of animism as a "premodern" religion. But one has a harder time

---

30. Yang, *Religion in Chinese Society*, 294–340.
31. This Charles Taylor would argue happened for "the West" (*A Secular Age*).
32. Yang, *Religion in Chinese Society*, 298.

calling Taiwan premodern with its skyscrapers and advanced semiconductor technology.

Moreover, the pervasive nature of folk religion and its blending with social institutions mean that it is a key part of Taiwanese consciousness. The conscience of a child growing up in Taiwan is as much shaped by modern-day politics as it is shaped by old folklore involving the supernatural. This does not mean that everyone is still "enchanted by the supernatural" (to use Taylor's terms) but simply that the "supernatural" has become part of an accepted experience of the people.

A gospel practice that involves the middle realm must directly address the forces of the middle realm. M.-H. Lin explains that there are scheduled parades of certain deities and that these parades are a spiritual analog to the patrol of police officers, which is meant to 「掃除惡煞安定人心」 ("get rid of evil [spirits] and calm the people's hearts").[33] If the gospel fails to do the same, it would be perceived as useless in Taiwan. Based on the interviews (e.g. Smoker Ang), demons and evil spirits are a real concern in many parts of Taiwan, thus a better theology and practice of exorcism are needed. The gospel must be seen as not just providing protection in the afterlife (i.e. going to heaven) but as protection in this life against the real/perceived forces in the middle realm.

One practical example is telling people about the power of Jesus's name to drive back any demons that may be attacking one's house or the power of prayer to do things that no spirits or deities could do. The charismatic churches in Taiwan are known for doing just those things. Judith C. P. Lin, in *The Charismatic Movement in Taiwan from 1945 to 1995*, explains the historical context for how this movement grew to be so successful and influential on the island today.[34] Using many primary sources (including oral reports), J. Lin, analyzes the works of people such as Pearl G. Young, Donald Dale, and Allen J. Swanson.[35] In this thorough historiography on the subject, J. Lin's work is very useful on a number of fronts. In relevance to this study, J. Lin shows the lasting theological influences of the aforementioned Christian workers on the island impacting theological thinking today.

---

33. Lin 林, *Dà Miào Chéng* 大廟埕, 443.
34. Lin, *Charismatic Movement in Taiwan*.
35. Lin, 94–100, 100–120, 146–50.

She also points out that the middle world of the unseen realm is normal in Taiwan. As such, J. Lin writes that most churches in Taiwan "have always understood the supernatural aspect of faith as recorded in the Scripture in a literal sense – which can be tasted and seen in the present day."[36] J. Lin contrasts this attitude of Taiwan with most churches in the United States, which shows "mistrust" and "disinterest," among other things when it comes to the supernatural aspect of faith.[37] She attributes the more widespread acceptance of charismatic teachings in Taiwan to the widespread acceptance of the middle realm in Taiwan.

J. Lin shows that in both charismatic and non-charismatic groups, power encounters are regularly practiced by Christians.[38] These include prayers for deliverance, miraculous healings, and, most of all, warfare with the demonic. These gospel practices that focus on the excluded middle teach the power of God, the way to pray, the danger of spirit-mediums, and multiple topics related to the lived reality of Taiwanese people in Taipei. According to J. Lin, this kind of approach has been taught in churches, especially since the 1980s. This study asks the question, How often is this approach used in initial gospel encounters with non-Christians compared to Christians in Taiwan? The follow-up question is just as important, Can this approach be used more frequently for initial (or entry-level) gospel encounters? In Taiwan, a gospel that adequately addresses the middle realm will see more responses.

The Gospel in Daily Life

If giving people good news for the middle realm is effective, what about good news in daily life? To explain what this means requires explaining the elements of this good news (i.e. gospel). Ray Comfort is one of the most famous street evangelists today. On the website of his organization Living Waters, Comfort lists multiple elements of the gospel, including discussions of God, the fall, Jesus, grace alone, faith alone, repentance, resurrection, and God's glory.[39] John Stott explains the gospel by categorizing it into five elements:

---

36. Lin, 247.
37. Lin, 247–48.
38. Lin, 250–51.
39. Comfort, "What Is the Gospel? Archives."

events, witnesses, affirmations, promises, and demands.[40] For Stott, the gospel event is historical at its core, gospel witnesses authenticate the message, gospel affirmations are theological statements about Christianity today, gospel promises relate to offers for both today and the future for all who would come to Christ, and gospel demands are what is required of the people today. It is interesting to note that the first four categories of the gospel are historical and doctrinal at their cores while the last one relates to the hearer's response. Comfort's categorization focuses on presenting the gospel to a non-Christian. Stott's categorization summarizes the New Testament picture. Both categorizations are theologically sound; the categorizations represent two main ways many theologians delineate gospel elements today.

Nevertheless, both categorizations miss something important to the Taiwanese context. In Stott's explanation of gospel promises, he talks about what the gospel promises to those who would accept and believe it. In it, he highlights forgiveness of sins in the past and new life in the present. These are again doctrinal statements that do not deal with *how* or *if* the gospel can help a person get a promotion, or whether the gospel can protect one's house from thieves, or whether the gospel can bring a romantic interest to a person's life. These are all questions raised by Taiwanese people in Taipei and answered by Guan Shengdijun, Earth God, and Yue Lao, in that order. Gospel promises do not seem to be close enough to the lived reality of the Taiwanese.

The missing component is the gospel in daily life. This must be differentiated from gospel living, which Stott includes as a gospel demand, and which many Christian teachers exhort. Whereas gospel living asks the Christian to live in accordance with the grace and responsibilities given to us, gospel in daily life asks the person (Christian or non-Christian) to turn to the gospel for the small things one encounters in daily life. When one's business is not doing well, what is the gospel's answer to that? When one lives in a dangerous neighborhood prone to crime, how does the gospel protect the person? When one is thirty-eight years old and yearns to get married but has zero romantic interests, where does the gospel come in? The easy answers of "have more faith" and "turn to Jesus" are not concrete enough to address these real concerns that people have.

---

40. Stott and Wright, *Christian Mission*, 62–76.

Perhaps for some Christians who have attended church for a while, they would start to understand how the gospel can apply in those specific situations. This work affirms that the gospel does implicitly address any and every situation in life, including the three mentioned. But non-Christians do not know what Christians know nor do they listen to sermons to find out. The research interviews show that many Taiwanese non-Christians looked at the abstract gospel as "irrelevant," "stupid," "arrogant," or even mistook it for another mystic chant. Until the gospel starts explicitly addressing situations in daily life, most non-Christians would likely still remain uninterested and unconvinced.

Chapter 2 discussed that folk religion in Taiwan should be described as living everyday lives with deities. For it is only in the concerns of everyday life that people seek out deities. Folk religion provides answers and concrete rituals for things encountered in everyday life. The essence of folk religion is not an abstract teaching or even a particular deity. The essence of folk religion is in how the unseen realm intersects with everyday living. In that way, cultural-religious expressions, folk customs, and special holidays with religious undertones (e.g. Tomb-Sweeping Day, Mid-Autumn Festival) represent the essence of folk religion, or at least the main expressions of it.

In Taiwan, one of the biggest roadblocks to the spread of the gospel is the popularity of folk religion. Folk religion in Taiwan provides a sense of security, situation specific assurances, an easy path of entry, and a familial approach. Deities are seen to protect and bless the whole family. Folk religion does not have complicated doctrines for people to grasp in order to be considered an adherent. The way to be a part of a particular folk religion is to visit the temple and *bài* the deity.

Abstract "gospel demands" or "gospel promises" do little for many Taiwanese. There are *some* Taiwanese for whom the gospel is powerfully convincing in its abstract form. What *many* Taiwanese non-Christians need is a more down-to-earth gospel that addresses their daily lives the same way that folk religion deities address their daily lives and felt needs. These deities do not address these needs as an implication or side-effect, but as their sole purposes. The only purpose of Yue Lao is to help people find romantic partners, the only purpose of the Earth God is to protect a piece of property, and the only purpose of Guan Shengdijun is to prosper businesses.[41] These are explicitly stated purposes, not implicitly suggested results of believing or adhering.

A contextual approach to gospel transmission for Taiwan must frame the LORD as better than Mazu in his protection of fishermen, better than Earth God in his protection of land, better than Guanyin in his compassion for people, better than Lord Superior Wen Chang in his concern for academia, and better than Yue Lao in his understanding of love.

What is suggested here is not to water down the gospel nor to make the gospel only about fulfilling the daily needs in a person's life. The gospel has eternal significance and brings the person into a relationship with the LORD. The gospel is also not about fulfilling one's desires, rather, the gospel is about fulfilling the desires of God. It can be easy to share about how the gospel can make one prosper, protect one's home, and bring a good mate. Taken to the extreme, this kind of prosperity gospel robs Jesus's focus on the kingdom, John's call to love, and Paul's admonition to live a life worthy of the calling we have received. The gospel is not about making our lives better; it is about being given new life in order to live for Christ now and unto eternity.

Even though the gospel has eternal significance, does the gospel nevertheless speak to our daily lives? The answer is most definitely yes. Teachings on the gospel's impact on daily life are often found in sermons or Christian evangelistic books. But in short gospel tracts, the gospel in daily life is often missing or downplayed. In a five to ten minute gospel presentation, the gospel in daily life is often ignored.

There is sometimes the mention of a life of discipleship and surrendering to Jesus as both Savior and Lord. There is sometimes also the mention of John 10:10 and the abstract abundant life that the LORD offers. These are good and useful *snippets* of the gospel in daily life, but not its full version. These short gospel presentations made to non-Christians often do not include how the gospel improves our daily lives in concrete ways. These truths are often only shared to the growing Christian who has already trusted Christ and must now continue their daily life. Why is it that to the non-Christians who are actively

---

41. It is more accurate to say that these are the only purposes for the majority of people. For example, Guan Shengdijun has developed a large enough following that there are some people who see him as near omnipotent. Disciple Wong saw Guan Shengdijun at Hsingtien Temple in such a way. For those people, Guan Shengdijun serves many purposes.

seeking ways to improve their daily lives, that aspect of the gospel remains unshared? Why must they turn to Mazu, Earth God, and countless others to find solutions when they need to only turn to Jesus Christ?

On the basis of this study, it is recommended that the gospel, when first presented to the non-Christian, must include aspects of the gospel in daily life in addition to abstract truths about the historical Jesus. This would help pave a more attractive initial entry way for the other aspects of the gospel. This method of gospel transmission uses language that Taiwanese people in Taipei can better understand. Especially in material that is shared *en masse* (e.g. gospel tracts, evangelistic essays, recorded videos), it is very easy for a non-Christian to misunderstand the gospel as only abstract truths about "eternal life" devoid of daily significance. Including "gospel in daily life" as an aspect to be shared at the first exposure is one step at helping to avoid misunderstandings.

These day-to-day issues are not secondary concerns that are addressed once the primary concern of "eternal life" is solved. These day-to-day issues are primary concerns to the Taiwanese people in Taipei. Coe Bei spoke of eternal life as "completeness." People like Coe Bei were not interested in living forever in some afterlife, but rather having "complete wisdom" along with other ways to have a more abundant life now. John 10:10b (ESV) says, "I came that they may have life and have it abundantly." Jesus's words here speak to the kind of complete, abundant life that Coe Bei desired. Phrases like this are very useful in Taiwan in conveying gospel truths about both this world and the next without detracting from either. Fishu framed eternal life as beginning from now and stretching on forever. Passages like John 10:10 fit Fishu's thinking and might have better appeal to more Taiwanese people in Taipei.

Take the example of Jesus Christ himself. While traveling across the first-century Roman world, Jesus encountered lawyers and tax-collectors along with lepers and prostitutes. The poor were especially attracted to Jesus. On at least two occasions, Jesus fed thousands of people with a few loaves of bread and fish. In John 6:1–15, Jesus fed five thousand people. The people were so transfixed on the material blessing of food that in John 6:25–59, food was all they would think about despite Jesus having repeatedly spoken of the bread from heaven. It is true that Jesus scolded people for thinking only of material things, but he still fed them, healed them, and defended them from attackers. Jesus had compassion on them.

Jesus encountered people in their daily lives with their daily needs. He answered them first not with abstract truth but with down-to-earth examples of how to live. Jesus spoke about how to deal with a Roman soldier asking a civilian to carry luggage or other items (Matt 5:41). Jesus spoke about paying taxes (Mark 12:17) and how often to forgive people (Matt 18:21–22). Abstract truth sometimes came with the fulfillment of daily needs and sometimes did not. Even in large-scale open-door meetings like the Sermon on the Mount, Jesus taught people how to act in daily life.

What are some gospel practices? It is important to begin an initial gospel encounter by answering the concerns of daily life. The end of the encounter can then intersect the LORD with those concerns. Instead of going through a rigid evangelistic manuscript, the Christian evangelizing person should consider starting by asking what non-Christian's main concerns are currently. It is important to discuss whether there are any issues in the non-Christian's life that is hard to solve. It is useful to find the last deity the person visited and the specific thing that was beseeched. Knowing the answer to these questions, the evangelizing person could then explain how the gospel can speak directly to the non-Christian's main concerns, how the LORD can solve that particular issue, and how the LORD can do even more than what the last deity could do. This approach to gospel transmission starts by understanding the needs of the person, then portrays the LORD as superior in every way to respond to those needs.

Sometimes, the LORD does not fulfill every felt need. But that does not mean the gospel does not speak on the subject. On the question of money, people seek Guan Shengdijun to get promotions. The gospel teaches people not to worry about money or promotions, but to "seek first the kingdom of God and his righteousness, and all these things will be added to you" (Matt 6:33). On the question of protection, the Earth God promises the well-being of one's apartment or house. The gospel teaches that God "will command his angels concerning you to guard you in all your ways" (Ps 91:11). On the question of romance, Yue Lao promises a date with a romantic interest. The gospel teaches us about love itself (1 Cor 13).

These are not comprehensive answers, but it is a start. It must be said that the good news of Jesus Christ (his life, death, and resurrection) must always remain in all gospel presentations. The gospel must not be "changed" or "watered down" to have better appeal to Taiwanese people in Taipei. However, these other elements regarding "daily life" must be in most (if not all) gospel presentations in Taiwan. It is through Jesus's teachings in life that we know how to live our daily lives. It is through Jesus's death on the cross that we become "adopted god-children"[42] who can beseech the LORD for the minor things in daily life. It is through Jesus's resurrection that we can overcome our limits and have a "surpassing mentality to face this life"[43] daily. The gospel can and must address daily life if it is to take root in Taiwan.

Summary of Gospel Transmission in Taiwan

The gospel has been circulating in Taiwan for many generations. These insights in light of local attitudes and lived realities strengthen existing gospel transmission efforts and serve as the foundation to build new gospel presentations. More than just the gospel encounter, the section on relationship networks has shown that sometimes one's whole environment needs to be impacted by the gospel. At its core, the Taiwanese gospel presentation must touch on the gospel in daily life. Without a stronger discussion of daily life, the gospel does not have the same appeal as folk religion in Taiwan.

---

42. Using Tattoo Ju and Genie's terminology of being a god-daughter of Mazu.
43. Using Curu's explanation about the implications of the cross.

CHAPTER 8

Conclusion

The title of this work is *Religiosity and Gospel Transmission: Insights from Folk Religion in Taipei*. In chapter 1, we explained the research problems as well as the objectives. In chapter 2, we discussed the definition of folk religion in a general sense and the nuances of folk religion in Taiwan. In chapter 3, we described the methodology used to conduct the qualitative interviews in Taipei, Taiwan. In chapters 4 and 5, we unveiled the findings of the qualitative research, helping to uncover local attitudes and lived realities. In chapter 6, we warned about some issues that one must be careful of when conversing with Taiwanese. In chapter 7, we proposed some positive approaches that one can use in gospel transmission. Here in chapter 8, we conclude our study with some practical gospel steps and recommendations for future research.

Gospel Steps

It seems from the interviews that multiple evangelistic approaches could be appropriate depending on the types of people encountered; a one-size fits all solution does not seem realistic. However, it is possible to summarize everything discussed in this study thus far and synthesize them into a list of gospel steps. These steps are specific to Taiwanese people in Taipei but have broader applicability to all of Taiwan with some modifications. These steps point out the transformation of the Taiwanese from a non-Christian to a Christian disciple-maker. This section divides the steps into two categories: (1) steps for the Christian evangelizing person and (2) steps for the transforming non-Christian.

Steps for the Christian Evangelizing Person

This section focuses on what the Christian evangelizing person should do. In these steps, the non-Christian takes on a less active role, with the Christian evangelizing person implementing most of the actions and bearing much of the responsibility. The following steps are suggested: (1) understanding, (2) dialoguing, (3) honoring, (4) suggesting, and (5) presenting.

Understanding

First, the evangelizing person must understand the worldview of the non-Christian. This includes how the non-Christian thinks, what folk religion means to the non-Christian, and other ways religiosity is conceptualized. We saw in chapter 2 that Chinese religiosity is characterized by ancient beliefs and highly diffused in society.[1] Folk religion in Taiwan is seen as part of Taiwanese culture, expressing "a value system in the spiritual world that people are unaware of but nevertheless apply in daily life."[2] The types of findings in chapters 5 and 6 also inform the evangelizing person about the attitudes and lived reality of the non-Christian.

This first step could potentially take the longest. It requires a person to either be a Taiwanese and have grown up in this country or be immersed enough in the culture and be aware enough about the literature to properly understand the best way to relate to Taiwanese people. This step is never truly complete because there are always more nuances to uncover. Furthermore, cultures and contexts are ever-changing. There comes a point when an evangelizing person must decide that they understand enough and start the second step.

Dialoguing

Second, the evangelizing person should now start dialoguing with one or several non-Christians. It is ideal, but not necessary, to do this in the context of friendship because the non-Christian is more likely to be honest with the evangelizing person. This avoids situations like the one with Pei-Pei where she was not honest with the street witnessing person. Honest dialogue would

---

1. Yang, *Religion in Chinese Society*.
2. Cheng 鄭, "Jìn wǔshí niánlái táiwān dìqū mínjiān zōngjiào zhī yánjiū yǔ qiánzhān, 近五十年來臺灣地區民間宗教之研究與前瞻," 127.

reveal the possible "sinned-againstness" of the non-Christian and allow the evangelizing person to empathize with that.

The dialogue advocated here is not just having a conversation. The conversational aspect is part of the dialogue, which is important to remember to avoid one-way harangues in a gospel presentation. More than having a conversation, a dialogue must include elements that Yong recommends in his pneumatological approach to theology and missiology. The evangelizing person enters into the experiences of the non-Christian, "crossing-over" into their world first. For example, if the non-Christian friend wants to go to a Yue Lao temple to beseech for a romantic interest, the evangelizing person can accompany this friend on the visit without doing the beseeching. After enough dialogues like these, the non-Christian is more likely to "cross over" into the Christian's world later.

One must be careful when dialoguing, especially when entering into the non-Christian's religious experiences. It is up to the evangelizing person to practice biblical discernment and rely on the Holy Spirit to decide how far is too far when crossing-over into the experiences of the religious other. The relevant section in chapter 6 gives some guidelines but the evangelizing person should consult with more seasoned Christians (e.g. the senior pastor of a church) to ensure that the evangelizing person stays true to the LORD.

Honoring

Third, the evangelizing person should find ways to honor the practices of the non-Christian. Recall Pastor Yeh's advice to find the root motivation of a practice like ancestral veneration and commend the positive aspects of it. As the interviews indicated, many Taiwanese do it to honor those who came before them. They do it because they have been taught, "When drinking water, think of the source." Yeh's warning was that ancestral veneration rituals are too deeply rooted in the Taiwanese ethos to be erased. Instead of working to erase the ancestral veneration rituals, the evangelizing person should honor them and work to transform them.

Ways of relating to deities could be honored too. Recall that Tattoo Ju treated Mazu as a family member and Mrs. Ting spoke of Guanyin as someone with great compassion. Their reverence for these deities, while misguided, does reveal a beautiful spirit of love and devotion. If guided toward the LORD, this same love and devotion would be great characteristics in a Christian.

Bringing the gospel into conversation with ancestors and deities allows the gospel to become more relevant to the non-Christian's existing context. This step is about embracing Taiwanese local attitudes about such things and figuring out ways to transform them. The goal is to honor the non-Christian's existing local attitudes as much as is theologically reasonable in order for the non-Christian to one day honor the LORD as much as is humanly possible.

Suggesting

Fourth, the evangelizing person should suggest to the non-Christian that the LORD is superior in every way. These suggestions should not start off as too strong. In the beginning, the evangelizing person could just talk about the many ways that the LORD has blessed their life. If the evangelizing person received a promotion recently, they could tell the non-Christian friend that this is because of the LORD's favor on their life.

When enough of these indirect suggestions about the LORD's superiority has been made, the evangelizing person can start becoming more direct in the suggestions. The evangelizing person can tell the non-Christian friend that the friend could start beseeching the LORD for a promotion instead of relying solely on a deity like Guan Shengdijun. In addition to making this suggestion, the evangelizing person should show the gospel in action. The evangelizing person should not just tell the non-Christian friend what to do, but do it together. The evangelizing person can take lessons with the non-Christian that improve career skills needed for a promotion. The evangelizing person can pray to the LORD together also. The key for a gospel in action is that the action must be felt in such a way that the non-Christian feels loved. Moreover, the LORD must be portrayed as extremely 靈驗 ("efficacious").

All the things that the evangelizing person suggest to the non-Christian in this step should be things that are focused on this life instead of the next life. Unless the non-Christian has a strong fear of death, the research findings indicate that the issues of this life are where Taiwanese give most of their attention.

Presenting

Fifth, the evangelizing person should present the superiority of the LORD. While the fourth step only allows the making of indirect and direct suggestions of the LORD's superiority, this fifth step makes it clear who the LORD is, what he offers, and what he demands. The omnipotent power of the LORD should be contrasted with the Taiwanese deities' more limited sphere of influence. The evangelizing person can start describing these deities as powerful spirits and demons in the middle realm to separate them from the LORD. Either way, the research findings indicate that power is a deciding factor for Taiwanese people in Taipei when it comes to their choice of deities and therefore must be mentioned here.

The evangelizing person could use the same analogy of a relationship of exchange that Taiwanese people in Taipei already use. The difference is that the evangelizing person can speak about the great exchange and the "incongruity" of grace.[3] It is in this step that the other truth claims that the Bible makes are presented. Discernment must still be practiced in sharing what is appropriate so that the non-Christian is not overwhelmed with information.

Information shared can include what the non-Christian needs to change. Especially if the non-Christian is an adherent of another religion, it is useful to tell the non-Christian how to cross this religious boundary from the other religion into Christianity. The evangelizing person should steer away from the language of conversion[4] but instead use the language of life transformation, utilizing centered set thinking in guiding the non-Christian toward the LORD. In this step, the non-Christian must hear the life, death, and resurrection of Jesus Christ along with their proper response of biblical faith to this truth. Without mentioning Jesus's work on the cross, this step is incomplete.

This fifth step does not translate to just one gospel presentation. If the non-Christian person is a friend, this fifth step (like every other step) could take years of interaction and hundreds of conversations. If the non-Christian is a stranger on the street, then the evangelizing person can only try his or her best to go through each step within the allotted time. While the steps are written with both possibilities in mind, the former situation is posited to have greater efficacy.

---

3. Barclay, *Paul and the Gift*, 72.

4. There are positive, helpful ways that the idea of conversion can be used both theologically as well as practically in gospel presentations. This warning only applies to the unnuanced idea of conversion as outlined in chapter 6, namely the type that Fan and Chen are dissatisfied about (see Fan and Chen, "Conversion").

Steps for the Transforming Non-Christian

The previous section focuses on the actions and responsibilities of the Christian evangelizing person. This section shifts the focus and turns to the non-Christian's role. There comes a certain point when the evangelizing person takes a less active role and instead takes up a supporting role. The steps here can overlap with the steps in the previous section because they are describing the same event of gospel transmission from two perspectives, the first from the perspective of the evangelizing person and the second from the perspective of the non-Christian. The steps are as follows: (1) beseeching, (2) *bài*-ing, (3) participating, (4) becoming, and (5) multiplying.

Beseeching

Recall from the fourth step in the previous section that the evangelizing person should suggest both indirectly and directly that the LORD is superior to the other Taiwanese deities. One way to do so is to ask the non-Christian to start beseeching from the LORD. The non-Christian does not have to renounce anything just yet. As described in chapter 6, the non-Christian can start by adding the LORD into the pantheon of deities in their lived reality. If the non-Christian currently beseeches from Yue Lao for romance, this person can start beseeching the LORD for romance in addition to Yue Lao. It is here that the non-Christian finds out how efficacious the LORD is.

Recall the story of Company Woman, who beseeched from Mazu, Earth God, and the LORD at the same time. She ended up thanking all three of them after her issue was resolved. At the time of the interview, she was still unsure about the place of the LORD in her life. However, instead of scoffing at Christianity like she used to, she started treating Christianity with respect, to the point that she admitted being more attracted to Christianity than any other religion she has experienced in the past.

It is true that the LORD must not remain as just one deity in a pantheon of deities. However, this is only the first step for the non-Christian. As a general approach, it is better to ease the person into Christianity. It is okay to let the non-Christian dwell in pluralism for a while. When the time is right, the evangelizing person can ease the non-Christian out of pluralism.

Bài-ing

Second, the non-Christian should *bài* the LORD more frequently. The non-Christian should try to *bài* the LORD not just when they need something, but also whenever they think of the LORD. The interview participants mentioned *bài*-ing deities when they happened to pass by temples. Genie mentioned *bài*-ing a deity at her office for five seconds at a time when she went in for work. The evangelizing person can remind the non-Christian to *bài* or pray to the LORD whenever the non-Christian passes by a church. The non-Christian can also be encouraged to do the same whenever an image of the cross is seen on someone's office cubicle or on a sign.

The idea is that the non-Christian should make interactions with the LORD a normal part of everyday life. The non-Christian should start treating the LORD as a friendly "neighborhood uncle"[5] who is available to help. Likewise, in small issues that arise as part of daily life, the non-Christian should seek the LORD for help either through divine intervention or granting of wisdom. Either way, the LORD becomes normalized in the mind of the non-Christian and in his or her lived reality. The evangelizing person should continue to preach the gospel in daily life to the non-Christian in any and all applicable situations.

Participating

Third, the non-Christian should start participating and experimenting with various Christian events and rituals. The evangelizing person can invite the non-Christian to various retreats that the church may hold or fun Christmas events that are entertaining for everyone. The point of participating in events like these is to build the relationship network that Curu said was so essential for her own Christian journey. These events help the non-Christian make many Christian friends and thus make becoming a Christian much more plausible. When the non-Christian becomes more open to Christianity, the non-Christian can be invited to Sunday worship services and small group discussions. These events allow the non-Christian to deepen their intellectual knowledge of Christianity.

As the knowledge increases, the evangelizing person should encourage the non-Christian to experiment with various things that the Bible teaches. For

---

5. Using Pei-Pei's terms.

example, both the evangelizing person and the non-Christian can practice fasting and prayer together, which can eventually replace Zen meditation. The non-Christian can also practice the morality that the Bible teaches, seeing firsthand what living as a Christian may feel like. Recall that Tour Guide Man spoke of becoming a religion's adherent as an unclear and long process. These kinds of experimental participation allow the non-Christian to do "religious practice" first (to borrow a term that many Buddhist participants used). In this way, the evangelizing person can invite the non-Christian to "taste and see that the LORD is good" (Ps 34:8). After enough time has passed (which varies depending on the person), the non-Christian would taste this truth and move on to the fourth step.

Becoming

Fourth, the non-Christian becomes a God-child, an 義子 (*yìzǐ*, adopted son or daughter) of the LORD (Eph 1:5). Recall that Tattoo Ju and Genie were god-daughters of Mazu. Genie in particular had to ask twice before she was accepted as Mazu's god-daughter. They saw being the god-daughter as a privilege. It is certainly rare in Taiwan because one has to pass a "ritual for adoption as god-daughter" for it to be possible. This perceived privilege makes this special identity all the more precious. Tattoo Ju admitted to not always taking the responsibility seriously. However, she and Genie both stated proudly that they tried to live up to this identity by being good people. They also said that they tried to interact with Mazu more frequently than their peers.

After the non-Christian has participated in enough Christian experiences, the evangelizing person must present this fourth step. Following the advice for how to present the gospel in the previous section, the evangelizing person must now wait for the non-Christian to make a response. Whether it is a decision, prayer, or ritual, the point is that the non-Christian must become a God-child. This is the point where the non-Christian becomes a Christian. This point is accompanied by various events and responsibilities. These include the indwelling of the Holy Spirit, the baptism of believers, and the moral living that befits a God-child identity.

Multiplying

Fifth, the new Christian must now multiply as a disciple-maker. The evangelizing person should continue to journey with this new Christian to help them "walk in a manner worthy of the calling to which [they] have been called" (Eph 4:1). Recall that in the interviews, behavior was an important aspect of faith itself and a key indicator of devotion. The new God-child must match his or her behavior with this new identity in order for other people to witness the change.

Just as the evangelizing person has walked with the transforming non-Christian through each of these five steps, so the transforming new Christian must walk these same steps with someone else. In this way, the new Christian fulfills part of Matthew 28:20 and continues the cycle pictured in 2 Timothy 2:2. After this step, the disciple-making cycle is complete.

Summary of Gospel Steps

We have examined five gospel steps that the Christian evangelizing person should take followed by five gospel steps that the non-Christian should take. These steps overlap in some areas to highlight the responsibilities of each side of the relationship. In rough chronological order, the steps look like this:[6] (E1) understanding, (E2) dialoguing, (E3) honoring, (E4) suggesting, (N1) beseeching, (N2) *bài*-ing, (N3) participating, (E5) presenting, (N4) becoming, (N5) multiplying.

Without the cooperation of the two parties, these gospel steps cannot be completed. Without the help of the Holy Spirit, they may step on each other's feet. It is thus a miracle anytime someone becomes a God-child. These gospel steps do not make the task of gospel transmission easy. However, the steps do make the task easier to follow. This study proposes that these gospel steps make up an efficacious contextual approach to gospel transmission in Taiwan. If followed, these steps will be a great help in the gospel taking root in Taiwan.

Recommendations for Future Research

We have looked at issues that are important to the Taiwanese context. We have looked at more concrete examples of what needs more attention in gospel presentations. This discussion helps the evangelizing person in Taiwan be better equipped to transmit the gospel with a more contextualized approach

---

6. "E" represents the evangelizing person's steps and "N" represents the non-Christian's steps.

and clearer understanding of the recipient's mindset. The main contribution of this work is to one's approach and understanding (i.e. what are the recipients like and how will they react?), not to the content of the gospel (i.e. what parts of the gospel needs to be shared in a complete gospel presentation?). For more complete treatment of all the essential issues in the content, different questions need to be asked and more research needs to be done. The following are four areas that could still use more work.

Perception of Folk Religion in Taiwan

There were multiple interview questions that dealt with how Taiwanese people in Taipei themselves interact with and perceive folk religion. One particular question asked the participants whether they thought folk religion had an overall positive or negative impact in Taiwan. Rich, detailed data were derived from that one question alone. Other questions helped reveal not just why people went to a deity, but also why they thought folk religion was such a critical part of Taiwanese identity. The scope of the study did not allow the researcher to tackle questions like these in depth. But future research in this area has the potential to reveal the nuances of the Taiwanese mindset in their perceptions of folk religion as culture and as religion.

Christian Conversion Stories Among Taiwanese

We have looked at Healthy Chen's story of how he became a Christian. We have seen glimpses of why the other research participants chose Christianity. It would be fruitful to expand on this topic and discover the stories of more Taiwanese people in Taipei. More systematic questions could be asked of their own experience of turning to Christianity. If the few Christian participants in the research generated such good data, imagine how rich the study would be if there are five times the number of participants.

More questioning needs to be done on the family of the participants too. Were they happy with the change in religious allegiance? What were the main struggles? Especially with folk customs and special religious holidays, how did the Christians deal with those? Did the Christians try to transmit the gospel to their family members? How did the Christians do so? What were successful tactics and what were unsuccessful? All these questions would generate more insight into gospel transmission in Taiwan.

Applicability Outside Taiwan

Another topic worthy of further study is how applicable this study is outside Taiwan. What would this contextual approach to gospel transmission look like in China? What are some elements that could transfer over to China's context? Due to them both being Chinese societies and due to having shared cultural and religious history prior to 1949, certain themes carry over well (i.e. importance of ancestors, focus on daily life, Confucian teachings) while certain themes do not carry over (i.e. cultural acceptance of folk religion, proliferation of temples and deity statuettes on the streets). What does other scholarship say on the topic and how can this be tested?

How does the contextual approach to gospel transmission transfer outside the East Asian context? We have mentioned many themes that could potentially be transferable. Do they apply in the United States? What does folk religion look like in the United States? Instead of people thinking in terms of folk religion, maybe they think in terms of folk Christianity. Is this what Nancy Ammerman, David Hall, and others are observing?[7] Future research can expand this contextual approach to gospel transmission in Taiwan and adapt it to other contexts as well.

Do people in a context like the United States only approach God to worship or do they go to him when they have a need? What are the contents of most prayers? In fact, why is it that "prayer requests" are more popular than "praises to God" when people have big or small group meetings in the United States? Are people in the United States as hungry for the gospel in daily life as Taiwanese people might be? Is there an itch that the prosperity gospel is scratching that evangelicals have not touched on enough? Would gospel presentations in the United States be more effective if they always included the gospel in daily life? These are all important questions that would require future research in the United States to ascertain.

Closing Remarks

Considering human nature, it is only a small stretch to imagine that the concepts uncovered in this study can be applied to multiple contexts with certain adaptions. After all, we have examined how a particular people view and

---

7. Ammerman, *Everyday Religion*; Hall, *Lived Religion in America*.

treat the unseen realm. We have looked at local attitudes and lived realities to find out that religion is often just another word to describe how Taiwanese people deal with everyday life. Furthermore, the gospel steps proposed in this chapter give a concrete and practical guide to a better approach to gospel transmission in Taiwan.

There are countless little boys and girls who, like this researcher, grew up with folk religion as their explicit religion or as their framework for religious thinking. To those people, folk religion is how they deal with everyday life. This work has proclaimed the good news that there is another way to deal with everyday life, a "gospel in daily life." Like 1 Thessalonians 2:4 (ESV) states, we have been "πιστευθῆναι τὸ εὐαγγέλιον" ("entrusted with the gospel").[8] This researcher will continue to do everything in his power to ensure the continued transmission of this gospel to the next generation of Taiwanese children so that more "God-children" can be born. It is in this way that the evangelization of the country can begin to be accomplished.

This work has contributed to strengthening the contextual approach to gospel transmission and thus helped the overall evangelization efforts ongoing in Taiwan. As Christians keep transmitting the gospel to other people, may they never stop thinking about the message that Jesus preached. May they never stop reflecting about the context of the listeners. The gospel is the ultimate good news, not just good news about the ultimate thing. Instead of turning to Mazu, money, or materialism in their daily lives, may everyone turn to the maker of the heavens and the earth. May the gospel in daily life point them in that direction.

It may not be possible to accomplish the evangelization of the world in this generation. But it is certainly possible for every generation to theologize about their actual work of gospel transmission, then entrust the task of gospel transmission to the next generation, and the next one, and as many as is needed until the Lord comes again. Until that day comes, this researcher will continue his gospel transmission task as an evangelist-theologian in his generation for his context. May you, the reader, do the same as God's chosen instrument in your generation for your context.

---

8. This is the phrase on the logo of Trinity International University.

Appendix 1

Chinese Terms and Names

Due to the nature of this research, a significant number of Chinese studies were consulted. The display of Chinese terms and names in English academic literature does not seem to have a standard yet. For example, Yale, Brill, and University of British Columbia display Chinese surnames first even in English. The Chicago Manual of Style 17th edition allows any order for the surname-first name display. However, many publishers and style guides remain silent on the issue. It is therefore important to specify the adopted convention and rationale for doing so.

Romanization

In Mandarin Chinese, there are five tones: four main tones and one neutral tone. Depending on the tone, a particular sound can be different words meaning completely different things. Most English literature ignores the tones when citing Chinese terms and uses a phonetic 拼音 (Pinyin), a kind of transliteration using the English alphabet. The researcher grew up with 注音 (Zhuyin), which uses Mandarin Chinese phonetic symbols like ㄅ ㄆ ㄇ ㄈ (Bopomofo). Pinyin spellings of Chinese terms or names are often alien to the researcher without clear markings of the tone. It is the same for many people who are familiar only with Zhuyin. Even with the right tone, a particular sound can still be different words. A good romanization system can help alleviate these issues.

Romanization of Chinese words is varied among scholars. The researcher has expanded on the practices of non-Chinese scholars, many of whom either use the Wade-Giles alone or Wade-Giles plus Pinyin.[1] But few include the Chinese characters, which make original language research unnecessarily cumbersome for those fluent in the language. Therefore, all Chinese words are introduced in three ways: (1) the original Chinese, (2) a phonetically accurate Pinyin with tonal accents, and (3) the English translation (mostly done by the researcher) or the popular English transliteration using the Wade-Giles form (if the term is a proper noun and different from Pinyin). This helps scholars with basic Chinese knowledge to continue research more easily. Subsequent uses of the word default to the pinyin. For interview transcripts from the field research, only the original Chinese and the English translation are included because including Pinyin serves no purpose there.

Words from Japanese, Greek, and any other language with non-Roman alphabets are introduced similarly. For example, in discussion of certain Greek words, the following are included: (1) the original Greek, (2) common transliteration, and (3) the English translation (mostly done by popular dictionaries like the BDAG). Subsequent uses of the word default to the transliteration. Italics are used in all cases of non-English words written in Roman/Latin script. Proper nouns like names of people (e.g. Yang), location names (e.g. Taipei), or special terms (e.g. Pinyin) are not italicized.

For certain words, the Chinese Pinyin instead of the English translation is displayed. The reason is to bypass preconceived notions of certain English words to more accurately portray the full range of the Chinese concept. A notable example is 拜 (*bài*, worship or a physical closing of the palms).

Chinese Names

In Chinese convention, the surname goes before the given name. However, to fit the standards of Trinity Evangelical Divinity School, the conventional English order of surname going last has been maintained for all Chinese names in this work.

When Chinese authors are mentioned, the Chinese is written first, with the English included in brackets for the first instance that it appears in the

---

1. Clart and Jones, *Religion in Modern Taiwan*; Fowler and Fowler, *Chinese Religions*.

work (e.g. "莊智超 [Tony Chuang] writes that . . .")). This order priority is out of respect for the original language. This order is preferred because this is how this researcher would like his name to be shown in another's work. Subsequent mentions of the same author in the same chapter are written in only English for simplicity (e.g. "Chuang prefers the term"). In the bibliography, the English name is written first, with the Chinese name put in brackets to conform to the standards of Trinity Evangelical Divinity School (e.g. Chuang [莊], Tony [智超]).

In some of the cases, Chinese authors write in Chinese for the Chinese population. These same Chinese authors sometimes write in English for the non-Chinese population in other parts of the world. In cases where Chinese authors have only written in English, their Chinese name are procured through internet and library searches. For a few of them, the Chinese name is not available for various reasons. These are the only cases that the Chinese name is left out of the citation (e.g. Raymond Fung).

Often, it is difficult to know the Chinese name just from an English transliteration, especially from non-standard Pinyin. This work has gone to such lengths to include more Chinese because this work, especially the bibliography, aims to be more useful for other scholars who are multi-lingual. If these scholars' Chinese names were shown, it would be much easier to peruse other works by Chinese authors in the original language. It certainly would have saved the researcher much time if other scholars writing in English had done the same. To this end, in the reference list, all Chinese works were written with the accented Pinyin, original Chinese, and an English translation. The translation is sometimes supplied by the author but most of the time translated by the researcher.

Chinese Quotation from Interviews

In the dissertation, many quotes were taken directly from the twenty-five qualitative interviews conducted. When the quotes were presented, the Chinese is displayed first, followed by the English in parenthesis. For example, a quote would be displayed as: Shi Gu said,「不像以前那麼嚴格」 ("Not as strict as before"). The quotations were displayed in this fashion for several reasons.

First, this allows the dissertation committee to be able to verify the quotation easily. As mentioned in the methodology chapter, the entire transcript of each interview is not translated. Including the quote in Chinese allows curious committee members to copy the Chinese phrase, then open the file of the participant, then search the phrase in the file, then view the bigger context. Google translate is adequate enough to at least get a rough understanding of the context. In other words, the first reason is to make sure this research has high confirmability.

Second, the Chinese was displayed first and the English second in parentheses because Chinese is the original language the research was conducted in. In many academic books, Latin or Greek would be provided with the English in parentheses as well.[2] It shows a respect for the original language, a respect that was mirrored here. For non-Chinese speaking people, it may feel unnecessary. It may even feel a bit annoying because these are not just words but entire phrases. But in an increasingly global world, this was an important step to take.

Third, in the study of English literature about Chinese religiosity, many books consulted do not use Chinese for their quotations and only listed the English translation. This researcher has often wondered what the original Chinese is and what is lost in translation. These scholars, by not providing the original language, makes it difficult for people to verify the work. Furthermore, it makes it difficult to appreciate the depth of insight or the beauty that may have existed in the way the author weaved the words in the original text.

Chinese Citations in the Reference List

In the reference list, several Chinese sources were cited in addition to English sources. For Chinese sources, as much information as possible was provided to help both bilingual readers and those learning Chinese. It has the added benefit of allowing people to find the books themselves. It was hard for the researcher to locate some books precisely because some scholars did not include

---

2. In many works in the field of New Testament Studies, the Greek is written in transliteration, not in the Greek letters. While not in the original typography, the transliteration still represents the original language.

the original Chinese. When the author included an English translation, the English translation was written first followed by the original Chinese. When the author did not include a translation, the researcher's own translation was provided along with a Pinyin version of the original title. This applies to the book or journal title, name of the series, name of the journal, and name of the publisher.

To help differentiate between which authors provided their own translations, the formats differ. For example, works with the translation provided look like: Pilgrimages, Sacrifice Offerings and Sociocultural Transformation 進香．醮．祭與社會文化變遷. Works without an author-provided translation look like: Mínsú Yǔ Xìnyǎng 民俗與信仰 [Folklore and Faith]. It is hoped that future scholarship across multiple languages will utilize a similar format to the one used in this dissertation. This should help scholars across all languages dialogue and converge more easily and more respectfully.

Appendix 2

Interview Protocol

A participant is only selected if they have personal experience with some form of folk religion (e.g. ancestral veneration, going to a temple).

The participant does not see the section headings or sub-headings; these are for the interviewer to categorize each big idea. There are three questions for basic information, which are used for statistics purposes. There are seven sections and an average of about three questions per section. There are eighteen questions in total; eleven are required, five are for Christians, and two are for a small sample. Explanatory remarks are included in each category to help guide the interviewer.

At the end of the interview, the interviewer thanks the participant for their help. The interviewer offers his email address to the participant so that they could send any questions or concerns the participant may have in the future.

Basic Information

This is information that helps categorize the participant for future data analysis purposes. The goal is to determine whether certain demographic factors influence views on "faith." The interviewer is to ask about specific practices that presume the presence of the supernatural. After all the interviews are done, a cross-reference of this information with views on "faith" and actual practices may reveal interesting data.

請問您的學歷是？您目前或最近的職業是什麼？ (What is your educational background? What is your current or most recent occupation?)

您是否有特定的宗教信仰？ (Do you have a particular religious affiliation?)

What Is the General Attitude toward the Unseen Realm?

The interviewer is looking for understandings of "faith" and religion, especially in the context of folk religion. To explore the mindset, the interviewer has to ask specific questions relating to specific practices. A question like "How do you express religiosity?" is too hard to answer. Some of these questions may elicit a response that points to understandings of "faith," religion, and believing in something. Those hints are what the interviewer is really looking for.

您有祭祖的經驗嗎？ (Do you have experience with ancestral veneration?)

[If there is prior experience] 為什麼您祭祖？ (Why do you practice ancestral veneration?)

[If there is prior experience] 您真的相信他們可以影響您的生活嗎？為什麼？如何影響？ (Do you really believe they can affect your life? Why? How?)

當我們祭祖，這意味著什麼？祭祖跟拜神明一樣意思嗎？還是只是尊敬他們，還是有其它意思？ (When we practice ancestral veneration, what does it mean? Are we worshipping them like deities, following their guidance, simply honoring them, or something else?)

一個人去世後有去另外一個地方嗎？這種信念的基礎是什麼？ (What happens when a person dies? What is the basis for this belief?)

您相信輪迴嗎？哪一種？為什麼？ (Do you believe in some form of reincarnation? What kind? Why or why not?)

[If participant believes in reincarnation] 您前世的行為會影響您現在的生活嗎？為什麼？如何影響？ (Do actions from your past life affect your present life? Why or why not? How?)

您算命過嗎？如果有，您最後一次算命是什麼時候？請詳細說明經驗，包括所採用的算命方法。 (Have you visited a fortune teller? If so, when was the last time you visited a fortune teller? Please elaborate on the experience, including the method of fortune telling that was employed.)

[If participant has sought fortune telling] 您是否真的想信他們會算對？如果是，您如何確定？如果不是，您為什麼仍要算命？ (Are you confident that they will tell you the right future? If yes, how can you be sure? If not, why do you still do it?)

What Does It Mean to Believe in a Deity?

The interviewer needs to find out how a person treats "faith" and belief. The interviewer probes in different ways what the person means by believing in a deity.

當朋友說「我拜媽祖」，您認為這意味著什麼？ (When a friend says, "I worship or believe in Mazu," what do you think that means?)

當一個人信媽祖，那個人到底在信什麼？比如說一位穆斯林教徒說信阿拉，他通常會信阿拉是真的，古蘭經寫的該跟隨的，之類的。那信媽祖的是信什麼？ (When a person believes in Mazu, what is this person believing in? For example, when a Muslim says he believes in Allah, he will normally believe in the reality of Allah's existence, that we should follow what the Quran says, etc. So, what do Mazu believers believe in?)

您現在正在拜哪位神明？ (Which deity do you worship or believe in right now?)

這個神明如何主宰/影響您生活？ (How does this deity dictate how you live or influence your life?)

你為什麼相信這位神明？ (Why do you believe in this deity?)

What Does it Mean to Be in a Religious System?

Are people in the "Mazu religion" when they go to a Mazu temple? What does it mean to officially be a part of a religion? What boundaries are crossed? What artefacts of the old religious system are left behind in the case of conversion to Christianity? These questions explore how useful categories and boundaries are for Taiwanese religious expressions.

「宗教」，「信仰」，和「拜」之間有區別嗎？它們有甚麼相關？ (Is there a difference between religion, "faith," and worship? Are they related?)

[If the person is a convert to another religion] 您目前的宗教系統主要的信念或儀式是什麼？ (What are some beliefs and practices that are key to your current religious system?)

[If the person is a convert to another religion] 現在您是[X教徒]，您跟以前有什麼不同？ (What is different for you now that you are a [term for converted religion's adherent]?)

[If the person is a convert to another religion] 在信奉新宗教後，您對民間信仰有改觀嗎？ (After converting to your new religion, do you view folk religion any differently?)

How Does Folk Religion Influence Understandings of Faith?

By inserting folk religion into the context, the researcher explores whether it affects the participant's answer.

您對台灣民間信仰有什麼看法？對台灣是正面還是負面影響？怎麼說？ (How do you view folk religion in Taiwan? Is it a positive or negative influence to Taiwan? How so?)

根據「KEYPO網路排名」，台灣人最愛拜的三位神明是媽祖，財神，和觀世音菩薩。您覺得這三個神明中哪一位最值得拜，就是最會推薦給朋友的？請解釋。 (According to "KEYPO internet ranking," the top three deities that Taiwanese people "like to worship" are Mazu, "God of wealth," and Avalokiteśvara. Which of those three deities do you feel is most worth worshipping or believing in, namely the one that you would most recommend to your friend? Please explain.)

您認為還有其他神明值得拜嗎？如果有，是什麼使這些神明在您眼中脫穎而出？ (Are there any other deities that you think are worth believing in? If so, what makes those particular deities stand out to you?)

當您聽到有人或有廣播說「信耶穌得永生」，您如何反應？您認為這句話是甚麼意思？ (When you hear a person or broadcast say a statement like "believe in Jesus for eternal life," how do you react? What do you think it means?)

是怎樣的人會被公認為很虔誠的［X教徒］？你可以形容一下這個人嗎？包括行為，思想，信仰，之類的。 (What kind of person would be considered a devout [term for converted religion's adherent]? Could you describe this kind of person, including this person's actions, thoughts, faith, etc.?)

What Are Some Chinese Terms Used to Describe Faith?

This question helps establish basic categories by finding out all the word choices that can mean the same thing. It provides data on whether current scholarly translations of religious literature match the understanding of the "average Taiwanese." It is expected that after a few interviews, the answer to this question can start to be repetitive and data saturation will happen. This question should be dropped at that point.

[Small Sample] 我們提到了「信」和「拜」這兩個字，我們還可以用什麼字來描述我們與神的關係？ (We mentioned the terms "believing" and "worship," what are some other words you use to describe your relationship to a deity?)

字可以互換嗎？這兩個字有什麼不同？ (Are the words interchangeable? What are the variations in meaning between the words?)

What Are Some of the Ways That 信 (Faith) is Used in Chinese?

This question helps establish the semantic range of the word 信 ("faith") in the context of everyday life. It is expected that the answer to this question will reach data saturation faster than other questions, at which time the question can be dropped.

[Small Sample] 您能解釋一下相信，信念，和信靠之間的區別和關係嗎？ (Can you explain the difference and relationship between [believe in], [belief], and [rely]?)

在宗教領域內與非宗教使用時，這些詞有什麼不同嗎？ (Are any of the words different when used inside versus outside a religious context?)

How Is Faith Understood by Taiwanese Christians?

The researcher talks to Christians to explore how their understanding of "faith" compares with other people. Whether their understanding turns out to be similar or different, it should provide for interesting analysis.

[If the person is not Christian] 您認為基督徒跟神的互動與您跟您的神明互動有什麼不一樣？有什麼相似的？ (How do you think Christians' interaction with their God is different from or similar to your interaction with your deities?)

[If the person is Christian] 在信仰這個議題上，在您成為基督徒前後對這個概念的理解有甚麼差異？ (On the topic of "faith," are there differences in your understanding of the concept before and after becoming a Christian?)

[If the person is Christian] 如今您是一位基督徒，試想在民間信仰裡頭，哪些是好的傳統，值得保留？哪些是不好的習俗，如何處理？ (Now that you are Christian, please reflect on your past practicing of folk religion. What are some good traditions that are worthy to keep? What are some bad customs, and how do we deal with them?)

Appendix 3

Details of the Coding Process

First Cycle Coding

The first cycle of coding is often called open coding or initial coding. Similar kinds of coding used in this stage include in vivo and process coding.[1] Many of the names of the codes created during first cycle coding were in vivo, which resulted in codes in both Chinese and English. For example, when one participant told the researcher that he saw religion as a stress reliever, his exact words were used for the code (i.e. "Reduce stress in life 減輕我們的煩惱").

Whether through in vivo or process coding, the idea is to code the contents first, which makes it more of a descriptive coding. Strauss and Corbin summarize the role of this stage as "concept identification."[2] This is not to be confused with identification of categories. During this stage, researchers are supposed to let the data guide the thinking and to see what concepts are emerging. It is here where researchers have to be careful of preconceived biases that may influence the concepts being recorded.

Coding for Key Words and Values

Codes were created using inclusion criteria that was developed. For example, the code "Ritual" was used when someone mentioned a ritual regardless of

---

1. Saldaña, *Coding Manual*, 55.
2. Strauss and Corbin, *Basics of Qualitative Research*, 87.

motivation or beliefs behind the act. The code "Belief" was used when someone mentioned a religious belief without specifying some kind of physical activity. It is possible for both ideas to be present in a participant's description of events. These kinds of codes are more descriptive in nature and help set the background of the participants' worlds. They all fall under the category of "Religious Environment."

First cycle coding included a wide range of selections, from single words (structural coding or splitter coding) to whole paragraphs (holistic coding or lumper coding). The goal of the coding done during this initial stage was to get a basic sense of the data and find key words that may be important to the research. The first run of coding was some descriptive coding and mostly in vivo coding, where the data was described using codes. For example, a key word that kept showing up was 拜 (*bài*, roughly translated to "worship"). This was a word that was used very often to describe interacting with deities. Analytic memos were made about the specific form of worship and what the term means in the context. However, during this first cycle of coding, there was not much analysis. New codes were created sparingly so as to have a more manageable corpus of codes after the first cycle.

The first cycle of coding was a good way of becoming familiar with the data. To move on to a more analytical and conceptual level after an initial run of coding, values coding was used. Values coding required not just looking for what the people were saying, but also what values their statements were reflecting. It was much more useful in answering the research questions of this study. Put simply, descriptive coding was used to set the background of folk religion in Taiwan and some of the general perspectives on what it entails. Values coding was used to determine the way Taiwanese people thought about religion in general.

Coding for Thinking and Believing

In conjunction with coding for values, coding was done for thought patterns, motivations, and religious understanding. A different kind of coding style was needed for that purpose. It was important to code not just to note what happened, but for the reasons that might be behind what happened. The code "Immediate need" was used when the participant attributed the reason for certain religious actions being performed to some kind of physical or emotional need experienced at the moment. For example, several participants listed going to the Yue Lao temple because they wanted to be in a romantic relationship. This was coded as "Immediate Need." Codes like this form the category of "Religious Motivation."

It was important to find out what the participants actually thought about the deities. Did they truly believe in them? If so, what do they mean by "believing in them?" Is that even a question in their minds? What kind of questions are they asking about different deities? All the data that answered questions like these were coded as "Believe In." This ended up forming a category of its own, leading to the creation of sub-category codes like "Choose to Believe," "Assumed as Real," "Just in Case," and others. This helped the researcher analyze how the participants thought about deities and what goes through their minds when they choose to interact with one particular deity more than others. Moreover, actions were often mentioned when one talked about a deity, which led to the existence of a significant amount of process codes.

Simultaneous coding was used; that is, having multiple codes within a single datum.[3] This allowed for formation of categories early on in the initial coding phase. For example, one interview included a section where the participant talked about how she treated Mazu. She used the term "worship" but also terms like "greeting." All the while, the concept was related to "believing in Mazu." The code "Faith in Deity" was used for the whole passage, with "worship" and "greeting" also applied to the same datum. Multiple meanings could be inferred from this datum. The intersections made for analysis that more easily interconnected different concepts to better form a nuanced Taiwanese worldview of religiosity.

Qualitative research methodology varies on the ideal number of codes, categories, and themes that should result from data analysis. Some advise having from fifty to three hundred codes, while others suggest having no more than one hundred. This should then result in anywhere between fifteen to thirty categories that eventually combine into five to seven major themes.[4] In the case of this work 237 codes were grouped into multiple categories, which resulted in the surfacing of seven major themes. These themes show up as the seven major headings in the chapters on findings. The development

---

3. Saldaña, *Coding Manual*, 94.
4. Saldaña, 25.

of the categories and themes happens during second cycle coding, the next topic of discussion.

Second Cycle Coding

During the second cycle of coding, first cycle codes are refined and sometimes changed. The idea is to relate codes to each other to reveal categories and sub-categories. Saldaña calls these eclectic coding and pattern/focused coding respectively.[5] As new categories emerge themes start to become apparent based on the categories that have the most connections. A popular coding style in the second stage is axial coding. Similar kinds of coding used in this stage include focused and selective/theoretical coding.[6] These coding terms have important nuances. However, they generally refer to refinement of existing codes rather than creation of brand-new codes. More precisely, new codes that may be generated come from existing codes rather than from the original data.

Coding for Categories

In the second cycle, all the existing codes that were generated in the first cycle were reexamined. Even before second cycle coding began, categories have already started developing. One reason was that it was hard to resist organizing codes by the third interview. The other reason was that by that time, there were 101 codes; without some form of organization, the codebook was too unwieldy. However, even though some sub-categories were formed during first cycle coding, the bulk of the core category refinement happened during second cycle coding.

This refinement started with a transitional stage involving a comprehensive review of the data before second cycle coding even began. Saldaña dedicates a whole chapter to this "after first cycle coding" as a way to illustrate its importance.[7] This process is included as second cycle coding because it was part of the process of category creation.

---

5. Saldaña, 74.
6. Saldaña, 55.
7. Saldaña, 211–32.

Code landscaping was done first, which was using a CAQDAS program to create a visual picture of the most common codes. The higher the frequency of occurrence, the bigger the box size the code becomes. See figure 19 for a visual picture of the top 100 codes when the codes were organized according to the research questions.

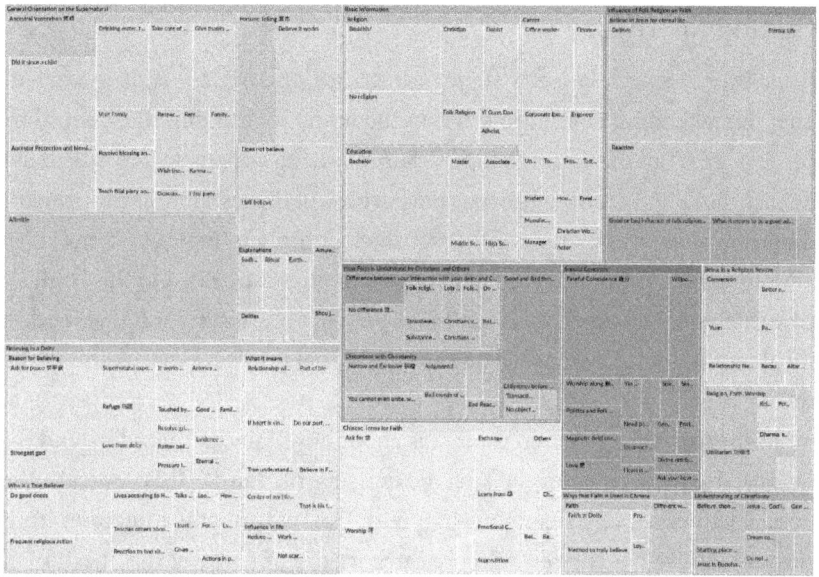

Figure 19. Visual picture of the most common codes for the research

This was not a concrete step in that it did not generate anything new; however, it helped the researcher get an idea of what may be the most important concepts. Some codes were given a more detailed look due to this while others were dropped altogether either because they were subsumed under another code or deemed redundant. For example, the code "Immediate Need" rose to the level of "categories," which was eventually renamed as "Utilitarian 功能性." That last code is seen as a sub-heading in the chapter on findings in the form of "Utilitarian Perspective of Deities."

The first concrete step was synthesizing the sub-categories formed in the coding done earlier and figuring out core categories in the data. This was one of the most important parts of data analysis. The goal of second cycle coding is to "develop a coherent metasynthesis of the data corpus."[8] To that end, the codes were organized into bigger categories as a way of "code mapping," which is defined as "how a list of codes gets categorized, recategorized, and conceptualized throughout the analytic journey."[9] The map progressed from a big list of multiple codes to a smaller list filled with many categories. Categories kept getting combined until there were only a few major categories.

Coding for Theory

After there were only a few major categories, theoretical coding started. Theoretical coding is used to develop theory by identifying the "central or core category" of the research topic.[10] Summarizing various scholars, Saldaña defines the central/core category as the purpose of the research, as the primary theme, and as "the major conflict, obstacle, problem, issue, or concern to participants."[11] Every category generated becomes integrated to this central/core category. This category is not the theory, but "an abstraction that models the integration, . . . a keyword or key phrase that triggers a discussion of the theory itself."[12]

In this case, the research topic was about how Taiwanese understand religion. The focus was on the specific concept of "faith." This central/core category thus served to explain what "faith" meant using the categories from the previous steps. The central/core category did not answer the question of how Taiwanese understand "faith." However, it did give the researcher the vocabulary to answer that question. Later in the data analysis, the vocabulary used to nuance this understanding of "faith" became more useful. At the end of the study, it became possible to create a contextual approach to gospel transmission based partly on this understanding. For a detailed explanation of the central/core category, please refer to the chapters on research findings.

---

8. Saldaña, 234.
9. Saldaña, 222.
10. Saldaña, 250.
11. Saldaña, 250.
12. Saldaña, 250.

Mixing the Stages

The above plan was formulated before coding began in earnest. However, it must be mentioned that the first and second cycles were not conducted in strict, sequential order. The categories started forming after coding a little over half of the interviews. Instead of waiting until the first cycle coding was fully done, coding for categories and formation of theories already began. In this way, first cycle and second cycle coding were mixed to some degree. Throughout the first cycle, coding continued primarily for key words, values, thinking style, and ways of believing. When second cycle coding began, the messy categories compiled during that cycle were refined and reformed into the headings that appear in the chapters on findings.

Bibliography

Ammerman, Nancy Tatom, ed. *Everyday Religion: Observing Modern Religious Lives*. Oxford: Oxford University Press, 2006.
Århem, Kaj, and Guido Sprenger, eds. *Animism in Southeast Asia*. London: Routledge, 2016.
Baer, Marc David. "History and Religious Conversion." In *The Oxford Handbook of Religious Conversion*, edited by Lewis R. Rambo and Charles E. Farhadian, 25–47. Oxford: Oxford University Press, 2014.
Barclay, John M. G. *Paul and the Gift*. Grand Rapids: Eerdmans, 2015.
Bates, Matthew W. Salvation by Allegiance Alone: Rethinking Faith, Works, and the Gospel of Jesus the King. Grand Rapids: Baker Academic, 2017.
Bauer, Walter, Frederick William Danker, William F. Arndt, and F. Wilbur Gingrich. *A Greek-English Lexicon of the New Testament and Other Early Christian Literature*. 3rd ed. Chicago: University of Chicago Press, 2000.
Berger, Peter L. *The Many Altars of Modernity: Toward a Paradigm for Religion in a Pluralist Age*. Boston: de Gruyter, 2014.
———. *The Sacred Canopy*. Garden City: Doubleday, 1967.
Bhabha, Homi K. *The Location of Culture*. 2nd ed. London: Routledge, 2004.
Bloomberg, Linda Dale, and Marie F. Volpe. *Completing Your Qualitative Dissertation: A Road Map From Beginning to End*. 4th ed. Thousand Oaks: SAGE Publications, 2018.
Bolton, Robert. "Taiwan's Ancestor Cult: A Contextualized Gospel Approach." *Taiwan Mission* 4, no. 3 (1995): 5–12.
Brown, Deborah A., and Tun-jen Cheng. "Religious Relations across the Taiwan Strait: Patterns, Alignments, and Political Effects." *Orbis* 56, no. 1 (January 2012): 60–81.
Burnett, David. World of the Spirits: A Christian Perspective on Traditional and Folk Religions. London: Monarch Books, 2000.
Chang, Hsun, and Benjamin Penny, eds. *Religion in Taiwan and China: Locality and Transmission*. Nankang, Taiwan: Institute of Ethnology, Academia Sinica, 2017.

Charmaz, Kathy. "Constructivist Grounded Theory." *The Journal of Positive Psychology* 12, no. 3 (2017): 299–300.

Cheng 鄭, Chih Ming 志明. "Jìn wǔshí niánlái táiwān dìqū mínjiān zōngjiào zhī yánjiū yǔ qiánzhān 近五十年來臺灣地區民間宗教之研究與前瞻 [Research and Prospect of Folk Religion in Taiwan in the Past 50 Years]." *Taiwan Historica* 臺灣文獻 52, no. 2 (June 2001): 127–48.

Chuang 莊, Tony 智超. "A Chinese Modernity: What Feng Shui, Ancestors, Mazu, Buddhism, and Mao Can Teach Us about a Different Kind of Secularization." In *Against the Tide: Mission Amidst the Global Currents of Secularization*, edited by Craig Ott and W. Jay Moon, 161–75. Evangelical Missiological Society Series 27. Littleton: William Carey, 2019.

Chuang 莊, Tsukung 祖鯤. *Christian Perspective of Zen and Dao* 說禪論道 — 基督教與儒、釋、道之對話. Paradise: Ambassadors for Christ, Inc 基督使者協會, 2009.

Clart, Philip A. "Chinese Tradition and Taiwanese Modernity." In *Religion in Modern Taiwan: Tradition and Innovation in a Changing Society*, edited by Philip A. Clart and Charles B. Jones, 84–97. Honolulu: University of Hawai'i Press, 2003.

Clart, Philip A., and Charles B. Jones, eds. *Religion in Modern Taiwan: Tradition and Innovation in a Changing Society*. Honolulu: University of Hawai'i Press, 2003.

Comfort, Ray. "What Is the Gospel? Archives." Living Waters, 3 June 2020. https://www.livingwaters.com/post-series/what-is-the-gospel/.

Denzin, Norman K., and Yvonna S. Lincoln, eds. *The SAGE Handbook of Qualitative Research*. 5th ed. Thousand Oaks: SAGE Publications, 2017.

Dong 董, Fang-Yuan 芳苑. "Táiwān Mínjiān Xìnyǎng Zhī Zhèngshì 臺灣民間信仰之正視 [Facing Seriously Taiwanese Folk Religion]." *Táiwān Shénxué Lùn Kān* 臺灣神學論刊 [Taiwan Journal of Theology] 16 (1994): 49–74.

Edwards, James R. *The Gospel According to Luke*. Pillar New Testament Commentary. Grand Rapids: Eerdmans, 2015.

Emmel, Nick. *Sampling and Choosing Cases in Qualitative Research: A Realist Approach*. London: SAGE Publications, 2013.

Fan, Lizhu. "The Dilemma of Pursuing Chinese Religious Studies." In *Social Scientific Studies of Religion in China: Methodologies, Theories, and Findings*, edited by Fenggang Yang and Graeme Lang, 87–107. Leiden: Brill, 2011.

Fan, Lizhu, and Na Chen. "'Conversion' and the Resurgence of Indigenous Religion in China." In *The Oxford Handbook of Religious Conversion*, edited by Lewis R. Rambo and Charles E. Farhadian, 556–77. Oxford: Oxford University Press, 2014.

Feuchtwang, Stephan. *Popular Religion in China: The Imperial Metaphor*. London: Routledge, 2001.

Flemming, Dean. *Contextualization in the New Testament: Patterns for Theology and Mission*. Downers Grove: IVP Academic, 2005.

Fowler, Jeaneane, and Merv Fowler. *Chinese Religions: Beliefs and Practices*. Brighton: Sussex Academic Press, 2008.

Fung, Raymond. "Evangelism Today: The Sinners and the Sinned-Against." In *Asian Christian Theology: Emerging Themes*, edited by Douglas J. Elwood, 200–207. Philadelphia: Westminster John Knox, 1980.

Gao, Shining. "The Impact of Contemporary Chinese Folk Religions on Christianity." In *Christianity and Chinese Culture*, edited by Mikka Ruokanen and Paulos Huang, 170–81. Grand Rapids: Eerdmans, 2010.

Gilbert, Greg. *What Is the Gospel?* Wheaton: Crossway, 2010.

Glaser, Barney G. *Doing Grounded Theory: Issues and Discussion*. Mill Valley: Sociology Press, 1998.

Glaser, Barney G., and Anselm L. Strauss. *The Discovery of Grounded Theory: Strategies for Qualitative Research*. Chicago: Aldine, 1967.

Goossaert, Vincent, and David A. Palmer. *The Religious Question in Modern China*. Chicago: University of Chicago Press, 2011.

Gupta, Nijay K. *Paul and the Language of Faith*. Grand Rapids: Eerdmans, 2020.

Gustafson, David M. *Gospel Witness: Evangelism in Word and Deed*. Grand Rapids: Eerdmans, 2019.

Gutiérrez, Gustavo. *A Theology of Liberation*. 15th anniversary edition. Maryknoll: Orbis Books, 1988.

Hackett, Conrad, and Timmy Huynh. "What Is Each Country's Second-Largest Religious Group?" Pew Research Center, 22 June 2015. https://www.pewresearch.org/fact-tank/2015/06/22/what-is-each-countrys-second-largest-religious-group/.

Hackett, Conrad, and David McClendon. "World's Largest Religion by Population Is Still Christianity." Pew Research Center, 5 April 2017. https://www.pewresearch.org/fact-tank/2017/04/05/christians-remain-worlds-largest-religious-group-but-they-are-declining-in-europe/.

Hall, David D., ed. *Lived Religion in America: Toward A History of Practice*. Princeton: Princeton University Press, 1997.

Halporn, Roberta. *Gods, Ghosts and Ancestors: The Ching Ming Festival in America*. Brooklyn: Center for Thanatology Research, 1997.

Harvey, Graham. *Animism: Respecting the Living World*. 2nd ed. London: Hurst, 2017.

———, ed. The Handbook of Contemporary Animism. London: Routledge, 2015.

Hatch, J. Amos. *Doing Qualitative Research in Education Settings*. Albany: State University of New York Press, 2002.

Hauerwas, Stanley. *Matthew*. Brazos Theological Commentary on the Bible. Grand Rapids: Brazos Press, 2006.

Hick, John. *A Christian Theology of Religions*. Louisville: Westminster John Knox, 1995.

Hiebert, Paul G. "Critical Contextualization." In *Anthropological Reflections on Missiological Issues*, 75–92. Grand Rapids: Baker Books, 1994.

———. "The Flaw of the Excluded Middle." *Missiology* 10, no. 1 (January 1982): 35–47.

———. "Sets and Structures: A Study of Church Patterns." In New Horizons in World Mission: Evangelicals and the Christian Mission in the 1980s: Papers and Responses Prepared for the Consultation on Theology and Mission, Trinity Evangelical Divinity School, School of World Mission and Evangelism, March 19–22, 1979, edited by David J. Hesselgrave, 217–27. Grand Rapids: Baker Book House, 1979.

Hiebert, Paul G., R. Daniel Shaw, and Tite Tiénou. *Understanding Folk Religion: A Christian Response to Popular Beliefs and Practices*. Grand Rapids: Baker Academic, 2000.

Hsieh 謝, Kuo-Hsing 國興, ed. *Pilgrimages, Sacrifice Offerings and Sociocultural Transformation* 進香．醮．祭與社會文化變遷. Táiwān Shǐ Lùncóng Mínjiān Xìnyǎng Piān 台灣史論叢 民間信仰篇 [Taiwan History Essays – Folk Religion Edition] 1. Taipei, Taiwan: National Taiwan University Press 國立台灣大學出版中心, 2019.

Hu, Anning. "Gifts of Money and Gifts of Time: Folk Religion and Civic Involvement in a Chinese Society." *Review of Religious Research* 56, no. 2 (June 2014): 313–35.

Hu, Anning, and Fenggang Yang. "Trajectories of Folk Religion 大廟埕 in Deregulated Taiwan." *Chinese Sociological Review* 46, no. 3 (2014): 80–100.

Idowu, E. Bọlaji. *Olódùmarè: God in Yoruba Belief*. London: Longman, 1962.

International Monetary Fund. "IMF DataMapper." International Monetary Fund, April 2021. https://www.imf.org/external/datamapper/NGDPD@WEO/OEMDC/ADVEC/WEOWORLD.

Jennings, Jr., Theodore W., and Tat-Siong Benny Liew. "Mistaken Identities but Model Faith: Rereading the Centurion, the Chap, and the Christ in Matthew 8:5–13." *Journal of Biblical Literature* 123, no. 3 (2004): 467–94.

Jiao 焦, Guocheng 國成, and Yanxia 艷霞 Zhao 趙. "'Xiào'de Lìshǐ Mìngyùn Jí Qí Yuánshǐ Yìyùn '孝'的歷史命運及其原始意蘊 [The Source Connotation and Historical Evolution of the Concept of 'Xiao']." *Qílǔ Xué Kān* 齊魯學刊 *[Qilu Journal]* 226, no. 1 (2012): 5–10.

"Jīdūjiào Sǐ Méi Rén Bài?! Qīngmíng Sǎomù de Xìnyǎng Wèntí ~mínsú Guóbǎo Lái Jiědá 基督教死沒人拜?!清明掃墓的信仰問題～民俗國寶來解答 [In Christianity, There's No Veneration after Death?! Tomb Sweeping Day and Faith Issues ~ Answers from a Folk National Treasure]." *Jīntiān Bù Jiǎnglǐ* 今天不講理 [Unreasonable Today]. Taipei, Taiwan: GOOD TV, 2 April 2020.

Jordan, David K. *Gods, Ghosts, and Ancestors: The Folk Religion of a Taiwanese Village*. Berkley: University of California Press, 1972.

Keller, Timothy. *Center Church: Doing Balanced, Gospel-Centered Ministry in Your City*. Grand Rapids: Zondervan, 2012.

Khong, Stephen. "Idol Removal." *Taiwan Mission* 4, no. 3 (1995): 22–23.

Kim, Sangkeun. *Strange Names of God: The Missionary Translation of the Divine Name and the Chinese Responses to Matteo Ricci's Shangti in Late Ming China, 1583–1644*. New York: Peter Lang, 2005.

Kraft, Charles H. *Christianity in Culture: A Study in Biblical Theologizing In Cross-Cultural Perspective*. 25th anniversary edition. Maryknoll: Orbis Books, 2005.

Kramer, Stephanie. "Key Findings: How Living Arrangements Vary by Religious Affiliation around the World." Pew Research Center, 13 December 2019. https://www.pewresearch.org/fact-tank/2019/12/13/key-findings-how-living-arrangements-vary-by-religious-affiliation-around-the-world/.

Kuo, Cheng-Tian. *Religion and Democracy in Taiwan*. Albany: State University of New York Press, 2008.

Leiter, Valerie. "A Bricolage of Urban Sidewalks: Observing Locations of Inequality." In *Disability and Qualitative Inquiry: Methods for Rethinking an Ableist World*, edited by Ronald J. Berger and Laura S. Lorenz, 13–28. Farnham: Ashgate, 2015.

Liao 廖, Kun-Tien 昆田. *Mínsú Yǔ Xìnyǎng* 民俗與信仰 [Folklore and Faith]. Xīwàng Xiàn Cóngshū Jìsī Xìliè 希望線叢書祭司系列 [Line of Hope Priest Series] 3. Taipei, Taiwan: Chuánshén ài wǎng zīxùn 傳神愛網資訊 [Passing God's Love Network Information], 2006.

Lin, Judith C. P. *The Charismatic Movement in Taiwan from 1945 to 1995: Clashes, Concord, and Cacophony*. Christianity and Renewal – Interdisciplinary Studies. London: Palgrave Macmillan, 2020.

Lin 林, Mao-Hsien 茂賢. *Dà Miào Chéng: Línmàoxián Táiwān Mínsú Xuǎnjí* 大廟埕: 林茂賢臺灣民俗選集 [Big Temple Courtyard: Selected Works of Lin Mao-Hsien on Taiwanese Folk Practices]. Taipei, Taiwan: Fēngráo wénhuà shè 豐饒文化社 [Abundance Culture Publishing], 2018.

Lin 林, Mei-Rong 美容. *Táiwān Mínjiān Xìnyǎng Yánjiū Shūmù* 台灣民間信仰研究書目 [Taiwan Folk Belief Research Bibliography]. Expanded ed. 增訂版. Taipei, Taiwan: Zhōngyāng yán jiù yuàn mínzú xué yánjiū suǒ 中央研究院民族學研究所 [Institute of Ethnology, Academia Sinica], 1997. https://www.sanmin.com.tw/Product/index/000754228.

Lin 林, Mei-Rong 美容, and Wei-Hua 緯華 Chen 陳. "Mǎzǔ Lièdǎo de Fúshī Lì Miào Yánjiū: Cóng Mǎ Gǎng Tiān Hòugōng Tán Qǐ 馬祖列島的浮屍立廟研究: 從馬港天后宮談起 [Temples Founded for 'Drifting Corpses' in the Mazu Islands: The Makang Mazu Temple as a Preliminary Case Study]."

Táiwān Rénlèi Xué Kān 臺灣人類學刊 [Taiwan Journal of Anthropology] 6, no. 1 (June 2008): 103–31.

Liu, Yi-Jung. "Religious Coping Methods of Taiwanese Folk Religion." *Journal of Religion and Health* 53, no. 4 (August 2014): 1138–45.

Lo 盧, Lung-Kwong 龍光. "Making Disciples in China." In *Making Disciples in a World Parish: Global Perspectives on Mission and Evangelism*, edited by Paul W. Chilcote, 77–83. Princeton Theological Monograph 162. Eugene: Pickwick Publications, 2011.

Madsen, Richard. *Democracy's Dharma: Religious Renaissance and Political Development in Taiwan*. Berkeley: University of California Press, 2007.

———. "Secular State And Religious Society In Mainland China And Taiwan." In *Social Scientific Studies of Religion in China: Methodologies, Theories, and Findings*, edited by Fenggang Yang and Graeme Lang, 273–96. Leiden: Brill, 2011.

———. "Secularism, Religious Change, and Social Conflict in Asia." In *Rethinking Secularism*, edited by Craig Calhoun, Mark Juergensmeyer, and Jonathan Van Antwerpen, 248–69. Oxford: Oxford University Press, 2011.

McKnight, Scot. *The King Jesus Gospel: The Original Good News Revisited*. Revised edition. Grand Rapids: Zondervan, 2016.

Merriam, Sharan B. *Qualitative Research: A Guide to Design and Implementation*. 3rd ed. San Francisco: Jossey-Bass, 2009.

Nadeau, Randall Laird, and Hsun Chang. "Gods, Ghosts, and Ancestors: Religious Studies and the Question of 'Taiwanese Identity.'" In *Religion in Modern Taiwan: Tradition and Innovation in a Changing Society*, edited by Philip A. Clart and Charles B. Jones, 280–99. Honolulu: University of Hawai'i Press, 2003.

Nakajima 中島, Michio 三千男. "Shinto Deities That Crossed the Sea: Japan's 'Overseas Shrines,' 1868 to 1945." *Japanese Journal of Religious Studies* 37, no. 1 (2010): 21–46.

National Statistics, Republic of China (Taiwan). "Latest Indicators." National Statistics, Republic of China (Taiwan), February 2021. https://eng.stat.gov.tw/point.asp?index=9.

Netland, Harold A. "A Christian Theology of Religions." In *Handbook of Religion: A Christian Engagement with Traditions, Teachings, and Practices*, edited by Terry C. Muck, Harold A. Netland, and Gerald R. McDermott, 19–26. Grand Rapids: Baker Academic, 2014.

———. *Christianity and Religious Diversity: Clarifying Christian Commitments in a Globalizing Age*. Grand Rapids: Baker Academic, 2015.

———. *Dissonant Voices: Religious Pluralism and the Question of Truth*. Grand Rapids: Eerdmans, 1991.

———. *Encountering Religious Pluralism: The Challenge to Christian Faith Mission*. Downers Grove: IVP Academic, 2001.

Ott, Craig. "Globalization and Contextualization: Reframing the Task of Contextualization in the Twenty-First Century." *Missiology* 43, no. 1 (January 2015): 43–58.

Overmyer, Daniel L. *Folk Buddhist Religion: Dissenting Sects in Late Traditional China*. Cambridge: Harvard University Press, 1976.

Paloutzian, Raymond F. "Psychology of Religious Conversion and Spiritual Transformation." In *The Oxford Handbook of Religious Conversion*, edited by Lewis R. Rambo and Charles E. Farhadian, 209–39. Oxforxford University Press, 2014.

Parrinder, Geoffrey. *African Traditional Religion*. 3rd ed. New York: Harper & Row, 1976.

———. *Africa's Three Religions*. 2nd ed. London: Sheldon Press, 1976.

Pew Research Center. "Religious Composition by Country, 2010–2050." Pew Research Center, 2 April 2015. https://www.pewresearch.org/religion/2015/04/02/religious-projection-table/.

Priest, Robert J. "'Who Am I?': Theology and Identity for Children of the Dragon." In *After Imperialism: Christian Identity in China and the Global Evangelical Movement*, edited by Robert R. Cook and David W. Pao, 175–92. Studies in Chinese Christianity. Eugene: Pickwick Publications, 2011.

Primiano, Leonard Norman. "Vernacular Religion and the Search for Method in Religious Folklife." *Western Folklore* 54, no. 1 (1995): 37–56.

Rambo, Lewis R. *Understanding Religious Conversion*. Reprint edition. New Haven: Yale University Press, 1995.

Rambo, Lewis R., and Charles E. Farhadian, eds. *The Oxford Handbook of Religious Conversion*. Oxford: Oxford University Press, 2014.

Redfield, Robert. *Peasant Society and Culture: An Anthropological Approach to Civilization*. Chicago: University of Chicago Press, 1956.

Robbins, Joel. "Anthropology, Pentecostalism, and the New Paul: Conversion, Event, and Social Transformation." *South Atlantic Quarterly* 109, no. 4 (Fall 2010): 633–52.

Ruether, Rosemary Radford. "Religious Identity and Openness to a Pluralistic World: A Christian View." *Buddhist-Christian Studies* 25 (2005): 29–40.

Saldaña, Johnny. *The Coding Manual for Qualitative Researchers*. 3rd ed. Los Angeles: SAGE Publications, 2015.

Scott, Janet Lee. *For Gods, Ghosts and Ancestors: The Chinese Tradition of Paper Offerings*. Hong Kong: Hong Kong University Press, 2007.

Shahar, Meir, and Robert P. Weller, eds. *Unruly Gods: Divinity and Society in China*. Honolulu: University of Hawaii Press, 1996.

Shaw, Rosalind. "The Invention of 'African Traditional Religion.'" *Religion* 20, no. 4 (October 1990): 339–53.

Shi 施, Zheng Ting 政廷. *Niànlì Shéngōng* 念力神功 [Willpower Martial Arts]. Taipei, Taiwan: Xiǎobīng 小兵 [Little Soldier], 2014.

Solomon, Robert M. "Making Disciples in Singapore: Challenges and Opportunities." In *Making Disciples in a World Parish: Global Perspectives on Mission and Evangelism*, edited by Paul W. Chilcote, 103–11. Princeton Theological Monograph 162. Eugene: Pickwick Publications, 2011.

Stark, Rodney, and Roger Finke. *Acts of Faith: Explaining the Human Side of Religion*. Berkeley: University of California Press, 2000.

Stein, Robert H. *Luke*. The New American Commentary vol. 24. Nashville: Broadman & Holman, 1992.

Stott, John, and Christopher J. H. Wright. *Christian Mission in the Modern World*. Updated and expanded ed. Downers Grove: InterVarsity Press, 2015.

Strauss, Anselm L. *Qualitative Analysis for Social Scientists*. Cambridge: Cambridge University Press, 1987.

Strauss, Anselm L., and Juliet Corbin. *Basics of Qualitative Research: Techniques and Procedures for Developing Grounded Theory*. Thousand Oaks: SAGE Publications, 2015.

Suga 菅, Kōji 浩二. "A Concept of 'Overseas Shinto Shrines': A Pantheistic Attempt by Ogasawara Shōzō and Its Limitations." *Japanese Journal of Religious Studies* 37, no. 1 (2010): 47–74.

Sun, Anna. *Confucianism as a World Religion: Contested Histories and Contemporary Realities*. Reprint edition. Princeton: Princeton University Press, 2015.

Sunstein, Bonnie Stone, and Elizabeth Chiseri-Strater. *FieldWorking: Reading and Writing Research*. 4th ed. Boston: Bedford/St. Martin's, 2011.

Taiwan Buddhist Tzu Chi Foundation [佛教慈濟慈善事業基金會]. "2019 Annual Report [2019 年度報告書]." Hualien, Taiwan, 2019. http://tw.tzuchi.org/financial/2019financial/.

Tamney, Joseph B. "Asian Popular Religions." In *Encyclopedia of Religion and Society*, edited by William H. Jr. Swatos. Lanham: AltaMira Press, 1998. http://hirr.hartsem.edu/ency/Asian.htm.

Taylor, Charles. *A Secular Age*. Cambridge: Harvard University Press, 2007.

Teppo, Anne R. "Grounded Theory Methods." In *Approaches to Qualitative Research in Mathematics Education: Examples of Methodology and Methods*, edited by Angelika Bikner-Ahsbahs, Christine Knipping, and Norma Presmeg, 3–22. Dordrecht: Springer, 2015.

Terwiel, Barend Jan. Monks and Magic: *Revisiting a Classic Study of Religious Ceremonies in Thailand*. 4th ed. Copenhagen: NIAS Press, 2012.

Thompson, Laurence G. *Chinese Religion: An Introduction.* 5th ed. Religious Life in History. Belmont: Wadsworth, 1995.

Tiénou, Tite. "The Invention of the 'Primitive' and Stereotypes in Mission." *Missiology* 19, no. 3 (July 1991): 295–303.

Tsai 蔡, Yen-Zen 彥仁. "Táiwān Dìqū Zōngjiào Jīngyàn Zhī Bǐjiào Yánjiū-Jiǎnjiè Yīgè Kuà Xuékē Yánjiū de Ànlì 臺灣地區宗教經驗之比較研究—簡介一個跨學科研究的案例 [Comparative Study of Religious Experience in Taiwan: A Case Study of Interdisciplinary Research]." *Rénwén Yǔ Shèhuì Kēxué Jiǎnxùn* 人文與社會科學簡訊 [Newsletter of Humanities and Social Sciences] 13, no. 3 (2012): 175–83.

Tsai 蔡, Yi-Jia 怡佳. "Yǔ Fú Xiāngyìng, Yǔ Shén Xiāng Qì: Táiwān Fójiào Tú Yǔ Jīdū Tú de Qídǎo Xiūxíng Tǐyàn 與佛相應，與神相契：臺灣佛教徒與基督徒的祈禱修行體驗 [Responding to the Buddha, According with God: Prayer and Religious Cultivation Experiences of Taiwanese Buddhists and Christians]." *Táiwān Zōngjiào Yánjiū* 臺灣宗教研究 [Taiwan Journal of Religious Studies] 15, no. 1 (2016): 51–78.

Tylor, Edward Burnett. *Primitive Culture: Researches into the Development of Mythology, Philosophy, Religion, Art, and Custom.* 4th ed. Vol. 1. London: John Murray, 1903.

Weiss, Robert S. *Learning from Strangers: The Art and Method of Qualitative Interview Studies.* New York: Free Press, 1995.

Weller, Robert P. "Matricidal Magistrates and Gambling Gods: Weak States and Strong Spirits in China." In *Unruly Gods: Divinity and Society in China*, edited by Meir Shahar and Robert P. Weller, 250–68. Honolulu: University of Hawaii Press, 1996.

Wong, Wai Yip. "Defining Chinese Folk Religion: A Methodological Interpretation." *Asian Philosophy* 21, no. 2 (2011): 153–70.

Wright, N. T. *Paul and the Faithfulness of God.* Christian Origins and the Question of God 4. Minneapolis: Fortress Press, 2013.

Wright, N. T., and Michael F. Bird. *The New Testament in Its World: An Introduction to the History, Literature, and Theology of the First Christians.* Grand Rapids: Zondervan Academic, 2019.

Yang, C. K. *Religion in Chinese Society: A Study of Contemporary Social Functions of Religion and Some of Their Historical Factors.* Oakland: University of California Press, 1961.

Yang, Fenggang. "Exceptionalism or Chinamerica: Measuring Religious Change in the Globalizing World Today." *Journal for the Scientific Study of Religion* 55, no. 1 (March 2016): 7–22.

———. *Religion in China: Survival and Revival under Communist Rule.* Oxford: Oxford University Press, 2011.

Yang, Fenggang, and Andrew Abel. "Sociology of Religious Conversion." In *The Oxford Handbook of Religious Conversion*, edited by Lewis R. Rambo and Charles E. Farhadian, 140–63. Oxford: Oxford University Press, 2014.

Yang, Fenggang, and Anning Hu. "Mapping Chinese Folk Religion in Mainland China and Taiwan." *Journal for the Scientific Study of Religion* 51, no. 3 (2012): 505–21.

Yang, Fenggang, and Graeme Lang, eds. *Social Scientific Studies of Religion in China: Methodologies, Theories, and Findings*. Leiden: Brill, 2011.

Yang, Fenggang, and Joseph Tamney, eds. *Confucianism and Spiritual Traditions in Modern China and Beyond*. Leiden: Brill, 2011.

Yao, Xinzhong, and Paul Badham. *Religious Experience in Contemporary China*. Cardiff: University of Wales Press, 2007.

Yao, Xinzhong, and Yanxia Zhao. *Chinese Religion: A Contextual Approach*. London: Continuum, 2010.

Yoder, Don. "Towards a Definition of Folk Religion." *Western Folklore* 33, no. 1 (Winter 1974): 2–15.

Yong, Amos. "A P(New)Matological Paradigm for Christian Mission in a Religiously Plural World." *Missiology* 33, no. 2 (April 2005): 175–91.

Zhai, Jiexia Elisa. "Contrasting Trends of Religious Markets in Contemporary Mainland China and in Taiwan." *Journal of Church and State* 52, no. 1 (December 2010): 94–111.

Langham Literature, with its publishing work, is a ministry of Langham Partnership.

Langham Partnership is a global fellowship working in pursuit of the vision God entrusted to its founder John Stott –

> *to facilitate the growth of the church in maturity and Christ-likeness through raising the standards of biblical preaching and teaching.*

Our vision is to see churches in the Majority World equipped for mission and growing to maturity in Christ through the ministry of pastors and leaders who believe, teach and live by the word of God.

Our mission is to strengthen the ministry of the word of God through:
- nurturing national movements for biblical preaching
- fostering the creation and distribution of evangelical literature
- enhancing evangelical theological education

especially in countries where churches are under-resourced.

Our ministry

Langham Preaching partners with national leaders to nurture indigenous biblical preaching movements for pastors and lay preachers all around the world. With the support of a team of trainers from many countries, a multi-level programme of seminars provides practical training, and is followed by a programme for training local facilitators. Local preachers' groups and national and regional networks ensure continuity and ongoing development, seeking to build vigorous movements committed to Bible exposition.

Langham Literature provides Majority World preachers, scholars and seminary libraries with evangelical books and electronic resources through publishing and distribution, grants and discounts. The programme also fosters the creation of indigenous evangelical books in many languages, through writer's grants, strengthening local evangelical publishing houses, and investment in major regional literature projects, such as one volume Bible commentaries like the Africa Bible Commentary and the South Asia Bible Commentary.

Langham Scholars provides financial support for evangelical doctoral students from the Majority World so that, when they return home, they may train pastors and other Christian leaders with sound, biblical and theological teaching. This programme equips those who equip others. Langham Scholars also works in partnership with Majority World seminaries in strengthening evangelical theological education. A growing number of Langham Scholars study in high quality doctoral programmes in the Majority World itself. As well as teaching the next generation of pastors, graduated Langham Scholars exercise significant influence through their writing and leadership.

To learn more about Langham Partnership and the work we do visit langham.org

www.ingramcontent.com/pod-product-compliance
Lightning Source LLC
Chambersburg PA
CBHW051537230426
43669CB00015B/2630